TEACHER EDUCATION

TEACHER EDUCATION

Dr. Jagdish Prasad Sharma
Reader, Teachers Training College,
Patna

CENTRUM PRESS
NEW DELHI-110002 (INDIA)

CENTRUM PRESS
H.O.: 4360/4, Ansari Road, Daryaganj,
New Delhi-110 002 (India)
Ph.: 23278000, 23261597

B.O.: No. 1015, Ist Main Road, BSK IIIrd Stage
IIIrd Phase, IIIrd Block,
Bangalore - 560 085 (India)
Tel.: 080-41723429
Visit us at: www.centrumpress.com

Teacher Education

First Edition, 2009

PRINTED IN INDIA

Printed at Balaji Offset, Delhi

Contents

Preface

Teacher education refers to the policies and procedures designed to equip teachers with the knowledge, attitudes, behaviours and skills they require to perform their tasks effectively in the school and classroom. There is a long-standing and ongoing debate about the most appropriate term to describe these activities. The term 'teacher training' (which may give the impression that the activity involves training staff to undertake relatively routine tasks) seems to be losing ground to 'teacher education' (with its connotation of preparing staff for a professional role as a reflective practitioner). Initial teacher education may be organized according to two basic models. In the 'consecutive' model, a teacher first obtains a qualification (often a first university degree), and then studies for a further period to gain an additional qualification in teaching; (in some systems this takes the form of a post-graduate degree, possibly even a Masters). The alternative is where a student simultaneously studies both an academic subject and the ways of teaching that subject, leading to a qualification as a teacher of that subject. Other pathways are also available. In some countries, it is possible for a person to receive training as a teacher under the responsibility of an accredited experienced practitioner in a school. Teacher Education in many countries takes place in institutions of Higher Education.

The curriculum for teacher education programme has to be flexible to include activities to promote physical, cognitive, social, emotional, linguistic and aesthetic development of children. It may also include resource mobilisation and management, use of community resources both human and material, enlisting community participation. Teacher

Education is a critical area in which adequate inputs and investments are to be made for developing not only human resources but also physical resources. Teacher Education is a continuous process, and its pre-service and in-service components are inseparable.

In this book the description and analysis of the subject is in the Indian context. It covers the syllabi of all the Indian universities on this subject in simple and lucid language drawing examples from the Indian society and Indian educational system. An attempt has been made to cover up most of the topics included in M.Ed. syllabus of the Indian universities.

—Dr. Jagdish Prasad Sharma

UNIT-I

Teacher and Education in the Emerging Society

The Teacher in Ancient India and in the Emerging Indian Society

India has a rich tradition of learning and education right from the antiquity. These were handed over generations to generations either through oral or written medium. The highly esteemed Vedas have come to down to us. They existed for nearly 2000 years before they were known in India. It was the knowledge of acoustics that enabled ancient Indians to orally transmit the Vedas from generation to generation. Institutional form of imparting learning came into existence in the early centuries of the Christian era. The approach to learning was to study logic and epistemology.

The study of logic was followed by Hindus, Buddhists and Jains, one of the most important topics of Indian thoughts was pramana or means of reliable knowledge. The Nyaya schools upheld four pramanas-perceptions of are liable by analogy or comparison, word (Sabda), and pronunciation of a reliable authority such as the Vedas. The Vedanta school added one more to it i.e. intuition. It is probably while studying the process of inference that the schools of true logic arose. Ancient Indian postulated syllogism though not as accurate as that of Aristotle. Yet, they recognize some of the major fallacies of logic like reduction and absurdum, circular argument, infinite regression, dilemma, and ignorance. In the field epistemology,

Jains contributed the most. There were not only two possibilities of existence and non-existence but seven more. Although the modern logicians might laugh at this pedantic system of ontological and epistemological reality they concede that the world is more complex and subtle than we think it to be. Regarding institutional form of education the first was the guru-sishya system.

According to sacred texts, the training of the Brahmin pupil took place at the home of a Brahmin teacher. In some texts the guru is depicted as the poor ascetic and it is the duty of the student to beg for his teacher. The first lesson that was taught to the student was the performance of sandhya and also reciting of gayatri. The family functioned as a domestic school, an asrama or a hermitage where the mental faculties of the pupils were developed by the teacher's constant attention and personal instruction. Education treated as a matter of individual concern, did not admit of the method of mass production applicable in industry. The making of man was regarded as an artistic and not a mechanical process. Indeed, the aim of education was the developing of the pupil's personality, his innate and latent capacities. This view of education as a process of one's inner growth and self-fulfilment evolved its own technique, its rules, methods and practices.

The thinking principle, Manana Shakti was reckoned higher than the subject of thinking. So the primary subject of education was the mind itself. According to the ancient Indian theory of education, the training of the mind and the process of thinking, are essential for the acquisition of knowledge. The chase counts more than the game. So the pupil had mainly to educate himself and achieves his own mental growth. Education was reduced to the three simple processes of Sravana, Manana and Niddhyaasana. Sravana was listening to the truths as they fell from the lips of the teacher. Knowledge was technically called Sruti or what was heard by the ear and not what was seen in writing. The second process of knowledge called Manana implies that the pupil has to think out for himself the meaning of the lessons imparted to him orally by his teacher so that they may be assimilate fully. The third step known as Nidhyasana means complete comprehension by the pupil of the truth that is taught so that he may live the truth and not merely explain it by word. Knowledge must result in realization. The admission was made by the formal ceremony Upanayana or initiation by which the pupil left the home of his natural parents for that of the preceptor. In this new home he had a second birth and was called Dvijya or twice-born. Besides these regular schools of instructions, there were special institutions for the promotion of advance study and research. These are called in the Rig Veda as Brahmana-Sangha, Academies of learned most its discussions hammered into shape the very language of the country, the refined language of Sanskrit (Samkrata) as the Vehicle of highest thought. These Academics were called parisads, there is a reference to the Pancala parisad in the Upanishads, in whose proceedings even kings participated, learning was also prompted by discussions at public meetings which were a regular of rural life, and were addressed by wandering scholars known as Carakas, These scholars toured the country to deliver public discourses and invite discussion.

What might count as earliest literary congress of the world was the congress of philosophers which was codification of Brahmanical philosophy by discussing the subject under the direction of the master philosopher, Yajnavalkya. In these deliberations at the highest level, a lady-philosopher named Gargi was a prominent participant beside men like Uddalaka Arni. Obviously, in those days women were admitted to the highest knowledge and did not suffer from any education disabilities. There was equality between the sexes in the filed of knowledge. The Rig Veda mentions women Rais called Brahmanavadinis. To begin with, in ancient India; the main subject was the Veda. The teacher would instruct handful of students seated on ground. For many hours daily they would repeat verses after verses of the Vedas till they attain mastery of at least one of them. To ensure correctness of memory, the hymns were taught in more than one way. Soon the curriculum was expanded. The limbs of the Veda or the six Vedangas were taught-the performance of sacrifice, correct pronunciation, knowledge of prosody, etymology, grammer, and jyotisha or the science of calendar. Also in the post-Vedic era, teachers often instructed their students in the six schools of Philosophy.

The writers of Smritis maintain that young women of upper class under went this kind of training. This is a doubtful contention. Princes and other leading Kshatriyas were trained in all the manifold sciences to make them fit for government. Most boys of the lower orders learnt their trades from their fathers. Some cities became renowned because of their teachers. Chief among them were-Varanasi, Taxila from the day of Buddha and Kanchi in the beginning of the Christian era. Varanasi was famous for its religious teachers. Taxila was known for its secular studies. Among the famous men connected with Taxila was Panini, the grammarian of the fifth or fourth century B.C.: Kautilya, the Brahmin minister of Chandragupta Maurya and Charaka one of the two leading authorities of Indian medical sciences. The institutions imparting Vedic knowledge that exists even today. There were also universities like Taxila and Ujjain for medicine and learning including mathematics and astronomy respectively. In the south Kanchi became an important centre of learning. Hiuen Tsang remarks that Vallabhi was as great as Nalanda and Vikramashila.

Although the Smritis maintained that a small number of students study under a single teacher, university turned towns came into existence like Varanasi, Taxila etc. At Varanasi there were 500 students and a number of teachers. The whole establishment was maintained by charitable people. Ideally, the teacher asked no fee, but the students repaid his debt by their service to the teacher. A Jataka story tells of how a teacher of Taxila treated well the students who paid him money while keeping other waiting. It is also interesting to note that in Taxila even married people were admitted as students.

Out of all the Universities, Nalanda and imposed structures. Eight Colleges were built by different patterns including one by the king of Sri Vijaya (Sumatra). One of the colleges was four storeyed high as stated by Hiuen-Tsang. Every facility existed for studying various kinds of subjects in the University. There were three great libraries as per Tibetan records. Nalanda attracted students not only from different parts of India but also from Tibet and China. The standards of examination were stiff, and only those who could pass the test prescribed by the dvarapandita or the scholar at the gate were admitted to this university. Also, for being admitted to the university, candidates were required to be familiar with old and new books. Nalanda was one of the earliest examples of residential cum-teaching institutions which housed thousands of monks devoted to learning, philosophy and meditation. Over 10,000 students including teachers lived and studied at the university. They came from various parts of the world apart from India, Central Asia, China and Korea.

Though Nalanda was primarily a Buddhist university its curricula included Hindu scriptures, philosophy and medicine as recorded by Hiuen-Tsang. Logic and exegetics were pre-eminent because these students were expected to enter into dialogue with visiting doctors of all schools. This compulsion of public debate made both teachers and students become familiar with all systems of thought in accurate summary. The university had also succession of brilliant teachers. Dharmapala was a Tamil noble from Kanchi in the south. Janamitra come from another country. Silabhadra, the saintly guru of Hiuen-Tsang, came from Assam and he was a converted Brahmin. A great achievement of the University was that it was able to continuously rejuvenate Buddhism in far off countries. Tibetan records mention a succession of learned monks who visited their country. It is also said that Sudhakara Simha went to China and worked there on the translation of Buddhist texts.

Education in Contemporary India

The infrastructure of the Indian school system is built to accommodate the educational goals and objectives of a national curriculum which has been adopted by many states in the country. The educational system provides for three independent tracks of schooling and examination. The ICSE (Indian Certificate of Secondary Education) schooling is affordable by the upper class Indians; CBSE (Central Board of Secondary Examination) is for students from families whose members serve in the defense services and central government agencies, and those generally in jobs that periodically require them to relocate to neighbouring states; and, the SSLC (Secondary School Leaving Certificate) is for people from both the middle and lower class of the society.

Even though varying in syllabi from state to state, the Indian school system is generally organized into the 10+2+3 pattern. This means that every child who enrolls in formal education will undergo basic education for 10 years (beginning the schooling from age 6), followed by 2 years of pre-university education (the junction between high school and graduate college education). This is then followed by 3 years of graduate education leading to the award of the Bachelors degree in the specific area of specialization, which may be arts, humanities, science, or commerce. Some specialization subjects such as engineering or medicine, require the student to study for 5 years before they are evaluated and the degree is awarded. Most students pursue for their postgraduate education in the various fields of education, sciences, management, engineering, medicine, and the arts disciplines.

Students enrolled at the elementary through secondary school level in state government managed schools enjoy free education. Vocational education is a progressive opportunity for talented students; in fact, this is one of the many avenues to encourage and motivate the disinterested children, and dropouts, to become educationally and scientifically literate. Formal education is compulsory and free for all young children up to the secondary school level. Beyond secondary education, the government-both the state and central-make available a few scholarships for the needy and deserving students. There exists, though, stiff competition to obtain any form of scholarship.

However, not everything in contemporary India can be labelled as "smooth sailing". After all, like any other developing or developed nation in the world India too has its own share of disequilibrating problems. The phenomenon of "brain-drain" of India's talented citizens to developed countries is one of the many debilitating factors that has pressured the nation to a slow pace.

Another factor, though not exactly a debilitating factor, is the problem of advancing the goals of literacy among the economically and socially disadvantaged. Children who come under this category are those who do not-or are not encouraged (by their kith and kin, and friends) to-attend formal schooling; and, even if they do, they dropout midstream. Both effects have many causative underpinnings, and research is proceeding in various segments. Not all recommendations that are implemented result in success; one of the major lacunae toward planning in any area including education is faulty implementation of the recommendations. Even so, with a determination to modernize and upgrade the education and instructional facilities and function, "India must run in order to more than just stand still, but there is ample evidence of sprinting, demonstrating a national commitment to educational progress

The Characteristics and Demands of Teaching Profession

Paradoxically, following the 86th Amendment of the Constitution which makes it mandatory for the State (government) to provide free and compulsory education to all children in the six-14 age group, and national rollout of the Sarva Shiksha Abhiyaan (Education for All) programme, never before has teachers' morale been so critical to national development in this country blessed or cursed — informed opinion is divided — with the world's largest child population (415 million).

Unfortunately the rising tide of teacher discontent and disaffection is swelling at a time when an unprecedented shortage of teachers is manifesting across the country. Suddenly as government and private schools, colleges and universities are confronted with an unprecedented teacher shortage, alarm bells are ringing in Indian academia, even if not in the sleepy warrens of the education ministries in New Delhi and the state capitals. In Karnataka, 23,000 teaching posts in government primary and high schools are vacant; in benighted Bihar, teacher vacancies number 2.3 lakh. The Unesco Institute of Statistics in its report Teachers and Educational Quality: Monitoring Global Needs for 2015 released in June, says that to meet the Millennium Development Goal of providing elementary education to all children by 2015, "India will need the greatest inflow of new teachers in the world — more than 2 million".

It's an indicator of the depth of the growing teacher shortage slowly overtaking India that the bourgeoning private schools sector, which hitherto attracted a perennial supply of best and brightest teachers, is also experiencing a faculty crunch. According to www.schooljobs.in, India's pioneer online teacher recruitment portal, 500 vacancies have been notified by private schools during the past three months. Moreover the appointments pages of national newspapers are increasingly attracting teacher recruitment advertisements with one school sometimes advertising for 15-20 teachers. Gone are the days of principals of top schools such as Bishop Cotton, Bangalore, Doon School and Delhi Public School boasting about piles of unsolicited job applications from highly experienced teachers on their desks. Today, for the first time ever, jobs are chasing teachers, rather than the other way round.

"Though government schools always had the problem of unfilled teacher vacancies because of budgetary problems, it's perhaps for the first time that private schools are confronted with an acute teacher shortage. This is largely because post-liberalisation, with the huge demand for people in the IT and BPO (business process outsourcing) sector, the number of young people entering the teaching profession has decreased dramatically. Moreover post 1991, India has witnessed a sharp uptrend in the promotion of private schools. These institutions which specifically cater to the aspirations of the country's growing middle class are mushrooming at a fast rate and have created an unprecedented demand surge for well-qualified teachers. But while the demand for teachers has shot up, supply has declined. According to a research, India needs 800,000 new teachers every year for the next three years if it's to make up the shortfall and cater to new student enrollments.

Indeed mushrooming private schools across the price spectrum is arguably the single most important factor contributing to the national teacher shortage crisis. Academic estimates indicate that the number of private schools in India has leapt from 50,000 in 1996 to 77,140 in 2006. In this meteoric growth trajectory, the rash of five-star 'international' schools springing up countrywide has attracted great public and media attention (India currently boasts over 100 international schools). Though these highly capital-intensive schools — which offer sprawling playing fields and sports facilities, wired classrooms, five-star residential accommodation and cuisine, and affiliations with the best national and international examination boards at annual tuition fees ranging from Rs.1-6 lakh — offer much better pay packets and working conditions to teachers than traditionally top-ranked CBSE and CISCE affiliated private schools, they too are encountering considerable difficulty in recruiting and retaining qualified teachers. The groves of academia are buzzing with stories of 'body snatching' of teachers by international schools — particularly principals' — emoluments beginning to match corporate salaries.

According to Anu Monga, principal of Bangalore International School (no. of teachers: 60; student enrolment: 250) and chairperson of the The Association of International Schools of India (TAISI). "International schools countrywide are experiencing a scarcity of competent teachers. Since international curriculums demand highly qualified and well-trained faculty, it's becoming increasingly difficult for schools to deliver internationally acceptable education without talented and committed teachers. We are aware of the unethical ways in which some international school managements are luring teachers from competitor schools. Therefore TAISI has decided to evolve a code of conduct for members with regard to recruiting teachers from member schools. But if international schools want to really reduce teacher attrition they must pay greater attention to continuous teacher training and development. Their focus has to be on motivating and retaining young professionals as teachers."

Although emerging teacher body snatching wars and unprecedented pay packages for the competent have prompted much head shaking and tuttutting among leftists and traditional academics, the entry of internationally benchmarked schools into the education sector has served the useful purpose of endowing the teaching profession with new social respectability. By awarding teachers superior working conditions, opportunities to use creative teaching methodologies, uncrowded classrooms, continuous teacher development programmes and most important, pay packets ranging from Rs.20,000-50,000 per month, the country's 100-plus international schools have made teaching a more attractive and profitable profession. And encouragingly there's a distinct possibility that the most idealistic — even if not the best and brightest — graduates of the country's 344 universities and 17,700 colleges may re-evaluate teaching as a career.

Promoters of the rash of five-star international schools offering leisure-resort style, landscaped, fully-wired campuses bristling with hi-tech equipment and teaching aids, have been brought down to earth with the growing awareness that the unique selling proposition of high-end academic institutions is excellent faculty, rather than luxurious infrastructure. Pressure from upmarket parents paying chastening fees of Rs.1-6 lakh per year upon managements to make good their promise of delivering a 21st century international education is beginning to tell. Consequently, faculty raids popularly known as body snatching have become de rigueur within the esoteric world of India's estimated 100 international and 9,500 upscale private schools. The rapid turnover of teachers in international schools is particularly painful for their high networth promoters as teacher training for international school curriculums —IGCSE and/ or the International Baccalaureate diploma — is very expensive. For instance the IB teacher-training programme averages Rs.25,000 per teacher and IGCSE Rs.15,000. Therefore the flight of a trained teacher is an expensive loss.

Yet better pay packets apart, a contributory cause of accelerated teacher migration from the new genre of capital-intensive five-star schools is the authoritarian command-control management style of first generation school promoters, usually businessmen-turned educationists. "This new generation of promoters not only lacks institutional management and teaching experience, they also tend to be too hands-on and interfere in everything from curriculum development, extra-curricular activities to classroom teaching styles. Experienced teachers and principals with numerous job options can't stomach this," says a Mumbai-based education consultant.

This newly emergent friction between promoters and high-profile headmasters is exemplified by the recent career graph of Dev Lahiri, former headmaster of Lawrence School, Lovedale. Following his exit from Lawrence Lovedale reportedly for refusing to toe the line of former Union HRD minister Dr. Murali Manohar Joshi, Lahiri was appointed the first principal of the upscale Selaqui School, Dehra Dun in 2003, which he quit, complaining about the ubiquitous presence of promoter Om Pathak on the school campus. The same year he signed up as principal of Kolkata's The Heritage School, which he quit again pleading irreconcilable differences with the promoter. Currently Lahiri is headmaster of the tried and tested 69-year-old Welham Boys School, Dehra Dun.

Certainly within the hitherto socially under-rated teachers community there is rising enthusiasm about the new developments in school education. Bangalore-based Preeti Vincent, a maths teacher who resigned from the Indus International School in 2004 to sign up with Bangalore International School, confirms that the emergence of international schools has changed the popular perception that teaching is a low-skills profession. Moreover it has given India's long-neglected teachers community a booster shot of new hope and excitement. "International schools value and recognise competent teachers, offer the best remuneration in the market and pay great attention to continuous teacher development and training with some of them even sending teachers abroad for training. However although the new international schools have redefined the role of teachers, very few involve them in curriculum development and decision making. Doing so is vital to motivating and retaining them.

Inevitably the prime target group of international schools and head hunting firms are under-paid teachers in the country's 8,097 CBSE and 1,502 CISCE affiliated schools. Given that even in the most highly-rated English medium schools, annual remuneration packages average a modest Rs.80,000-120,000, teachers from these schools are flocking to international schools where twice this pay is common. This teacher exodus to five-star schools has forced CISCE and CBSE schools to raise pay and incentives to retain their most experienced faculty who are being targeted — often harassed — for recruitment.

But if despite substantially improved pay packages and service conditions, private schools in India are experiencing an accelerating teacher shortage, this is a global phenomenon. Most western countries, especially the US and UK, are also reporting rising teacher vacancies -- particularly of maths, science and English teachers. In the US there are an estimated 22,000 vacancies for school teachers. Therefore the emerging teacher crisis in private schools in India is also connected with intensifying recruitment of private school (government school teachers are an altogether different genre) teachers by school managements and local governments in these countries. Currently there are over 25,000 secondary school teachers from India abroad.

The emerging shortage of teachers is not peculiar to upmarket independent schools. Even schools at the bottom of the private education pyramid are complaining of teachers being lured away by the BPO industry and other sectors of the economy. These mostly English-medium unaided schools which comprise the largest group in the private school sector catering to children from lower middle class families, are affiliated with state examination boards and charge annual tuition fees ranging between Rs.5,000-10,000. Since they keep tuition fees low and affordable, teacher salaries are abysmal by 21st century standards — typically between Rs.3,000-5,000 per month. The BPO industry, which is growing at 56 percent every year and offers start-up monthly remuneration of Rs.10,000-15,000, has been quick to discern this unhappiness over pay and working

Yet if private schools are experiencing teacher shortages for the first time in post-independence India for demand-pull reasons, their problems — and ability to resolve them — pale into insignificance when compared with faculty shortages in the country's estimated 1,000,000 government-run primary and secondary schools. By a curious and typically Indian anomaly, government school teachers enjoy 30-50 percent higher pay than private school teachers. But even with teachers' pay pegged at above market price, for years the country's Central and state governments which are running huge fiscal deficits have neglected to appoint additional teachers. Consequently most of the 31 states of the Indian Union have thousands of teacher vacancies in government schools. In Uttar Pradesh 61,437 teachers' posts are vacant, in Karnataka 13,500 new teachers need to be appointed, while in Bihar there's a massive deficit of 2.3 lakh teachers.

Fortunately because of public pressure to meet the target of the Sarva Shiksha Abhiyaan (Education for All campaign) which was launched in 2001 and followed by the Right to Education Bill, 2006 that guarantees free education to every child between six and 14 years, state governments have been compelled to make provision for recruiting new.

Yet perhaps the most disturbing fallout of the creeping teacher shortage nationwide is crowded classrooms and single teacher schools. India already boasts one of the highest teacher pupil ratios in the world: 1:60 (according to World Bank data) and over 200,000 government schools have only one teacher who conducts multigrade classes simultaneously. Consequently poor learning outcomes which is a defining characteristic of Indian education is certain to remain an unresolved problem. "In some states like Bihar and Uttar Pradesh the teacher-pupil ratio is 1:62. To halve this ratio or at least reduce it to a more manageable 1:40, we need to aggressively recruit teachers. While para teachers are good as a stopgap arrangement, they should be replaced by regular well-trained teachers.

Against this backdrop of the bewildering mess which has been made of the chronically under-provided education system, it's hardly surprising that India's youth are reluctant to enter the teaching profession — synonymous with shabby, crowded classrooms; dilapidated infrastructure (toilets, water, libraries, laboratories), unsympathetic parents and lack of social respect. "Regrettably teaching no longer attracts committed and talented young people. It's right at the bottom in the hierarchy of professions. If we want to attract talented youth into the profession, teaching needs a complete makeover. It has to be repackaged as a stimulating, interesting and well-paying profession. You can't pay a teacher as much as you pay your domestic help and hope to provide quality education.

Yet at bottom, India's pernicious teacher shortage crisis is a problem of quality, rather than quantity. The country's estimated 20,000 teacher training institutions (including government and private sector Montessori, D.Ed, B.Ed and M.Ed colleges) which churn out 300,000 teaching graduates every year, are lumbered with outdated curriculums delivered by de-motivated faculty. "In terms of the number of B.Ed postgraduates, India has a sufficient annual output. But how many of them are sufficiently trained to be effective in their classrooms, is the moot point. Ninety percent of B.Ed postgrads are under-qualified and need further training before they can be allowed to handle classes independently.

The upshot of all this is that in the final analysis, with the 86th Amendment to the Constitution having endowed all of India's estimated 375 million children aged six to 14 years free and compulsory education, the Central and state governments have no option but to re-order their spending priorities and raise their combined annual education outlay from the current 3.5 percent of GDP to 6 percent as was presciently recommended by the Kothari Commission in 1966.

Even as post-independence India's establishment stands indecisive at a historic crossroads in the new millennium, the education system is in the throes of an unprecedented crisis characterised by enormous teacher shortages, crumbling institutional infrastructure and deplorable learning outcomes. If a radical re-ordering of national spending priorities is not undertaken expeditiously, India's much-trumpeted demographic dividend could soon morph into a demographic disaster.

Teacher Education in India: An Auxiliary Perspective

India is a vast heterogeneous country in terms of culture, environment, language and the genealogical diversity of the people. Heterogeneity has, therefore, resulted in diverse educational goals. A majority of the schoolage population (approximately 70%) consider schooling to be merely a literary program i.e., reading, writing, arithmetic; 5% utilize education for its ascribed status. An important 25% pursue education for a career or simply to earn a living in a world that places a high degree of importance on academic status. It is basically this 25% of the student population which happens to exploit all opportunities the system has to offer. Innovations, modernization and improvements in schooling has had a positive impact. That a majority of India's school children are on the periphery of educational modernization is an ethical issue for which one cannot provide easy solutions.

Renewed Innovative Endeavours

Toward improving the quality of teacher education in India during the seventh Five Year Plan (1986-1990), many innovative endeavours were (and continue to be) enthusiastically pursued. These innovative efforts could be broadly classified as: 1. National endeavours, and 2. Regional endeavours. Following are the highlights of each.

National Endeavours

During 1986, the Department of Education under the Ministry of Human Resource Development (MHRD) made a national effort especially involving many classroom practitioners, in documenting the National Policy on Education (NPE) (MHRD, 1986a). Among the major thrust areas was teacher education. Emphasizing the usefulness of educational technology, the innovative use of satellite instruction television programs and the PMOST (Programme of Massive Orientation to School Teachers) at both the elementary and secondary levels were launched from 1985-1987, and continues to be popular among many educators across the country. The educational responsibilities at the national level by the central government's department of education are activated through specific organisations such as:

(a) The National Council for Educational Research and Training (NCERT). The organisation conducts research, pre-and in-service teacher education programs throughout the country;

(b) The National Council of Teacher Education (NCTE). Under the aegis of specific Task Force groups, both the NCERT and NCTE network at the organisational and academic levels to increase the participation of the regional centers. The priority areas in each Task Force have been detailed in the Policy (synonymous with Programme) of Action (POA) (MHRD, 1986b). The POAs are documents that serve as a guideline for all regional educational endeavours;

(c) The National Council for Women's Education (NCWE). This organisation promotes programs to encourage women to pursue education at all levels-formal, informal and non-formal. Working with the regional centers, the NCWE has made significant strides and has been quite successful in its efforts to provide a complete education to girls even beyond the secondary school and graduate levels; (d) All India Council for Technical Education (AICTE). This organisation concerns itself with the development and implementation of effective technical education programs in the country; and,

(e) The National Council for Science Education (NCSE). Along with the other organisations, the NCSE works to enhance and promote the quality of science and technology education. "Science and technology have in fact assumed so much importance that while individuals look for scientific solutions to even their day-to-day problems, nations depend upon an adequate number of technical personnel for overall development" (Anand, 1983).

In addition, the central board of education promotes the pursuit of vocational education especially among the physically and mentally handicapped. Special education programs are often a part of the elementary, secondary, graduate and postgraduate teacher education curriculum. Educational technology and innovate methods in teacher education and science education has received considerable attention from the

Central Institute of Educational Technology (CIET), the State Institute of Technology (SIET), and regional Technical Teachers' Training Institutes (TTTI). Mukhopadyay (1985) has detailed a superior documentary on the subject; summarizing the content of the publication is beyond the scope of this article.

Regional Endeavours

Unlike the NCERT, the endeavours of such state and regional level organisations as the State Educational Research and Training (SERT) and the District Institutes of education and Training (DIET) are more specific. The endeavours are pragmatic and directionally oriented toward the dissemination of tested and effective classroom practices; testing, evaluation and implementation of successful teaching-learning techniques; and other application-oriented ideas through pre-and in-service workshops for both elementary and secondary school teachers.

For instance, in the area of methods of teaching the functional aspects of many didactic models are brought together into an eclectic presentation. Some models that are considered include inquiry synectics, advance organizers, jurisprudence, principles of cooperative learning and problem solving, discrepant events, and so forth. Thus, in the place of a single approach to instruction, an extracted combination of effective approaches that are well-linked in terms of predetermined educational goals-for example, to be able to address a diverse audience of learners who exhibit different methods and speeds of learning-continues to be extensively practised in the country's classrooms and teacher education colleges. 'Model Blend' is the term that was given to this eclectic approach to instruction. In current educational parlance, this is known as 'instructional module', and it has been a successful innovation at the teacher education level. Indeed, the effectiveness of instructional modules at the Bachelor of Education (B.Ed.) degree level has been amply established by research.

Education, a Sub-system of the Social System

Education is a sub-system in the wider social system. Although it has a separate identity and, upto a limited degree, functions autonomously, it has linkages with the economic, political, religious, and other sub-systems which exert powerful influence on the goals and instrumentalities of the educational subsystem on the one hand and on its autonomy on the other. The economic sector has to find funds for education, for the later can rarely pay its own way. Power interests define and redefine the goals of education and from time to time seek to assign to it new instrumental rules. In several parts of the world education has cut its umbilical cord placed in religion, yet denominational institutions still continue, and otherwise also religion plays a role in determining the ideological overtones of at least some components of education. Education can rarely free itself from social and cultural norms and has to relate itself to the ferments within the society. The state of health of one sub-system casts its shadows on the health of the other. In this respect education is especially vulnerable; while its intrinsic worth is universally recognized, it is also subject to many diverse pressures because of the multiplicity of instrumental roles that it is called upon to play. It has to deal with something of a paradox when on the one hand it has to transmit the cultural heritage and tradition, and on the other, has to function as a prime mover of change. In point of fact, the educational subsystem is not the only agency offering education, to begin with, the domestic group, the neighbourhood, and the peer group have important educational roles and the educational process continues beyond the formal school stage through books, mass media, cultural, political, and religious intercourse, and interpersonal contacts of a wide variety. The formal education system has to take account of early socialisation and has to anticipate future educational processes.

Qualities of a Good Teacher

1. *Confidence:* Belief in ourselves despite setbacks. Teachers encounter situations all the time that could be considered setbacks. Kids can be cruel, to each other and to teachers. They can have attitudes, especially teenagers. I've had teachers to were obviously nervous when they taught. Others were shy and only half

committed to their subject. But the best teachers laughed off their mistakes: chalk breaking, books dropped, VCRs not working. Where some teachers were flustered, the good teachers shrugged and went on about the lesson, sometimes even joking about the mess up. These teachers knew they were human and knew mistakes happen. They didn't take things personally and let problems get them upset.

2. *Patience*: Some of my best teachers could have helped students through a mental breakdown. Not that they had to, but that they were so patient, they could have gone the distance. Many a time I, or classmate, would just not be "getting" a particular concept. My best teachers were those who were willing to keep explaining, knowing that eventually it would make sense. They were willing to wait until a distraction calmed students down, or abandon a lesson entirely if it was clear material needed to be revisited. The best teachers just stuck with it, willing to do what it took, no matter how long it took.

3. *True Compassion for Their Students:* I'm sure we've all encountered a bad teacher who didn't care what our excuse was. Certainly, some excuses weren't valid, but many were. The best teachers cared about their students as individuals and wanted to help them. They had a sixth sense when a student needed extra attention and gave it gladly. They didn't expect students to leave thoughts of the outside world at the door to the classroom. They took the time to discuss subjects outside their teaching, knowing that sometimes lessons can still be taught without following the textbook. Good teachers were willing to speak up for us to other teachers, if need be. They cared about us beyond the walls of their classroom.

4. *Understanding:* Good teachers had understanding-not only the sixth sense mentioned above, but true understanding of how to teach. They didn't have a rigid technique that they insisted on using even if it didn't

help us learn. They were flexible in their teaching style, adapting daily if need be. They understood the little things that affected our ability to learn; the weather, the temperature in the classroom, the time of day. They had an understanding of human nature and the maturity (or lack thereof) of teenagers. Good teachers knew that we hated to be called "young" and therefore pre-judged. They treated us as real people, not just "students."

5. *The Ability to Look At:* life in a different way and to explain a topic in a different way. There are many different learning styles. Not everyone gets a subject as taught by every teacher. I've taken subjects (chemistry for instance) many times, at many different levels, by many different teachers. I took College Organic Chemistry three times from three different teachers. I can tell you from experience that it was more the skill of the third teacher than the third time taking the class that allowed me to pass. Bad teachers only look a subject matter one way. They teach based on how they learn. This works for some people, but fails for others. The good teachers are ones that are able to teach to different learning styles. If students don't understand a subject, they teach it a different way. Instead of looking at abstract formulas, they explain with images what the formulas represent. This requires a through understand of their subject, as well as the ability to consider that subject in different ways, which not all teachers are able to do.
6. *Dedication to Excellence:* Good teachers want the best from their students and themselves. They don't settle for poor grades, knowing it reflects upon their ability to teach just as much upon a student's ability to excel. The best teachers encourage the sharing of ideas and offer incentives (like not having to do homework for a day) to get students to think outside the box. They don't tolerate students' badmouthing other teachers, doing their best to point out that other teachers are human

too. They encourage students to be good people, not just good memorizers of text. They want students to learn and be able to apply what they learned, not just be able to pass tests.

7. *Unwavering Support:* The best teachers know that everyone is able to do well if they have the right teacher. They don't accept that a student is a lost cause. They encourage if you are frustrated and provide true belief that you can get the material. They stand up for individuals against other students, not allowing for in class taunting. Sometimes, they even extend this outside the classroom, although taunts in the hallways are very hard for teachers to combat. The best teachers are there if you need extra help and even encourage it.
8. *Willingness to Help Student Achieve:* The best teachers are those that don't stop teaching when the bell rings. They hold extra sessions for SAT prep, they reach out to students after class. They know that some need extra attention or assistance, and they don't act like it's not their job. They take that job seriously and know they aren't just employed to get students to be able to do higher math, but do well in life. They realize that achievement isn't just a good grade on a test, but a feeling of accomplishment with mastering a subject; they are willing to work with a student for that feeling.
9. *Pride in Student's Accomplishments:* The best teachers let you know they are glad you got a good grade or made the honour's society. They smile and tell you that you did a good job. They tell other teachers about how you did as well. Outside you may feel embarrassed, but inside you are glowing. The best teachers don't single out the best students either. They celebrate the accomplishments of everyone, knowing that everyone is capable to doing well. They are upbeat and positive, focusing on how a student did well, not how well they taught. They may know that it was the strength of their teaching that helped a student to achieve, but they act as if the student is completely responsible.

10. *Passion for Life:* The best teachers aren't just interested in their subject, they are passionate about it. They are also passionate about many other things. They praise good weather and smile when they take a few minutes to discuss last night's episode of a popular TV show. They have a energy that almost makes them glow and that you want to emulate as much as possible. They approach tasks with a sense of challenge rather than routine. They take the universe's curve balls and turn them into fun (if possible). They are human, certainly, but they make you feel that there is always a reason to keep going. Things will get better no matter how much they appear to suck at that moment.

Ability of a Teacher

A. Organizer – in the classroom involves the careful organisation of tasks and activities that the learners are to be engaged in, direct the learners in the roles and tasks they will undertake, to tell the students exactly what they need to do and how they should do it.

B. Guide – having organized the activity and instructed the learners as to their roles, you will remain discreetly on hand to act as a guide in case some learners do not fully understand the exercise.

C. Motivation – you may find that some learners are resistant to the type of learning that you would like them to engage in. You will be sometimes called upon motivate the learners and to get them interested in the activity.

D. Monitor – the teacher will often have to act as monitor, just like being alert on what's going on in the classroom.

E. Assessor – checking and deciding when and how to give feedback.

F. Tutor-on a one to one basis, giving individual attention, guidance and helping students to learn more efficiently.

G. Facilitator – to encourage students to communicate with each other.

H. Controller – being in complete control of the class.

The Changing Teacher-Taught Scenario

The teacher and the taught represent the two most significant components of the educational sub-system. Over the decades the class base of both has changed. Second and first generation learners are now flooding the institutions of learning. They bring with them a variety of problems with which the existing pedagogy cannot cope.

First, in increasing number, teachers are drawn from groups which do not have a tradition of literacy and learning. The social background and cultural orientations of the learners and their instructors pose a new set of problems to the educational process.

Second, education has now been brought within the orbit of the demand for social justice and is claimed as a matter of right. Coping with the demand for equality of educational opportunity is difficult enough; but when the demand for equality of results is added to it, the problem becomes infinitely more complex.

Third, education cannot be inflexible in respect of its ideology and content and has to be responsive to the urges and demands of different sectors impinging on it. A series of questions arise in this context: What do the guardians expect from the education of their wards? What are the perceptions of learners from different strata regarding the objectives and methods of education? How do different interests in society exert visible and invisible pressures on the educational system to tilt its advantages towards them? What are the latent and manifest functions that the elite, which supports the educational system, expects it to perform?

Fourth, what about the unintended consequences of education? How are these, to be managed so that they do not become dysfunctional to the larger objectives of society? These, questions are important and feeble-minded handling of them pushes the educational system into a state of disarray. Adequate answer to them have to be found so that the educational system, being sensitive and vulnerable to them, does not lose its sense of direction and purpose.

Finally, in many countries of the 'Third World,' education is viewed as an aspect of power and even of profit. The implications of the power and profit motive in the organised educational endeavour have not been examined sufficiently and in depth. If the educational system is moving like a massive but rudderless ship, it is because some of these critical issues have either not been faced or faced halfheartedly. Much of the value chaos in the contemporary educational system can be attributed to this failure. The world-view and value constellations of the teachers in India today present a series of ambiguous and blurred images and contradictory and conflicting values.

World-View and Values

In this context 'world-view' is taken to mean the summation of the shared outlook of a society regarding the past, present, and future of the human order and Its components. It takes account of both qualitative and quantitative dimensions, it attributes or assumes quality in the elements of the order and its processes and often tends to translate quantity into quality. It may also evaluate quality into aggregate quantity terms. Basic questions with which it is concerned are those of relative primacy of principles over persons, of natural (including social) over super-natural order, and of man-made objectives and conditions over non-man-made objective and subjective conditions. Thus, a consideration of world-view implies assumptions regarding what the human order was in the past and why, what it is now and why, and what it would be in the future and why. It may also envisage conscious intervention to set desirable sailing direction so that human destinies can be controlled and piloted towards a preferred and desired future. By value we shall mean a preference quality in action. Values have normative overtones, but they often lack the sanctions that go with social norms. They attribute quality to different modes of behaviour along a continuum—from the most desired to the least desired (and also the undesired). They may be explicit or implicit and there may be a significant gap between the ultimate and the proximate values. In proximate terms, the choices may be situational and pragmatic although they, may be at variance from the ultimate desired action, which may continue to be articulated and cherished. They form a part of the cognitive universe and encompass within them aesthetic and evaluative elements. They provide guides to behaviour without being rigidly prescriptive. Often there is a hierarchy of values and the permissible range allows different levels of choices. Some values may be universal to a society, others may be specific to particular groups and categories. Nonetheless, a social order cannot be conceptualised without a scheme of values. In reference to teachers it may be asserted that while they will share some general societal values they are likely also to have a set of values which are specific to their professional category and its cultural role definition.

Desired World-View of Teachers

In the grim context of today's India, it would be useful to start with an inventory of the elements of world-view and values, which are considered desirable and necessary in those who belong to the-teaching profession. We shall examine later how far the existing reality approximates to this normative model. Absence of a fit between the two will necessitate deep causal analysis and indications of possible remedial action. For a country of India's cultural heterogeneity, social complexity, economic inequalities, and ideological differentiations, unanimity in respect of all values is not possible nor perhaps even desirable. 'The area of personal belief has therefore to be omitted from this discussion. However, a consensus is needed on some premises and in respect of some core socio-political as well as academic values. Let us first list some of the desired elements of the world-view of teachers as a category.

- First, principles should have primacy over persons. This should be based on some universal norms as against particular considerations of status and station or considerations of caste, class or sex.
- Second, in the scheme of social action the accent should be on rationality rather than on obscurantism. Super-natural powers should at best feature in personal beliefs and their hold on arenas of public policy and action

should be gradually minimized and ultimately eliminated. Creative rationality should emerge as the key force.

- Third, man should be viewed as capable of gaming mastery over the physical universe. In exploiting its resources, however, man should recognize some outer limits and in the process, he should not destroy the delicate harmony and balance of nature.
- Fourth, the necessity of freedom for all human beings has been theoretically established. A subjective ethos and objective conditions for the realization of genuine freedom, however, remain to be established,
- Fifth, freedom without equality makes little sense. Equality of creative expression is a must not only for individuals but for their collectivities of different orders. Grant of equality should not be reduced to a ritual act; conditions conducive to its realization must be consciously promoted.
- Sixth, cultural differences persist and will continue to persist for they have deep-rooted functions. There should be no cause for alarm. In fact, they, may even be, maximized; what need to be minimized are economic disparities and cultural deprivations.
- Seventh, man is a product of history, but in many significant ways, he has also been its author. An increasing interventionist role should be envisioned for him, if for nothing else, for his own survival. Henceforth, lie shall have to learn to define his role as an architect of his destiny.

Values rooted in personal belief can be left out of consideration so long as they do not clash with national and social values that need to be promoted, urgently. The fact that individually held values get, directly or indirectly, consciously or sub-consciously, projected on the educational scene and into educational offerings, does not need to be reiterated.

Democracy, secularism, and social justice have been enshrined in the Constitution as the three most important national values. One car legitimately have some doubt about the honesty of such articulation and indeed the approach towards their realisation can be faulted on many scores, but there can be little, doubt that on the awareness level, they have been accepted as core values and enjoy a consensus at least among large sections of the elite. It is difficult to estimate how far they have percolated down to common citizens. Ritualistic acceptance of these values by the teachers will not do these must inform and inspire their teaching. The concept of the autonomous individual must be expanded with reference to his rights and obligations. The class room itself should become an example of a participative community. It is possible for one to be secular in profession and non-secular in practice. Such 'duplicity must be exposed and genuine secular habits of thought and action promoted. Faith in social justice would necessitate debunking of all discriminatory practices based on ethnic or caste considerations', religion or sex. The gospel of egalitarianism is much more than mouthing some high-minded slogans. An attitude of caring for and sharing with the deprived and the underprivileged, need to be inculcated. If one accepts social justice as a value, one should learn to be appalled by the enormity of injustice meted to various section and categories of the community everyday and protest about it. The acceptance of these core values should be judged not by their formal enunciation but by the praxis they generate.

To these three, let us consider adding three more national values in our general scheme of values there is emphasis on past-present orientation; instead, the shift should be towards a present-future orientation. This does riot imply negation of history, but it certainly involves rejection of harking back to the past more often than is really necessary. What concerns us most in existential terms is the living present and to-be-lived future. For the baffling problems of present, history may have new answers; new maladies re-quire new remedies. These must represent a creative response to the challenges that we face today. At the same time it is necessary that in solving today's problems we do not morgage the future. Options that offer temporary relief today but endanger human survival a few decades later are no solutions it is important, thus, that we examine the problems of today in a present-future perspective. The second value that is to be added involves the rejection of the passivity principle. Servility and compliance have to be ruled out. The autonomous individual is an active individual. His consciousness should be extended to enable him to critically examine the goings on in society and to judge the rights and wrongs of it. He should riot stop at judging, he must learn to do something about the rectification of the wrongs. The third related value has a hearing on the cultivation of what has been called the scientific temper. The overt and convert dimensions of this temper need to be worked out meticulously.

Despite the erosion of his influence, the teacher continues to be an opinion leader of considerable power. His faith in these core values is necessary if the younger generation is riot to start on a shaky foundation of beliefs, misbeliefs and disbeliefs.

Teacher as Professionals and their Professional Ethics

Acquisition, Transmission and Addition of New Knowledge

In the knowledge industry, especially in the teaching profession, one has to acquire and also add to fund of existing knowledge. The teachers additionally have to transmit knowledge to the successive generations of students who come under their mentorship. A good teacher, thus, has to equip himself with the major growth points in his speciality or sub-speciality, demonstrate adequate communicational skills to transmit the knowledge he has acquired, and continuously strive through his research endeavours to create new knowledge. Ideally a balance has to be struck between acquisition, transmission, and addition. This calls for a passionate devotion to knowledge in these three dimensions.

For a teacher, acquisition of knowledge alone would be a selfish and unproductive pursuit if it is not followed up by the transmission function. Teaching is not to be viewed as a mechanical process. It is not enough to tell the students what one knows about a subject. There is an element of high creativity in teaching. The plus factor requires creation of enquiring and questioning minds. A competent teacher would not promote excessive dependence of the students on the teacher; instead, he would generate a self-learning and group learning processes. Routine teaching gets an element of inspiration when the individual research of the teacher and his instructional role get organically linked. Through this process a good teacher gets to be a better teacher, if not always an inspired teacher. Creativity thus emerges as a central value in the teaching profession.

Social Relevance

Knowledge in itself is important, but at some stage one has to ask the question: knowledge for what? Knowledge, thus, has to be socially relevant and useful. To invest a social purpose into education, the teaching-learning process must aim at sharpening the problem-solving capabilities of the learners. Socially useful knowledge will therefore involve coming to grips with the pressing problems of the day as well as their multidimensional causal analysis and possible pathways for their solution. Application orientation will have to be accepted as a value, if the ideal of creative teaching is accepted.

Extension-organic Links with Community

The notion of a scholar leading a cloistered or ivory tower existence, devoting oneself only to reflection 'and research, is dated. Extension is now regarded as an important aspect of the educational process. The isolation of the academic, thus, has to be broken. He must develop organic linkages with the community. In a simplified form his knowledge should become a part of the cognitive universe of the common people and more than that, this knowledge should contribute to improving the quality of life around him. It is erroneous to believe, that the academic 'Knows best in which areas of knowledge he should reflect and carry out his investigations. Organic linkages with the people will bring useful feedback and provide the academic with new perspectives that will equip him better to determine the themes for reflection and research. A shift from individual-centred research and study to people-oriented academic endeavours is indicated. If knowledge and its gains have to have a wide spread, this has, to be incorporated as a central value of the teaching profession.

Irrelevance of Some Knowledge and so Continuous Renovation and Innovation

The criterion of relevance necessarily brings us to a consideration of the irrelevance of some knowledge. The size of knowledge industry being what it is, knowledge is growing at a very fast pace. It is now said to double itself every five years. This brings us to a knotty problem; what was good and useful teaching twenty years ago may be out dated and practically useless today. The teacher has to make some critical and effective choices; the deadwood of knowledge has to be chopped off and modern, uptodate and relevant knowledge emphasized. Continuous renovation and innovation in the knowledge field, thus, emerges as an important value. A good teacher can never rest on his oars; mentally be has continuously to be on the move.

Decolonisation of the Third World Mind

A related point needs, consideration here. Perceptive observers of the academic scene in the Third World have noticed that the academia in these countries suffers from a captive mind syndrome. A decolonization process of the minds of the academics has not seriously been taken in hand. Standards of scholarship are set by high prestige centres of learning abroad and much of Third World scholarship emulates it, The attitude of our scholars is one of servile adoption.

In consequence, our recognition and reward system is distorted. There is evidence of quest for chasing "international standards", which may be meaningless in our own national context. Decolonisation of our academic life, therefore, should emerge as a value. This is not a plea for raising iron or bamboo curtains or for barring the free flow of knowledge internationally. What is indicated is the reed for cautious thought geared to promoting an intellectual tradition that emphasizes posing of right and relevant questions and devising methods of finding answers to them efficiently 'and economically. This task has to be incorporated in the value system of our academics.

Cultivation of Excellence

The central value of academic life must be the cultivation of excellence. This fact is implicit in the foregoing argument. Excellence is an attractive and easy term, but so far it has been poorly defined. Accepting cultivation of excellence as a core value, we must proceed to define it precisely and work out a set of indicators that leave little room for equivocation and doubt.

Freedom and Responsibility

A propitious climate for true academic growth requires freedom of enquiry. The operating culture of academic life, when burdened with authoritarian management and bureaucratic procedures, inhibits the growth of ideas and corrodes the cultivation of excellence. Little thought appears to have been given so far to evolving a suitable philosophy of management of the academic enterprise. Such a philosophy would permit the individual academic freedom to question, to doubt, to dissent, and to deny. At the same time, this freedom cannot divest itself from social responsibility.

Importance of Freedom to Work Together

Great spurts in knowledge require concentration of ideas and collaboration of effort. The contribution of lone workers has been significant but major breakthroughs at the present state of knowledge will be possible only if teams pursue problems in harmonious working relationship. This brings us to two important values —one, freedom of enquiry, and two, fostering a true team spirit for the attainment of stipulated scientific objectives.

Critical Awareness and Articulation of the Tradition

Men of knowledge, of necessity, are transmitters of the heritage. This function cannot be questioned. However, orientation to the heritage may differ and the explicit or implicit purposes for which it is transmitted may also not be the same.

The core 'value in this context will therefore emphasize critical awareness and articulation of the tradition.

A Social Consciousness to Undertake Social Criticism

Finally, the academic is not a passive observer of the social scene. Whatever his speciality or subspeciality, he is also an analyst social trends. The analyses have an evaluative dimension. He has of necessity to emerge as a critic of society—its trends and processes. His criticism will be worthless if it is only negative in character. An academic with a social consciousness will also illuminate pathways to progressive action. A social consciousness unafraid to undertake social criticism, thus, has to be emphasised as a Value.

Problem Solving Approach and Emergence of New Social Order

The world-view and value system outlined in the foregoing pages represent a somewhat idealistic conceptualisation, but it is not the projection of an unrealizable utopia. An elite sector, such as the one represented by the teachers, has to function as the prime mover and, pace setter of change. Unless it defines its goal and performs its role with conscious determination, society at large is likely to surrender itself to the negative forces at work. Exertions of the academic profession in the right direction bold out hopes not only of problem-solving but also of the emergence of a new social order.

Problems in Teacher Education: Suggestions to Remedy the Problems

Making of a teacher differs significantly from making, say, of an advocate or a surgeon. The teacher is more than a mere skilled performer in a branch of his profession. Of course, he must have the best of skill in accustoming the pupil to the austere joy of mastering a difficult theme, be it quadratic equation or the, equation E-MC ^{2} or any other theme. But, in the end, when the frontiers of knowledge change, the importance and even the validity of what is learnt may not survive. What survives is the discipline of learning and the values acquired in the process. Whatever be the topic a teacher teaches, the ultimate values of his professional endeavour bear on the habits, of living and thinking and enjoying life, the art of life-on what the pupil loves and, cares for. Thus the teacher fashions the life of the pupil-which is the one single theme of all of education. Skills in teaching are, no doubt important, but they do not take the teacher far. An otherwise unashamedly dissolute teacher may teach effectively; he also influences lives of the pupils no less, but sadly. Contact with great and good teachers as also with great ideas is the foundation of moral and spiritual education. The most effective weapon of a teacher is the silent power of example; it matters in the end and always. It is, therefore, necessary that teacher education should aim not at merely cultivation of professional skills but in making of man, a man of high character and noble vision. This consideration brings to teacher-education a very different purpose and responsibility which are not equally relevant to other professional education.

Effectiveness

It is this concern which influences us in suggesting a unique type of organisation which will necessarily perform functions analogous to those of the professional bodies such as the Indian Council of Medical Education and Bar Council, but which, in addition, will be vested with responsibility of stimulating and organising thinking on the fundamental problems relating to philosophy and practice of education and their bearing on the problems of human values as well as those of national development and international solidarity.

We are not unaware of the magnitude of the problem of teacher education; the large number of teachers that need training of different kinds and different levels (including the university level) and at different periods in their career. The entire process has to be viewed as a whole in a well conceived and integrated fashion and with sensitiveness to the intellectual and human values which we have emphasised in this report.

The National Council for Teachers' Education, which was established under Resolution of the Ministry of Education dated the 21st May, 1973, was an important item in the direction of promoting a systematic reflection and action in regard to all matters concerning teacher education. But the role of this Council has been only advisory in nature. Thus the results have not been very effective. The reports of the four regional study teams appointed by this Council in February, 1978, have revealed several glaring deficiencies in the functioning of teacher education institutions at both elementary and secondary levels, and they reinforce the necessity of evolving a mere effective machinery or agency.

Lack of Adequate Facilities

Most of the teacher education institutions suffer from lack of adequate facilities, and they do not adhere to the norms regarding physical facilities or provision of adequate staff. Colleges of education are generally either understaffed or the staff are under-qualified. There are serious curricular deficiencies, and evaluation in teacher education is far from satisfactory. There is no uniformity in the duration of teacher education. This is particularly so in the case of teacher education related to the elementary level. In some States, there is only one-year programme while in others it is of two years' duration. Moreover, due to various reasons, academic sessions for B.Ed. are delayed, and in some cases, effective teaching lasts only for three to six months, although the number of working days in a teacher education institution is expected to be at least 220 in a year.

Many private colleges have sprung up and in a number of degree colleges, teacher education courses have been instituted without ensuring the availability of suitable facilities and qualified staff. Even capitation fees are being charged, thereby commercialising teacher education.

In this context it would be pertinent to refer to the reports of the enormous corruption not only in seeking admission to teacher training institutions but also in passing the examination with inadequate or even proper training. The teachers who have gone through this polluting mill and profited by it can hardly be expected to stand for high principles of rectitude and correct behaviour.

Relevancy

In about 15 universities, correspondence courses leading to the award of B.Ed. and M.Ed. degrees have been started. But serious questions are being raised as to whether such correspondence courses are really relevant in a field where a personal contact between the trainer and the trainee is extremely important, and where the major objective is making of the man in the teacher and not merely a technician. These questions require an urgent answer in view of the fact that the number of students both in regular colleges and in correspondence courses has considerably increased.

There is in our country a backing of untrained teachers in several States. And since there is no manpower planning in teaching profession, it is difficult to suggest any rational policy which States can follow in regard to the intake of fresh student-teachers.

Curriculum

A key problem associated with the content of teacher education courses is that teachers are both perceived as and trained to be transmitters of information from textbooks, rather than as professionals who can teach students to think, find answers and understand concepts on their own – a conceptualization which provides continued impetus to poor quality schooling. [6] Changing the latter, therefore, demands substantial attention to the content and process of teacher education. Existing teacher education programmes do not encourage students to reflect on their own experiences and assumptions, which otherwise would be a way for teachers to set aside their own biases and beliefs. Instead, assuming that the latter can be easily set aside, these programmes 'fail to empower the teacher as an agent of change...' Warning against such thinking, as a Unesco report on EFA notes, 'both in developing and developed countries, there is a temptation to lower teacher training standards'. As the Yashpal Committee Report points out, existing programmes of teacher education are inadequate to deal with the (poor) quality of teaching and learning, implying that programme content should be revised, keeping in view the changing requirements of school education. 'The content of this (B.Ed.) programme should be restructured to ensure its relevance to the changing needs of school education...

Lack of Professionalism

In theory, teachers are required to be reflective practitioners – professionals who are domain experts in both subject content and the 'how' of teaching. 'Teaching' is thus thought of as a profession, and not merely a vocation or skill. Their role as professionals is what allows them to adapt to the needs of the classroom as they teach, innovating with teaching practice, pedagogical approaches, the design of teaching learning material, and similar such issues which collectively determine the quality of teaching and learning in the classroom. Yet, other sectors of the economy that see their work as a profession have somewhat different standards of initial and ongoing training.

A counter-argument often advanced is that of numbers, according to which it is not feasible to train a few thousand teachers through a handful of resource persons. Yet, this argument holds only so long as we continue with the model of a one-shot, camp-type training. Were the system to display some degree of flexibility, it is not hard to envision that trainings held across the year would allow successive groups of teachers to be trained by the capable teacher-educators and, moreover, allow for regular feedback between the same group of teachers and teacher educators when they meet each other on successive occasions.

Selection of Right People

Many reports have advocated the importance of attracting capable and interested men and women to the teaching profession, rather than allowing teaching to be relegated to the bottom rung of potential employment avenues. A number of considerations such as existence of a desirable career path, opportunities for continuous professional development and learning, and appropriateness of selection procedures (including quality of applicants) must be accounted for at a policy level while deciding the fate of school education. Yet, as has been often remarked, teaching as a profession in India has plummeted from the ranks of a desirable occupation to one which is taken up as a last resort, when all other avenues are unavailable. This is particularly so in an era when contractual teaching is replacing teachers as recognized professionals, or employees of the state. Contractual appointments of teachers has ensured that teaching becomes a low paid profession, resulting in an extreme casualization of the profession. This experience highlights the need for teacher education courses and institutions to recognize the profile of persons who become teachers, and structure content accordingly.

It seems obvious that urgent measures need to be taken to:

(a) introduce effective changes in the teacher education curriculum, particularly with a view to providing a powerful orientation towards value-education,

(b) suggest a rational duration for pre-service and in-service teacher training programmes;

(c) suggest effective methods of evaluation of trainees; and

(d) suggest measures for the maintenance of standards of teacher education and to meet various deficiencies and avoid evils which are prevalent in the field of teacher education.

The Central Government should create a National Organisation which would have adequate powers and functions to ensure that the teachers who would be incharge of the care of the children, adolescents and youths of our country are not only well-trained in professional skills related to their subjects of specialisation but will also have effective personality and character capable of providing the needed guidance and inspiration to the growing minds and hearts of the young, as also a wide vision of our country and the world serving as a sure basis for patriotism, international understanding and voluntary optimism for a peaceful, progressive and glorious future.

The need for such a national organisation arises from three important considerations.

Firstly, the National Council for Teacher Education which is already a national organisation, has expressed the view that it lacks authority to implement its resolutions and that it should be reconstituted as an autonomous statutory body for accrediting of teachers' training institutions at all levels in the country and to function effectively in this regard with the universities and State Governments.

Secondly, there is a need in the country to establish and/ or to support certain pace-setting value-oriented institutions for teacher education, atleast one in each State and Union Territory which would serve as models and which would ensure State-level research and experimentation in teacher education. These pioneering and pace-setting value-oriented institutions should be rational in character and they should embody national policies in regard to teacher education.

There should thus be a national body charged with functions and powers to establish and conduct these pace-setting value-oriented institutions. Thirdly, the evaluation of teacher-trainees, which needs a radical change, can be effectively handled, if the proposed national organisation is empowered to hold National Public Examinations which would reflect high and competent standards.

The aims of the proposed Council should be:

i) To keep under review the institutions and programmes of teacher education in the country at all levels and to maintain high standard of teaching, research and examinations in the field of teacher education with a view to developing attitudes, skills and personality which would reflect the image of the teacher embodied in this report.

ii) To establish and to maintain

a) Institutes of Teacher Education-designed especially to educate the staff of the colleges of teacher education in India; and

b) pace-setting model institutions of teacher education, preferably one in each State which should be utilised as centres for radiating new ideas and values in the region on the lines recommended in this Report.

iii) To provide aid, financial, material and human, and advice necessary for coordination and maintenance of high standards of teaching, examination and research and to stimulate thinking on problems of teacher-education.

iv) To function as an accrediting authority with powers ton recognise or derecognise teacher training institutions and degrees awarded by them.

v) to conceive of and implement programmes of strategies for bringing the existing teacher education institutions to conform to the aims and objects laid down by the Council.

vi) to organise preparation of variety of resource material including material for audiovisual aids and use of educational technology necessary for promoting high standards of work in teacher training institutions.

vii) to perform such other functions as may be conducive to the realisation of the aims and objectives of teacher education visualised by the Council on the lines recommended in this report.

viii) to organise or support seminars, conferences, symposia as also to set up committees and penals for the promotion of the objectives, functions and activities of the Council.

In addition to the present composition which consists of the Union Minister for Education as the President and 40 other members representing State Governments, University Grants Commission, All India Council for Technical Education, Planning Commission, National Council of Educational Research and Training, Ministry of Education, Central Advisory Board of Education, 13 experts and a Member-Secretary, there should be an executive body consisting of a full-time Chairman and five full-time members, all appointed by the Central Government, and it should have the power to appoint standing committees and other committees for carrying out various functions and responsibilities. The Member-Secretary of the Council will also be Member-Secretary of the executive body. The Chairman and Members should be eminent educationists, teachers and educational administrators.

The proposed national organisation should be in charge of implementing the valueoriented programmes of teachers' training. The first step in implementation will be to prepare the educators of teacher-educators. For this purpose, selection should be made from among those candidates who are willing and competent to undertake a special programme of training. The trained educators should have the possibility of being appointed in the pace-setting value-oriented institutions as also in other institutions of teachers' education.

Teacher Educators can Only Improve Teacher Quality

The very fact that teaching is a profession entails that teaching is a specialized activity for which specialized knowledge/ training is required through specialized institutions. A good institution will produce individuals who will be devoted to the profession and make their mark in the activities organized by them while going to the field. If examples with respect to engineering and medical institutions in India and abroad are considered, one will agree that the onus of getting good teachers lies on the institution that prepares the professionals. Further the institutions alone do not matter much; it is the teachers in the institutions who produce desired individuals. Teacher educators are responsible for producing quality teachers. Harvey (1993) and Atwood (2007) point out that Quality processes tend to focus on 'core' aspects of education such as learning-teaching and course organisation. In other words teacher educators' way of organizing theoretical framework, practical sessions and skills development programme affect the future teachers. The activities suggested during training are carried to the classroom teaching in the schools. Researchers like McAffrey et.al. (2003), Rivkin et.al. (2005) and Rockoff (2004) found that teachers have a significant impact on the achievement of the students. However, research studies are jejune to provide answer to the question if the teacher educators directly affect the teachers' classrooms behaviour or management of activities in the schools. Reasons for this could be many.

Teacher educators have never taken the aspect of professionalism very seriously. They have been criticizing the process of teacher education rather than providing answer to problem faced by them. However, NCTE was established in 1993 by the Act of parliament to give the tinge of professionalism to teacher preparation programme. Unfortunately instead of mending the system it caused some damage to the programme of teacher education. Obvious reason was lack of insight on the part of teacher educators to provide a good model of teacher education. Till date they have not been able to envision a good model of teacher education programme. Existing teacher education problems were further aggravated by the privatization of teacher education institutions. Teacher educators never accepted the private enterprise in teacher education programme though they had been party in recognizing the private teacher education institutions (through NCTE) for the sake of fringe benefits bestowed by the private players. The situation deteriorated to such an extent that at particular time a committee was constituted by the Ministry of Human resource Development to scrap the regulatory body of teacher education (NCTE). The situation was saved after a great hue and cry made by some right thinking teacher educators to reverse the decision. The developments like these have made it mandatory for the teacher educators to put their heads together and give a little thinking to their role in the changed set up under Liberalization, Privatization and Globalization.

Contribution of Teacher Educators

The teacher educators have much to contribute to the development of quality amongst the teachers. It is high time that they understand their role rather than simply criticize the system in the name of NCTE. If they do not contribute, they will move from the current marginalized status to the one of irrelevance. They will have to respond at both conceptual/ empirical and pedagogical levels (Liston et.al. 2008).

The first and foremost thing is that they will have to accept the existing realities of the world. Privatization has entered educational system and they cannot deny it at any cost. A large number of men and women aspire to get degree or diplomas in teacher education to join teaching or jobs similar to teaching. The existing teacher education colleges or the University departments of education cannot accommodate all the aspirants. The nation at such a juncture will have to depend on private participation in education system of the country. Further the Mass Education does not Necessarily Mean the End of Quality. Simply harping on the tune of deterioration of standards due to the gap in demand and supply will not serve any purpose. Teacher education programme in India has never been based on demand and supply phenomenon. There has always been a good number of participants who never joined teaching after earning a degree or diploma in education. It has generally been observed that objective of many women in getting admission to teacher education programme has been to earn a certificate for future employment. Many women join teaching even after a decade of getting professional degree in wake of their personal or family problems. In such a situation there is a need to draft teacher education courses that have totally specialized knowledge, specialized skills and inherent code of ethics. It can be done by having good theoretical base. Instead of depending on Philosophy, psychology or such other subjects they should bring up a body of knowledge that the future teachers start philosophizing or thinking psychologically to find solution to their classroom problems. Also the teacher educators should start devising the knowledge akin to the discipline of education. For example over the years the education has developed its own vocabulary like learning styles, thinking skills etc.

Secondly, the teacher educators will have to delve on specialized skills that add quality to the professional functioning. Such skills mean having hard, technical expertise along with softer interpersonal capabilities. Skills of quality teaching and quality assessment are most desired. Quality teaching skills involve the process of making students work hard and become independent learner. For example posing a problem before the learners and helping them find solutions to these problems is a skill and such skills need to be developed in the teacher trainees. Similarly the teacher trainees have to be trained in quality assessment procedure. This type of assessment requires the trainees to assess the students with respect to their thinking process and learning styles. In the same manner, the skills related to feed back have to be developed amongst future teachers so that the feedback is accepted open mindedly by the students and they improve upon.

Thirdly teacher educators should envision functions other than teaching by making teacher education degree/ diploma broad based with respect to changing times. Many dimensions with specializations will have to be added since the future teaching will not be limited to classroom teaching alone. Students will not depend upon teachers to seek knowledge about subject matter. They will be finding better transmitter of knowledge in media. However, they will not be able to negate the teachers.

They will require help of the teachers to solve their day-to-day learning or behavioural problems. The students who will not be able to have access to schools will look for teachers get self learning material to suit their learning styles. Not only students, even the parents of the students will seek indulgence of teachers in achieving their aspired goals. Above all the future schools will be having trauma centres on their campus and will depend upon teachers' skills to solve various issues related to behavioural problems of students. All such issues cannot be ignored by the teacher education programme if it has to suit the demands of the society. Therefore teacher educators will have to design course curricula to accommodate such functions of the teachers. Specializations like Public Relationing, Parent Counselling, Behavioural Therapy, Developing e-learning material etc. will have to be included in the course curricula of teacher education. All such dimensions have to be added to the teacher education courses if these courses have to exist in the future. Otherwise there is very likelihood that these courses will loose their credibility to the global societal needs.

Fourthly, the whole nature and process of teacher education will have to be worked out differently. Existing teacher education programme is divided in to different academic papers and sections. Usually the academic papers are Principles of Education and Educational Psychology etc. While teaching these courses, the teacher educators emphasize information aspect only (having no relevance to classroom teaching or school problems). The student teachers are never taught 'how to use the information for solving problems related to school education in general and teaching in particular'. Keeping in view the limitations of discipline oriented approach the teacher educators should visualize Problem oriented approach. A comprehensive list of various problems faced by various functionaries be developed through field based working. The student teachers should be asked to find out workable solutions to the problems. The purpose of teacher education should be development of problem solving skills rather than imparting knowledge alone. This is possible by having flexible, experience based, process oriented teacher education programme; wherein the student teachers are trained in analysing the problem, developing hypotheses, collecting relevant data and drawing conclusions. Later the student teachers discuss these conclusions with large group to work on the solutions in simulated set up. Such a Project based teacher education programme will help in establishing credibility of teacher education programme. Let the apex institution like NCTE work with a vision to metamorphose the existing teacher education programme.

Fifthly, the teacher educators will have to organize their research as per the needs of the society and the market forces. Liston et.al. (2008) in his editorial pointed out that "Teacher quality research emerges from different conceptual lenses, some less familiar to educators (e.g., labour economies). It is important to grasp varied theories of action implied and to analyse assumptions and values in different research designs." To put it in simpler words, it connotes that research process and research problems in education should be such that these solve societal problems from different angles. For example the society in India at present is being faced with problems like violence by schools students, sex linked problems at primary stage, aspiration of parents that their child should lead the class in every activity, going for tuitions even at pre-primary level, etc. The answer to such problems is not simple. It involves knowledge of sociology, psychology as well as economics. The teacher educators need to get all essential knowledge to take up the issue and find workable solutions. After all it is the teacher educators who teach about the nature of the child and work directly in the field.

Conclusion

In short it is suggested that instead of criticizing or finding faults with the Apex body of teacher education (NCTE), let the teacher educators work with a vision and extend helping hand to the NCTE. The objective of the NCTE is to produce quality teachers. Since the NCTE does not have its own staff, it depends totally on the services rendered by teacher educators employed in the Universities and colleges. Also the personnel heading NCTE belong to us. They had been part of the Universities or colleges. The major question is – should we criticize our colleagues because all of us are unable to visualize and perform our own role? The role of teacher educators today is to mend the existing system with vision to help teacher education grow as a profession and produce quality teachers for schools.

Reorienting Teacher Education for Sustainable Development

National Council for Teacher Education (NCTE): India is a signatory to the Agenda 21 of the United Nations Conference on Environmental Development (UNCED) Rio, Brazil, 1992. An important outcome of this Conference was the adoption of the Declaration and Recommendations of the Tbilisi Intergovernmental Conference on Environmental Education organised by UNESCO and UNEP held in 1977. It was resolved to reorient education towards sustainable development. What is sustainable development and how it can be implemented by using the instrumentality of education was clarified by what is given in the following paragraph:

Education, including formal education, public awareness and training should be recognized as a process by which human beings and societies can reach their fullest potential. Education is critical for promoting sustainable development and improving the capacity of the people to address environment and development issues. While basic education provides the underpinning for any environmental and development education, the latter needs to be incorporated as an essential part of learning. Both formal and non-formal education are indispensable to changing people's attitudes so that they have the capacity to assess and address their sustainable development concerns. It is also critical for achieving environmental and ethical awareness, values and attitudes, skills and behaviour consistent with sustainable development and for effective public participation in decision-making. To be effective, environment and development education should deal with the dynamics of both the physical/biological and socio-economic environment and human (which may include spiritual) development, should be integrated in all disciplines, and should employ formal and non-formal methods and effective means of communication.

Recognising that countries, regional and international organisation will develop their own priorities and schedules for implementation in accordance with their needs, policies and programmes, the following objectives were proposed:

a. To strive to ensure universal access to basic education, and to achieve primary education for at least 80 percent of girls and 80 percent of boys of primary school age through formal schooling or non-formal education and to reduce the adult illiteracy rate to at least half of its 1990 level. Efforts should focus on reducing the high illiteracy levels and redressing the lack of basic education among women and should bring their literacy levels into line with those of men;

b. To achieve environmental and development awareness in all sectors of society on a worldwide scale as soon as possible;

c. To strive to achieve the accessibility of environmental and developmental education, linked to social education, from primary school age through adulthood to all groups of people;

d. To promote integration of environment and development concepts, including demography, in all educational programmes, in particular the analysis of the causes of major environment and development issues in a local context, drawing on the best available scientific evidence and other appropriate sources of knowledge, and giving special emphasis to the further training of decision makers at all levels.

Although school textbooks of languages, science and social sciences, which were written after the National Policy on Education (1986/1992), contained environmental concerns, the teaching by and large has been bookish and the above objectives have remained elusive. The problem can be traced to the teacher education programmes. In a vast country like India the teacher education till very recently had remained unregulated. In order to appreciate the role of teachers in reorienting education towards sustainable development it is necessary to understand teacher education system in the country. The pre-service teacher education programmes in India are tied up with common structure of school education. The school structure comprises of 8 years of elementary stage followed by 2 years of secondary stage and 2 years of senior secondary stage. Courses of teacher education are, therefore, offered stage-wise.

Teacher education for the elementary stage is being carried out at about 800 institutions, which offer courses of two-year duration and are open to candidates who have passed the senior secondary examination at the end of the 12th year of schooling. As the 32 states/union territories have been determining the profile of their elementary education, certificates of teacher education for the elementary stage issued by the State Departments of Education have as many as 28 different names. Some of the names of elementary teacher certificates are BTC (Basic Teaching Certificate), D.Ed (Diploma in Education), TTC (Teachers' Training Certificate), JBT (Junior Basic Training), and there are many others.

Teacher education for the secondary stage is being carried out at about 900 institutions. The course commonly called B.Ed (Bachelor of Education) is generally of one-year duration and is open to graduates. Affiliating universities, which also determine the curriculum, award the B.Ed degree. As there are more than 200 universities in the country, the course contents of teacher education programmes for the secondary teachers though appear similar but are generally different. It should, therefore, only be expected that teacher education programmes in the country have wide diversity. In such a scenario some unifying structure to teacher education could be introduced after August 1995 with the setting up of the National Council for Teacher Education (NCTE).

In this article urgency of reorienting of teacher education for sustainable development is made out by first highlighting that the life on Earth is under threat and what can be achieved through a paradigm shift in teacher education. The common impression about teacher education is that it has remained unchanged for a very long time and is not found relevant to the citizenry now required in the national and also the global contexts. The principal concern of the humankind now is that Earth has come under threat because of the lifestyles of its six billion human inhabitants.

Plants and animals provide the food that sustains human life. The earth and all its living organisms supply all the raw materials for human activities. Through economic activities natural and physical resources are converted into products and services which have more direct and immediate utilitarian value. Invariably, fall out of human activities have been contamination of environment with heavy metals, pollution of natural resources such as lakes, rivers, subsoil water and even the air we breath. As the economic activities have been associated with development, not much attention was given to their effects on the environment, although they have caused havoc in the form of serious illness, damage and death in humans and other biological species. Many of the species that evolved during the long history of Earth have become extinct and many are on the verge of becoming extinct. It is unfortunate that in the name of development and man's selfish pursuit for improving his quality of life grave harm has been caused to the rich biodiversity of Earth. Such wanton actions of human beings are all the more disturbing because life, as is known to us, seems to exist only on the planet Earth and in none of the other planets of the star Sun. Therefore, the blame for this state of affairs is being put squarely on the reckless lifestyles of people in both developing and developed parts of the world. It is certain that unless human activities are regulated so as to ensure sustainable environment, not only interests of other species but also of generations of human beings yet unborn would get harmed. The planet Earth would become increasingly less inhabitable.

In the Brundtland Commission's report, "Our Common Future", sustainable development has been given the definition "*meeting the needs of the present generation without compromising the needs of future generations*". In this context it has become imperative to reorient the thrust of education and that of teacher education towards adoption of a sustainable lifestyle. In operational terms it would require that children when they are at school might have to be made aware of the threat to their life and that of other species because of the environmental degradation, and social inequity and poverty caused by the attitude and conduct of their elders.

Unless every one accepts wholeheartedly the necessity of living in harmony with all forms of life and adopts a lifestyle that will leave the world a better place than what one inherited, the beautiful process of evolution of life on Earth will receive an adverse setback. This can be brought about through the process of teaching-learning of the conventional school subjects such as languages, science and social sciences. Introduction of a separate school subject of environmental studies may not be required. Only teachers have to adopt pedagogy of *learning through thinking*. It is a process of learning in which learners construct their own knowledge by asking questions, problem solving and taking decisions based on their own judgement. Learning of topics such as the natural world, effects of human activities on environment and trends in population growth etc.

should not be allowed to get reduced to mere bookish knowledge for passing tests. Instead through understanding, children may be helped in internalising the concern for adoption of a sustainable lifestyle.

One of the Fundamental Duties is *"to protect and improve the natural environment including forests, lakes, rivers, wild life and to have compassion for living creatures"*. Fortunately, in the school curricula although environmental science has not been made a separate school subject, yet its concerns permeate appropriately at all stages of school curriculum. School textbooks of languages, science and social science contain environment concepts. The NCERT study on Environment in School Curriculum has shown that environmental concerns have been introduced sequentially from local to global in its textbooks of the primary and upper-primary stages. Also, the Bharati Vidyapeeth Institute of Environment Education and Research, Pune has confirmed the NCERT findings. This institute took up a research study on status of infusion of environment concepts in school curricula, a part of the India Environment Management Capacity Building Project. A content analysis of the science textbooks of standards 1 to 10 of the Maharashtra State has been carried out. From the matrix that has been constructed it comes out clearly that by and large textbooks contain prominent environment related concerns. A detailed scrutiny of these textbooks has brought out that treatment of concepts can be improved by contextualising the learning materials and by using the everyday use vocabulary instead of unfamiliar scientific and technical terms and by improving illustrations.

Where we lose out is that in spite of the constitutional concern, in reality, the teaching-learning tends to be mechanical. Reasons for it are not hard to understand. Only a few teachers know in letter and spirit what is expected of them to teach how to teach that. The end result is that instead of ensuring *learning through thinking* their pupils memorise questions and answers.

This state of affairs can be attributed to mismatch between what is learnt by would-be teachers at the stage preceding their teacher education and what is expected as prerequisite by the teacher education curriculum, which gets compounded because of inadequacies in their teachers who prepare them for the teaching profession.

It has already been mentioned that although school curricula have undergone several changes during the past 25 years, the curricula of teacher education have remained practically static. Also, teacher educators have seldom been given in-service support and they have remained insulated in their own world. This isolation is perhaps because there are few programmes directly addressed to preparing professionals for stage specific teacher education. Many persons end up becoming teacher educators more because of their circumstances and rarely because they exercised a prior option for entering into the career of teacher education.

How can this impasse be broken? To achieve it, concerted efforts may have to be made at several levels of formal education. The first step will be to identify profiles of teachers for different stages of school education for achieving the curriculum objectives effectively. Also, if teachers have to assume their changed role of facilitators and promoters of *learning through thinking*, responsibility of assessment of their students will have to be shifted from the system of common public examinations to making it the direct concern of the teacher. This is necessary for breaking away from the mindset that the principal objective of teaching is to coach students for performing well in public examinations and entrance tests for admission to professional courses. It is a common knowledge that all such assessments generally test speed of recalling facts and answering questions as per the pattern known to examinees in advance.

Let us assume that this radical shift in schooling process will take place, though gradually. The changed role of teachers will determine the stage specific profiles of teachers. The next step will be to design suitable curricula for teacher education courses for preparing teachers as per the identified profiles. The logical implication of such a bold step on teacher education will be that curricula of teacher education programmes will now be determined by the requirement of the changed concerns of schooling. It should not cause surprise if the desired content and process of teacher education are found not to resemble much with what is familiar to most of us.

After taking care of these steps pertaining to curriculum renovation, the next challenge will be to prepare a cadre of professionals who can take care of the new curricula of teacher education. It will be crucial that all the steps described above are inter-linked by agencies that generally work in isolation. The universities will be expected to give a fresh look to their M.Ed programme and give it a professional status. Different M.Ed courses for preparing teacher educators for different stages of school education will have to be designed and offered by the universities and their affiliated colleges. These courses could be M.Ed (elementary) for preparing teacher educators for elementary teacher education institutions, M.Ed (secondary) for preparing teacher educators for secondary teacher education institutions and M.Ed (physical education) for preparing teacher educators for institutions engaged in preparation of physical education teachers, etc.

The programme outlined above may take some time in coming into place. We cannot wait until this happens. Strategies for supporting 4.6 million teachers who are in service have to be worked out. Also, there are about 30,000 teacher educators in the country who are involved in pre-service education of teachers. They will have to be given support for reorienting pre-service education for preparing such teachers as will be able to make their pupils appreciate the concern of sustainable development and influence their lifestyle.

Is the inertia of the system so daunting that it will deter attempts for changing it? Initiatives that can overcome the inertia and that can influence the school system in the right direction have to be found. A possible way out perhaps lies in using the advanced information and communication technologies in all facets of school education. By electronic packaging of learning resources for offline access and using online networks it may be possible to reach out to even to those teachers who have remained unreached so far. This is where experts have to come in. They may take up projects for developing software for self-learning of environment concepts. Software will have to be prepared for each school stage and made available in regional languages.

The NCTE is going to launch a major initiative called "Teacher Support". The backbone of this project is the appreciation that what we want the entire school system to do are already being carried out by a vast number of gifted teachers. The NCTE has planned to tap good classroom practices and make them available to teachers and teacher educators.

I will like to close this article with the hope that fires of talent which are simmering in the length and breadth of our country as they occasionally become visible in the form of creative performances of our students and teachers now need to be stoked by the vast pool of talent in our teachers. The glow of knowledge will show the direction for using the resources of our planet in providing a better quality of life to each person and at the same time leaving the world in a better condition than ever before.

The Major Concerns of Teaching Profession

But what is empirical situation? What are the explicit and implicit value? articulating themselves in the visible and invisible concerns of the teachers? To be sure, one finds a great deal to cause concern and at the same time much that gives hope.

Security Value

Security value appears to be paramount in the concerns of the organized teaching profession. Their struggles are for better and higher salary scales, automatic and additional avenues of promotion, enhanced dearness allowance, continuance of examination remuneration, provision for more faculty housing or increased house rent allowance, and liberal loans for house-building or for buying scooters and cars. There is nothing inherently wrong in these demands the teacher is surely entitled to a reasonably comfortable standard of life and to a respectable social status, but when agitational methods ignore and sacrifice the interests of the learners or tarnish the image of the teacher in the eyes of the learner, thus incapacitating the teachers from performing many specific roles, the situation begins to cause worry. The public at large, especially the thinking section of it, would evince greater sympathy for the teachers' cause if they assert themselves equally for raising academic standards, promoting academic excellence and showing willingness to do whatever is necessary for the purpose. It is unfortunate that on some of the major crises of higher education the organized and vocal section of the academic profession maintains a tantalizing silence. This is a distortion that needs to be corrected.

Attitude towards Work

During the Commission's visits to the colleges and universities, another feature of the educational scene came to light, and this is the wide prevalence of private tuition in colleges-which is not just of one or two students who find it difficult to get along without the assistance of a teacher, but large scale tuitions from which some teachers earn much more than their salaries. The overtone of this practice is that in many cases tuition does not result in intensive coaching but in assistance towards disclosing of question papers or in enhancement of marks. This is a very painful reality, but it is difficult to gather information of this kind from questionnaires. However, the other fact, repeatedly mentioned by parents, students and conscientious teachers, was that many teachers took their duties lightly, did pot prepare their lectures, dictated notes which they had themselves made years or decades ago, cut their classes, and paid little attention to the difficulties referred to them by their students.

Attitude to Reform

It is obvious that no educational reform has a chance to survive if teachers do not support it in adequate measure. A lukewarm, or sometimes cynical approach on the part of teachers often dooms a reform. An initiative for change coming from 'the rank and file teacher or from his organisation is something unknown in our country. But refusing to take a stand on the minimum number of working days is a non-learning ethic that is being, promoted Institutions of higher learning today are often symbolic of indiscipline. Student indiscipline is followed by karamchari indiscipline and even the teachers have often joined forces with them. Who should then assume the responsibility of setting things right? A sizeable section of the teaching community does not take its obligation to students seriously. If curricula are out of date, and ineffective teaching methods reduce education to an uninspired routine, or if the learning needs of first generation learners are given no thought or if standards of judgement of academic quality in education and research become diluted in the spirit of " sab chalta hai" (everything goes), who indeed is morally responsible? Again, when in recruitment or promotion organized demands are weighted in favour of mediocrity or even non-performance, the teaching profession, with pursuit of excellence as one of its cherished values, abdicates responsibility.

From time to time, an elite section of the academic protest against inroads into the legitimate autonomy of educational institutions to take all decisions, particularly about their internal functioning, through the prescribed university bodies. This is a heartening sign, but at the same time there is a section of teachers who, for petty gains, invite political or bureaucratic intervention sometimes by allowing situations to arise where delegations or dharnas specifically seek intervention from ministers, parliamentarians or political parties. Not many in power can resist such temptations.

Organized opinion and strength of the teaching profession has not demonstrated conspicuous capacity to take a bold and determined stand, against erosion of the autonomy of the university system. We must clarify however that we are not advocating the autonomy of the ivory tower. Today our universities and colleges have to have numberous links with the community, developmental activity in the region, research institutions and industry etc.

Hence the university is part of the total system, and it cannot remain aloof from the research educational and developmental activity on the whole. Boards of studies, boards of research and councils for extension activity would naturally have non-teacher professionals, scientists or even relevant government operatives represented on them.

Creativity and Research

Pursuit of excellence, creativity and research are acclaimed to be central to the value system of the teaching profession. With regard to students, it is most important that taking things merely on the basis of authority, without sufficient questioning and examination, is to be discouraged and a positive effort should be made to cultivate an enquiring mind, an exploratory and experimental approach, and an urge to reflect and introspect. This cannot be done if the teacher cannot set an example, or if the teacher himself is dogmatic, opinionated and unimaginative. Only a creative person can excite the often dormant qualities of imagination and speculation among students, and can turn them on for creative activity from the writing of stories or poems to great works of art and science. In regard to creative work by teachers themselves, it may be said that it not only contributes to effective teaching but also enables either academic or social problems to be solved, in both cases spreading the benefit of the research far and wide. Involvement of teachers in researches relevant to regional or national development may in fact raise the prestige of educational institutions and bring them resources from hitherto untapped agencies. Teachers may In turn use students in a carefully planned manner to undertake dissertations in higher classes, or projects and studies in lower classes, to create a data base and an analysis of the same to sharpen their creative talent and at the same time provide the back-up for objective grassroots planning of social and economic development. There are tremendous opportunities, but what is the reality?

Self Perception and Regulation

We have discussed the crucial role of the teacher in influencing young minds on the question of values, and we have analysed the values that have to be inculcated if society has to be held together and if it is to progress towards the goals we cherish. We are also aware that it is easy to make idealistic demands from the teachers on the basis of human and social relations which prevailed a thousand or more years ago. But in our view, it cannot be denied that the teacher has a special position because of his mission or his duty or professional responsibility. He cannot afford to get lost in the norms of social behaviour which happen to prevail-because who then will show us direction or pull us out of the morass? As a man devoted to learning, to ‘he pursuit of truth in his creative endeavours, and hence being in a position to see farther than many others-as a social critic, the teacher has to struggle for the propagation of the right values. Therefore, we believe that teachers should be the first to introspect, and scrutinise their own value system so as to raise it to the highest moral level, and they should not shirk from imposing severe restraints on themselves in order that their word may have effect and their Conduct may set an example which others may follow.

It is shocking that nearly half the teachers think that only a few of their co-professionals have personal integrity and devotion, or pursue for academic excellence or even have commitment to students' welfare or community service. Absence of scientific temper is even more conspicuous for both categories of teachers. Obviously, if teachers are to be the inevitable instrument for dissemination of value-oriented education, they will have to reform themselves by their own effort.

The questionnaire also explored what the teachers, students and the community consider to be unacceptable behaviour on the part of a teacher. Here a number of questions were asked and people were asked to rank them in the order of repugnance. Partiality in assessment of students was considered to be the worst behaviour by 71.4 per cent of the community in universities, and instigating students against other colleagues was considered as the worst by the college community.

Teachers own responses are indeed very healthy 80 per cent or more teachers considered it against professional ethics to earn money by publishing “bazaar notes”, teaching from notes prepared long ago, dictating notes instead of lecturing, favouritism in grading, skipping classes, instigating students and undertaking tuitions to earn money. In fact instigating students against other teachers had the highest position amongst undersirable activities both for college and university teachers, the second position going to dictating notes instead of teaching.

These healthy opinions could be the basis of spelling out what can be defined as unacceptable behaviour. It would be better if professional associations of teachers took the initiative in giving final shape to such a definition because they should be interested in protecting the honour of their members. But reluctance to do so would naturally lead to such behaviour being defined by the authorities and then we would have only ourselves to blame.

It is shocking that nearly half the teachers think that only a few of their co-professionals have personal integrity and devotion, or pursue for academic excellence or even have commitment to students' welfare or community service. Absence of scientific temper is even more conspicuous for both categories of teachers. Obviously, if teachers are to be the inevitable instrument for dissemination of value-oriented education, they will have to reform themselves by their own effort.

Many other endeavours are being researched, tested, evaluated and those that merit implementation are gradually incorporated into the educational curriculum. A detailed documentation is beyond the scope of this article; however, the following are a few examples. Distance education (see Parmaji, 1984); Values education; Environmental science education (ESE) (Sarma, Rao & Patnaik, 1985); Computer assisted instruction (CAI) (Monahty, 1985); School-based inservice education and training (SBINSET) (NCERT, 1988a); Teaching of English as a second language (TESL) (NCERT, 1988b); Socially useful productive work (SUPW) (Ruhela, 1983). The educational enthusiasm in the country is encouraged by the prospects and potential for a strong Indian society in the 1990s and beyond. In fact, "with quantitative expansion of educational facilities, there is now a greater emphasis on qualitative improvement" (Reed Information Services, 1991).

A Central government Bill has recently been drafted to provide the National Council of Teacher Education (NCTE) with statutory status. The main functions of the NCTE will be to prepare norms, standards, and guidelines for teacher education; to provide for essential links among concerned agencies and their proposed programs; and to advise the Central and State governments, University Grants Commission, universities, and allied educational agencies regarding priorities, policies, plans and programs (MHRD, 1992).

Summary

The NPE has done a commendable task in bringing together many educators at both the national and regional levels, promoting a spirit of cooperation toward implementing the national curriculum. In fact, the NPE does indicate a triangular network between the educational policy, school curricula, and teacher education (Taylor, 1991b; Ginsberg & Chaturvedi, 1988).

Many colleges in the country are striving for excellence in providing a quality education for the citizens, and to increase the literacy rates (Yadav, 1990). Women's education has steadily enhanced in its quality of programs for girls and women at all levels of education; during the Eighth Plan period, foundation professional courses are planned to promote the objectives of gender equity issues.

UNIT-II

Training Institutions

Various Levels of Training—Pre-primary

Teaching is a highly noble profession, most suited one especially for women. Teachers are always a boon to society. Through their intelligence, patience and wisdom, they attempt to not only hone the learner's intellect and aptitude but also, create a well-rounded personality.

Teaching has an influence in developing ones mind and character and also gives the satisfaction of having sparked the light of knowledge and dispelled the clouds of ignorance. As this field is so vast having areas of specialisations, different skills and type of training are required for different levels. Areas of specialisation include teaching at nursery schools, middle schools, high schools, colleges, universities, institutes, special schools etc. Each level calls for a different expertise. If you love to be with children, teaching at schools would be a good option, but if you want to be with young adults, it is better to look at the college or university level. Good teachers can bring out the best in every student. They are the ones who make a difference in the lives of their students. Rousing students from their apathy and watching their curiosity grow is one of the biggest rewards of teaching.

Comfortable hours of working and paid vacations are considered to be the main reasons behind the popularity of teaching as a profession. However, teaching when compared to other professions is less lucrative but it is the mental satisfaction attached with the profession that draws the attention of individuals. Education is the basic necessity to any society. According to a Tamil poet, the deeper we dig, the more we discover. The role of teacher also involves the character building of the taught apart from designing and implementation of the curriculum. Teachers cause desirable and anticipated revolution in the society silently. In short, a teacher inspires and shapes the destiny of the nation in class rooms. Realizing the above facts, the teaching profession is considered as the noblest profession in India. Educational institutions shape a person's orientation towards social action and try to overcome the constraints due to the inequality, poverty and social structure. Being a developing nation, it may be relevant for Ethiopia to understand the Educational system of other countries. In this context an attempt has been made to discuss the basics of the educational system and teacher training in India with special reference to the state of located at the southern tip of the Indian peninsula.

The structure of education in Tamilnadu is based on the national pattern of 10+2+3, (also 10+2+4 and {10+2+Respective professional course duration} patterns does exist) consisting of five years of primary and three years of upper primary/middle school education for the age groups of 6-11 and 11-14 respectively both put together as primary elementary education, followed by secondary and higher secondary education of two years duration each. The entry age in standard 1, which is also called as class or grade, is 5 plus. There are also pre-primary classes for the age group of 3-5. After secondary or high school education, a student can join higher secondary course or industrial training institute (ITI) or polytechnic college. The higher secondary school certificate enables the students to pursue their studies either in universities or colleges for higher education in general academic stream leading to bachelors' degree like B.A., B.Sc., B. Com., B.C.A., and B.B.A. (of 3 years course duration) and technical and professional courses such as B.E., B. Tech., B.D.S, (of 4 years course duration) and M.B.B.S., B.P.T., B.L., and E.T.T (elementary teacher training). After graduation, the student can pursue, post graduation or masters degree course of either two years duration (or) three years duration. Students can also join the professional courses like B.E.d. or B.L. after under graduation. On completion of post graduation a student may work for M. Phil. or Ph.D. degree.

Primary

They are broadly classified into two categories namely nursery or Montessori school teachers and primary school teachers. The teachers at this level play a very important role in society as they are largely responsible for molding the young impressionable minds. Theses teachers mainly deal with children in the age group of 4-10 years. As the child comes out of the protected environment of his home for the first time and is away from his parents, these teachers are a parent substitute. What a child learns and experiences during his early school years can shape the child's view about himself and the world around him which would later play an important role in his success at school work and also his personal life making him a good social being. Therefore the nursery and primary school teachers are responsible for the social, emotional and intellectual growth of children.

Upper Primary School Teachers

At the upper primary school level the teacher's are responsible for students in the age group of 11-13 (classes 6-8). They help children to develop their use of languages, explore mathematical ideas and introduce them to history, geography, science and creative arts. They also train the students in physical education, music, reading, elocution, dramatics art and craft. Creative techniques in teaching are used for lower classes, for older students the teaching is more formal including regular home work and tests.

Secondary and Higher Secondary Training

The secondary and higher secondary school teachers specialize in one or two subjects and teach those subjects to all age groups in secondary and higher secondary schools. They prepare the students for the 10th grade and 12th grade examination (conducted by either State Board or National Board.

Further a student has choice to register with either the State Board or the National Board). More emphasis is given on imparting knowledge of the subjects and these teachers play an important role in the overall personality development of the students.

Training of Primary, Upper Primary and Secondary Higher Secondary Teachers

The basic educational qualification to enter into an elementary teacher training school, which offer training to those who later become primary and upper primary school teachers is a pass in 12th grade. The training extends for a period of two academic years. The admissions to such training schools are made on merit basis among those who have applied for the training. There are more than 774 elementary teacher training schools in Tamilnadu and the total in take of the students is roughly 4380 per academic year. It is to be emphasized here than nearly 600000 students appear for the 12th grade examination and only less that 0.008% of these students join in elementary teacher training schools per annum. Therefore, according to this statistics, the majority of the students who seek admission in elementary teacher training schools normally have an interest and affinity towards teaching profession. Thus they become teachers by choice and not by chance.

The academic qualification for the entry in to a college of education is a bachelor degree in any one of the subjects taught in the secondary school level. Students with postgraduate degree in any one of the subjects taught in higher secondary school level, are also eligible for the admission in a college of education. The program is of one year duration leading to the degree of bachelor of education B.Ed. B.Ed. degree holders with an undergraduate degree become qualified to teach their concerned subject for 9th and 10th grade students in a secondary school and those with postgraduate degree are qualified to handle 11th and 12th grade in a higher secondary school. Totally there are 22 B.Ed. colleges and 3180 B.Ed. graduates come out as secondary and higher secondary teachers per annum. Any education oriented program has to have emphasis on both the principles of education and the mode of impart of knowledge. For example a B.Ed. program with chemistry as a major subject has to revolve around the means and modes related to impart the knowledge of chemistry and practical training at or up to secondary or higher secondary school level for which the concerned resource persons are required to be well equipped with a proper graduation, post graduation degree in science (B.Sc./ M.Sc.) with chemistry as the main subject having appropriate combination of allied science subjects (such as, physics and mathematics, physics and biology, geography and geology and likes). Needles to mention that these two programs (i.e.) B.Sc. and B.Ed. can neither be amalgamated nor can be acquired simultaneously as they are not only two different graduation programs under different eligibility requirements but also pertain to two different faculties (i.e.) science and education respectively. However, when these two degrees are acquired, they become contingent to each other as the former will enrich in "what to teach" and the later will help in "how to teach and impart". Obviously knowing 'how to teach' without acquiring 'what to teach' becomes meaningless.

When India was in the early stages of independence there was dearth of Indians for various jobs connected with the building of infrastructure of the nation. Post graduates, graduates and diploma holders were just snapped as soon as they come out of the institutions. Even under such a demanding situation the required academic eligibility to become primary, upper primary and secondary school teachers was not compromised and diluted, as the lives of younger generation and hence the development of the nation is entrusted to the safe hands of a teacher. Then the Indian planners in the field of education were fully aware of the fact that if fountain head is polluted containers can not be free from contamination.

The salient features of a teacher training institution whether it is elementary school teacher training or college of education, are as follows:

- There is a rigorous and very serious training.

- The teacher trainees should compulsorily stay in the hostel attached to the institution.
- The institution will be situated in rural area, as far as possible away from the urban area.
- There are supervisors to monitor the day-to-day activities of the trainees.
- The students are trained to get up early in the morning and to do some physical exercise to keep them physically and mentally fit.
- Dress code for the trainees will be strictly followed.
- Every day before the breakfast there will be a prayer for 15 minutes
- Very strict rules and regulations regarding the discipline of the trainees will be followed. Any trainee found not abiding by the prevailing rules and regulations will be terminated from the institution after sufficient warring.
- In the evenings, a group of students will be engaged in playing games and the other group of students will be working in the kitchen garden of the institution from where they get part of vegetables and greens. These groups will be exchanged once in a week.
- Study hours will be strictly maintained in the evening after dinner under the supervision of the instructors from (06.00 to 08.00) P.M.
- Certain primary and upper primary schools will be attached to elementary teacher training schools and secondary and higher secondary schools will be attached to college of education where the trainees will have teaching practice periodically through out the period of their study.
- In order to develop the trainees as good administrators and to bring out their leadership qualities in them various committees like mess committee, purchase committee, recreation committee, accounts committee, games committee etc. are formed among the students to look after the day to day affairs of the hostel

- The members of various committees will be exchanged cyclically once in a month to ensure the transparency both financial as well as administrative.
- To create political awareness among the trainees, mock-parliament will be conducted every week, where a group of trainees will assume the role of ruling party and others should act as the members of the opposition party. The subject for the debate will be either the important political incident of that week in the nation or the institution or the hostel.
- In order to develop the practice of savings and regulating their expenses each and every institution will have a mini bank known as Sanjayeka Savings Bank which will be operated by a committee of students and supervised by a teacher.
- There will be a cooperative store in the institutions managed by the students where the students can purchase their needs cheaply.
- Days of national importance like Independence Day, Republic Day and Teachersm Day should be organized and celebrated by the trainees in a grand manner.
- Free medical camps should be arranged periodically which will be sponsored by the philanthropists. Trainees will take all efforts to bring the suffering to the camp and get treated.
- The trainees should also be provided a special training in first aid and are deployed to serve the people in the event of national calamity like cyclone and flood. May be this develops the necessary patience and service oriented attitude which are the two eyes of a teacher.

Generosity is the most important to human beings in general and teachers in particular. Lord Rutherford, the Nobel Prize winner who discovered the presence of nucleus in an atom, had been one of the outstanding examples of teachers who had taken interest in the work of his students. Instead of trying to attract more attention to his own work, Rutherford identified and motivated a number of his student researchers who made note worthy discoveries in the later period. This essential quality of generosity is developed in the minds of trainee teachers so as to share their knowledge with the students generously and whole heartedly. Any profession is inherent with certain discomforts depending on the nature of the profession, and it is applicable to teaching profession also. But during the training period they are made to understand the discomforts of the profession which is an essential part of discharging any profession. "Devotion to profession is the highest form of worship of God", says Swami Vivekananda. They are trained to devote themselves to their profession gradually.

Water never assumes or imposes a shape. The formless one alone can have so many forms representing zero-ego state. The trainee teachers are gradually brought to such a state of zero egoism over the period of their training. Any growth would be considered complete only when it is associated with the growth of spiritual component in human being. Science can not answer every thing, for example, the questions regarding love, faith and beauty. However science and spirituality are similar in their quest to understand the secrets of life. During the training period students acquire spiritual understanding of life to a certain degree which is necessary not only to maintain emotional equanimity while experiencing difficulties but also to be generous, to critically analyse things and tend towards zero ego state. Chinese philosopher Confucius says "I hear, I forget; I see, I remember; I do, I understand. The trainees are provided practical training in almost all fields pertaining to education and social life. As Confucius says, as they do, they understand and follow.

The nature of training that one undergoes in such a teacher training institution transforms him not only as a good teacher but also a good citizen, administrator, substitute for parent and social worker. The trainees are made to realize that they are supposed to live up to the reputation and expectation of their profession. After graduation, they come out knowing fully well about the significance of their profession in the society and that they are entering in to a more responsible phase of life in which they need to have more commitment and discipline.

Technical Teachers Training

Even though often less acknowledged, the importance of a good teacher is enormous in India. They play a vital role in the overall development of the students. Not only are they responsible for imparting academic knowledge, but are also responsible for inculcating the right values and principles to their students. The importance of teachers is especially enormous during the formative years of children when they first join school. Therefore it is very important to have professionally qualified teachers to ensure the right development of students. At present there are several colleges and institutes offering Teacher's Training Courses in India. Since the needs of the primary students are different from the secondary students, the primary teachers and secondary teachers are required to take up different teacher's training courses. Therefore there are different teacher's training institutes offering:

- Basic training certificate (BTC)
- Junior basic training (JBT)
- Nursery Teacher's Training (NTT)
- Diploma in Education (D.Ed),
- Primary teachers training (PTT),
- Bachelor in Education (B.Ed)
- Other teachers's training courses.

Basic Training Certificate (BTC)

The quality of the education system plays a major role in the development of the country as it builds up the human resource of the future. But the sustenance of a vibrant educational system depends to a large extent on the quality of teaching at the elementary level. In order to improve the quality of the teachers, the government of India has set up various institutes that provide Basic Training Certificate (BTC) after the successful completion of a course in teacher's training. The institutes providing Basic Training Certificate (BTC) courses are set up in almost all the states in India so that maximum number of teachers can avail the training and help improve the quality of education in India. The basic training certificate courses in the field of education are increasingly becoming popular as recruitment boards of primary teachers in various Indian states regard the BTC as a part of the minimum eligibility criteria for appointment of primary teachers.

There are several institutes that offer Basic Training Certificate (BTC) Courses in India for teaching at the elementary stage. On completion of the Basic Training Certificate (BTC) Courses from an institute in India, one can apply to various primary schools.

Junior Basic Training in Education

The concept of JBT-Junior Basic training in India is a result of the realization that education received at the elementary level shapes the human personality in more ways than one. It is therefore in the interest of the students that they be taught by trained teachers who can develop the cognitive skills and also take care of the emotional needs of the students. The junior basic training Institutes (JBT) have come up in India mainly to train the teachers who are actively engaged in imparting education to the tender aged children.

Eligibility and Admission Criteria for JBT-Junior Basic Training in India

In some of the states in India the JBT or Junior Basic Training course is conducted for a period of two years. Entrance test is also conducted for the admission of students to this course. Apart from the government institutes there are quite a number of private institutes that conduct junior basic training courses in India. A certain number of seats are also kept reserved as per the rules and regulations mentioned by the government. Students who have passed their 12th standard board examination or equivalent are eligible for taking admission in this course. In some of the states in India a minimum percentage of 50% marks in 10+2 examination is essential for the students willing to join this course. Candidates with a bachelor's degree seeking admission to this course should have a minimum percentage of 45% marks. Candidates should be between seventeen to twenty eight years of age. Five years maximum relaxation in the upper age limit is given to the reserved category candidates.

Junior Teacher's Training Certificate Courses

As schools bring together students from different sections of the society, training of teachers is very important so that they can take care of the differential needs of the students. Junior teacher's training certificate courses are designed to impart training to the teachers so that they can make the students confident enough to face the challenges of the future. Teachers trained through JTTC are expected to be actively engaged in the whole process of producing enlightened citizens of the country.

Elementary Teacher Education (ETE)

Elementary Education refers to the education imparted to children between the age group of 4 to 14 years. The education system in India is supposed to be the second largest and well-developed after America but in the rural areas, the number of drop-outs at the elementary level is quite high. The government, however, is taking steps to enhance the scenario and has been creating programs that would make education easily accessible to everyone and also ensure that they continue with higher education. In order to strengthen elementary education in India it is also essential to provide proper training to the teachers entrusted with the duty of educating the students. There are quite a number of institutes that conduct elementary teacher education (ETE) in India.

Elementary level education lays the foundation of learning in a child. It is, thus, very important that teachers acquire proper training in order to handle children at the elementary level. The course includes all the major aspects of the field of study. Apart from the theory part, teachers also go through practical training courses. However, candidates willing to pursue an elementary teacher education course in India need to fulfil the admission criteria as mentioned by the respective institutes. Candidates who have qualified their 10+2 examination or equivalent from a recognized board with the minimum percentage of marks are eligible for admission to this course. The growing need for trained teachers for the proper functioning of the schools have compelled private institutions to start various courses in elementary teacher education in India.

Primary Teacher's Training (PTT)

Well-trained teachers are capable of improving not only the quality of education in India but also the quality of life as they are actively engaged in building the human resource of the future. Primary Teacher's training is even more important as elementary education plays a very important role in a person's life. As they need to take care of the emotional needs along with developing the cognitive skills of the students primary Teacher's training is regarded as essential. Because of theses reasons Primary Teacher's training (PTT) is made compulsory in various states for appointment as primary teachers.

On this page we have tried to cover the institutes in India that offer the Primary Teacher's Training (PTT) courses.

We have tried to provide as accurate information as possible while compiling this list of PTT institutes in India. However, if you come across any discrepancy or error, do write to us about it. We would welcome any kind of feedback that will improve the quality of this page-a page that concentrates on providing the best information on PTT institutes in India.

Diploma in Education

As elementary education plays a very important role in a person's life and also in the development of the nation, the need to train the teachers is increasingly been realized. In India there are different institutes that provide Diploma in Education, D.Ed. This diploma in education would help the teachers in developing their cognitive skills and also in taking care of the psychological needs of the students. The D.Ed-Diploma in Education, India is gaining popularity as various states have made it compulsory to have D.Ed to be eligible for appointment as teachers. Many institutions offering D.Ed-Diploma in Education in India Teacher training in India is offered through a number of institutions across the country. The various institutions offering D.Ed-Diploma in Education, India include the following:

- Adarsh Junior College of Education, Maharashtra
- Adhyapak Vidyalaya, Junior College of Education, Mumbai
- Basic Training Institute, Raipur, Madhya Pradesh
- District Institute of Education & Training, Ambala, Haryana
- Hindu College Of Education, Haryana
- Padmashree Academy for Creative Teaching, Bangalore.

Qualification: For admissions to the D.Ed-Diploma in Education at various institutes in India, the minimum qualification required is completion of 12 years of basic education. Also 50% is the minimum marks required in the qualifying examination to be eligible for Diploma in Education.

Bachelor of Education, B.Ed

Teachers play a very important role in a student's life. It is, to a great extent, the teachers who decide the shape a student's life will take. So, it is very necessary to be adequately equipped with resources that will make the teacher a perfect role model to the students. To achieve this, Bachelor of Education or B. Ed was introduced, which will teach a person about teaching and the various aspects associated with teaching.

Once a person completes the Bachelor of Education (B. Ed) coaching or training, then he is awarded with a B. Ed degree.

There are some important reasons as to why one should opt for B. Ed course. After training one becomes efficient in teaching subjects of his specialization on the basis of accepted principles of learning and teaching. The course develops skills and widens understanding so that one can impart quality education to his students. The course also teaches about the attitude and makes him skilled in coming up with innovative teaching techniques. One becomes more competent in understanding psychological principles of growth and development and individual differences of the students he teaches.

There is a separate section in this course where the candidate learns to guide the children and counsel them in solving their personal and academic problems.

Top B.Ed colleges in India: If anyone is willing to have a strong foundation of teaching, it is always prudent to seek admission in some of the reputed B. Ed colleges in India.

Among them are:

- Jamia Millia Islamia, Maulana Mohammed Ali Jauhar Marg, New Delhi
- A.G. Teachers College, Ahmedabad
- Himachal Pradesh University, Department Of Education, Shimla
- D.M.College of Teacher Education, Imphal
- Andhra University, Visakhapatanam
- University of Bombay
- St. Xaviers College of Education, Patna
- College Of Teacher Education, Kozhikode
- NSS Training College, Pandalam.

Indian Universities offering B.Ed course Correspondence courses: Besides the above mentioned colleges, there are some universities which offer integrated course on Bachelor of Education.

- Annamalai University
- Bangalore University
- Jamia Millia Islamia Institure of Post Graduate Studies and Research
- University of Kerala, Institute of Distance Education
- University of Madras
- Maharishi Dayananad University
- Mother Teresa Women's University

- Patna University
- SNDT Women's University.

The demand for qualified and trained teachers all over the country has made the students choose B. Ed to ensure a good teaching job.

M.Ed (Master of Education)

As the education sector is attracting adequate attention in the age of structural adjustment and economic reform, Master of education (M.Ed.) is increasingly becoming a preferred career course for many Indians. This has also helped in the growth of the M.Ed. Career Colleges in India. The M.Ed Courses in India are generally pursued after the successful completion of the Bachelor of Education (http://www.indiaedu.com/b-ed-colleges/index.html) (B.Ed.) courses. It is a Post Graduate degree course offered at most of the District Institute of Education & Training (DIET) centers across India. In India M.Ed (Master of Education) is mainly offered by institutions that are recognized by National Council of Teacher Education, New Delhi. It is a government body in charge of improving and implementing teacher education programmes in the country. It is essential to pursue the M.Ed. courses if you are interested in pursing a teaching career. M.Ed. is considered an important course as it helps the students to learn the education systems and patterns more profoundly and comparatively. In every state in India there are several institutions that offer Master of Education courses. The eligibility criterion for admission to this course is that candidates must pass their Bachelor of Education B.ED from a reputed institution in India.

Technical Teachers' Training Institute (TTTI)

Technical Teachers' Training Institute, Chennai is a resource institute established by the Government of India for quality improvement of technical education in our country and in the Southern region in particular.

Technical Teachers' Training Institute, Chennai is a model human resource development Institute for planning, designing, developing, organizing and evaluating quality training programmes, research studies and learning packages for technical and vocational education, industry and community. The Institute strives continuously and vigorously to further enhance its sensitivity to environmental changes and reach greater heights of excellence through active collaboration with national and international agencies on Projects and Programmes aimed at quality improvement of technical education systems.

About TTTI

The Technical Teachers' Training Institute (TTTI), Chennai, was established in 1964 by the Government of India as a key catalyst institution for ensuring quality in technician education in South India comprising the states of Andhra Pradesh, Karnataka, Kerala and Tamilnadu and the Union territory of Pondicherry. The mandate of the Institute is to take initiatives to offer need based HRD programmes through appropriate modes and develop curricula and instructional resources. It will also foster research and offer consultancy and extension services for the total development of polytechnics and other technical and vocational institutions, the Directorates managing these institutions, business, industry and service sectors and the community at large. In carrying out these, the Institute will collaborate with national and international agencies interested in and/or deriving benefits from technical and vocational education including business, industry and service sectors. TTTI, Chennai an autonomous organisation has made substantial and significant contribution towards improving the quality of technical education in all its aspects. Though during the initial stages the emphasis was on training of teachers, over the years the emphasis has gradually changed to assisting the state governments and the polytechnics in the region towards improving their education process and products. This has led to diversification of the Institute's activities to suit the requirements of the clientele system.

Special Teacher Training Such as Physical Education, Music, Teaching the Handicapped

CPED Institutes: While the Sports Authority of India and sports authorities of different states provide extensive support to the secondary schools for organizing sports event, emphasize on considerable improvement of mental as well as physical health of a child through training in extra-curricular subjects such as Physical Education since the initial days of schooling. Kids are thus given adequate training in Physical Education apart from general academics in the schools in Gujarat since the elementary level. Thus, jobs for Physical Education instructors are aplenty in this state. One can go for a lucrative career option in Physical Education training after acquiring requisite skills and knowledge in the field. Several institutes across the country offer certificate, higher certificate and diploma courses in Physical Education. Anyone interested in studying CPED-a higher certificate course in this field, he will find many options in.

Features of CPED Institutes in India

Several Physical Education Colleges and Education Colleges in India offer higher certificate course in this field. Interestingly enough many education trusts conduct this course. While the eligibility criteria for admission to this course is a pass in 10+2 level with a minimum of 45% marks for the general candidates, it is 40% for the applicants who have taken part in the sports events at state or National level.

Music Teacher

True, the prime significance of music lies in its unison with inner chords of our life, creating a harmony that often translates us from the immediate din and bustle of life to a state of relaxation and enjoyment. But it would be rather novice to say that the significance (or utility) of music ends here. It is rather the beginning point. Apart from all the lengthy speculations as to the utility of music and so on and so forth, music today has turned out to be a great career option. With the immense growth in the entertainment industry, career in music is increasingly turning out to be a lucrative option. Before approaching any further, let us have a brief look as to what music precisely is. Singing, Instrument Playing, and Dancing-all three of these arts are elements of music. Singing refers to expression of music vocally; Instrument playing means expression of music with the aid of instruments; and Dancing expresses music with the aid of body movements. These three are broadly the fields in which a person can pursue to build a career in music

Career as a music teacher has become customary with Public and private schools. In the preparatory schools, kids are made to grow a sense of affinity towards singing, playing instruments, body movements and dancing, the act of listening in general, and experimenting with the various music patterns.

The middle, junior, and high schools appoint music teachers for singing, instrument playing, several instrumental as well as choral events, production of musical theatrical events, and the like.

Secondary schools have proper courses on theory and history of music, relation between music and other arts (including the connection between music and literature) which sees a large proportion of music professionals being recruited in the schools as music teachers.

The Higher Educational Institutions have options for music teachers with specialization, such as in Theory of Music, Music history, Literature and Music, Performative Music, Music Composition, Music Therapy, etc.

There are also several music teachers who are Self-Employed. That means, instead of getting recruited in some school or like institutions, they teach privately. Such private music teachers often have their studios at some office building or music store. Many also take to teaching music as a part time career option. However, to be a music teacher one needs to have proper professional training and should posses some degree in the concerned field, preferably from some reputed institute.

Professional Courses in Music

Music as a career option has increasingly been becoming popular in India. Various colleges and universities all over the country are offering professional courses in music. As a matter of fact, almost all states in India have one or more universities that offer specialized courses on music. Besides there are several music schools that only concentrate on music (unlike the universities where music is only a part of the extensive types of courses on offer) and create students who will fit perfectly in the professional world of music. For instance, Dakshini is an institute in West Bengal, based in Kolkata, which offers course on the various aspects of the songs of Rabindranath. This includes both vocals and the theory of this particular genre of songs. People possessing certificate from this institute, for instance, have high chances of making it big in the professional world; be it as a performer, or some other related job. Courses offered include vocals as well as instrumentals. There are also centers that give certificate on various software courses that are nowadays so vital, especially for the recording chores. Some of the known professional courses in Music are:

- B.Arts (Hons) Music
- B.Arts (Visual Art/Music/Dance & Drama)
- B.Arts Music
- B.Arts in Tabla
- B.Fine Arts in Sitar
- B.Fine Arts in Tabla
- Certificate course in Music
- Certificate course in Music & Dance
- Certificate course in Music Appreciation & Music
- Diploma in Music
- Diploma in Sitar
- Diploma in Tabla
- M.A Music
- M.Phil in Music
- Ph.D in Music.

Preparation of Special Education Teachers: Present Status and Future Trends

Educating children with special needs who may not benefit from regular school education calls for changes in curricula, classroom arrangements, provision of aids and appliances, additional finances and appropriate teacher preparation. Preparation of special teachers in India has many problems which need to be addressed. This paper critically analyses the process of preparation of teachers of children with special needs in India, and makes suggestions to improve this process.

All school going children, whether they are disabled or not, have the right to education as they are the future citizens of the country. Some children with special needs may not benefit from regular classroom education due to various reasons including disability. In such a case, it is only appropriate that they be provided with education in some other meaningful way. This entails changes in curricular decisions and classroom arrangements, provision of aids and appliances, arrangements for finances and above all, appropriate teacher preparation. The preparation of regular school teachers at primary and secondary levels is more or less streamlined in India, while the preparation of special teachers still faces problems related to the role of teachers in the different service programmes for people with disabilities, and the competency levels of teachers in terms of the ability to teach children with a single disability and those with multiple disabilities. These issues are further linked to teaching in integrated schools and special schools. The most important aspect of this situation is the economics of developing such a large task-force of personnel to meet the needs of persons with disabilities, whose prevalence is usually quoted as 'one in ten'. According to the National Policy on Education, 1992, the number of school going children with disabilities in India is reported to be about 12.59 million (1). It is in this context that this paper critically analyses the process of preparation of teachers for children with special needs.

Global Scenario

A survey on the situation of educational provision for children with special needs by UNESCO (2) illustrates the types of programmes offered in different parts of the world. The analysis of information from 63 countries that responded to the survey shows that special day schools, special classes in regular schools and residential schools, in that order, provide special education. Early childhood special education programmes, being of recent origin, are provided by only one fourth of the countries surveyed. Integrated and inclusive education are emerging trends practised in very few countries, in the form of support teaching in regular classes and establishment of resource room facilities. Most countries do not have a separate vocational education programme. However, in another UNESCO report, it is seen that about 11 countries have separate vocational training institutes and 6 have them as part of the upper secondary or secondary schools (3).

Apart from the programmes described above, special education is a major component of community based rehabilitation CBR programmes in developing countries, and requires trained personnel for effective delivery of services. For instance, in countries like South Africa a two year training is provided to people with 10 years of schooling to work as special education teachers in CBR programmes (4) and in Zimbabwe, training is provided to community rehabilitation technicians and volunteers for the same purpose (5). Though the process, model and approach may vary, all CBR programmes worldwide have the common objective of enabling persons with disabilities to receive assistance within the existing structures of education, health and social services. This is expected to promote the participation of people with disabilities in the various developmental programmes, and is an enormous task that requires specific manpower preparation to meet its objectives.

Special Educational Services in India

The service provisions in India for persons with disabilities are more or less similar to the global scenario. However, a majority of the services, including special schools, are concentrated in urban areas. There are more special schools for school going children than vocational training centres or integrated schools. Of late, a number of CBR programmes have been initiated to deliver services closer to the homes of people with disabilities.

Teacher's Training for Physical Education

The UNESCO report of 1995 on teacher training was analysed for types of training, duration and the organisations offering them (3). Out of the 63 countries, only 48 have given adequate information on teacher training programmes. An analysis of the available information revealed that in 26 countries, general teacher training included some elements of special education, and that special education training is offered at the diploma level in 7 countries, at the degree level in 15 countries, at both levels in 3 countries. Detailed information on the availability of special education training programmes is not available, but the criteria for becoming a special education teacher are reported by 15 countries. Thirty nine countries have reported in-service training programmes on special education for both regular and special education teachers on a regular basis.

In India, a majority of the teacher training programmes are one year diploma courses after high school education, run by non-governmental organisations. There are about 6 university level programmes in the country leading to the B.Ed. degree after graduation. In the past, great variations were noted in the content, process and evaluation of the teacher training programmes run by the non-governmental organisations in India. The constitution of the Rehabilitation Council of India (RCI) brought about some changes in these aspects of teacher training programmes. RCI is currently making efforts to streamline the teacher training programmes in terms of syllabus, infrastructure and staff pattern, to assure the quality of training. It is now essential that higher level programmes also have uniformity in content and process, according to the directives of RCI in collaboration with Department of Education, Ministry of Human Resource Development. The syllabus for university level programme (B.Ed.-Special Education) has been already standardised by RCI, while the M.Ed. syllabus is in the process of standardisation.

People with disabilities are provided education and training in different settings such as regular schools, special classes in regular schools, special schools, vocational training centres,

CBR projects, and so on. Hence the staff involved in these programmes, including the special education teachers, are required to have different skills and knowledge depending on their client's needs, to provide individual based training. It is questionable whether the pre-service programmes to train special educators prepares them to function effectively in all the above these programmes. Hence a short in-service programme can be planned to help the staff to gain expertise in the areas that have not been covered in the pre-service training programme. A study by Narayan, Rao and Reddy (6) showed that special teachers of visually handicapped children could acquire the skills to identify children with mental retardation and to train them in basic skills, with one week's intensive training. This short training also instilled confidence in the teachers to handle children with mental retardation in addition to children with visual handicap.

Training of teachers in a single disability as against multi-category disability, is a point of discussion in many fora. Many question the quality and adequacy of training people in more than one disability. However, as reported in the National Policy on Education (7) both have their merits and demerits. Gartner and Lipskey (8) pointed out that non-categorical teacher training equips teachers to deal with more than one disability, which in turn bridges the boundaries between general education and special education. However, single disability training is also needed on a limited scale because the children with severe and profound disabilities cannot be easily integrated, and need special education in segregated settings.

A majority of the training programmes in India focus on a single disability. But a single disability teacher training programme is not economically viable since appointing special educators for small groups of 4 to 5 children with single disabilities would be very expensive. Hence, it is necessary to have a teacher training programme which enables the teacher to manage all disabilities. As the current trend in special education is integrated education and inclusive education, there is also a need for reorienting the general teacher training courses. Jangira (9) states that the assumption among most professionals is that general teachers cannot be trained to meet the educational needs of children with disabilities. He points out that this assumption is baseless as there has been no research conducted in this area. However, in order to provide training effectively to children with disabilities in different service programmes, single disability teachers, multi-disability teachers and regular teachers with special education skills would all be required. Therefore, different types of teacher training programmes will need to be planned, with variations in content, process and duration.

Training for Master Trainers

To train the teachers at various levels with diverse needs, well qualified and experienced master trainers are required, apart from well equipped departments of special education in universities. It is essential that master trainers are certified special educators in the respective disability, who further have higher qualification to be at a faculty level, in order to ensure quality in teacher preparation. The current scenario in India reveals that there are few universities which have departments of special education, not all of them have suitably qualified staff, and some have positions that have been vacant for a long time due to non-availability of trained persons. The world trend is towards universities having departments of special education training, and this trend needs to be followed in India as well. All universities must have departments of special education with courses at degree and postgraduate levels to enable preparation of master trainers in special education. This would also automatically lead to research in special education through M.Phil. and Ph.D. programmes. The national institutes should collaborate with the universities with this aim, to upgrade the quality of special education on the whole.

In-service Training Programmes

The field of special education has grown tremendously in the past few years, demanding frequent updates for the professionals. Periodic in-service training programmes for teaching professionals to keep them abreast of the developments worldwide and to equip them to face the challenges of changing trends, is of paramount importance. Such programmes are needed for all levels of staff from classroom teachers to master trainers. Periodic short term programmes varying from 2 weeks to 3 months, based on the need, should be made mandatory for all trained professionals.

The Tasks Ahead

Keeping in view the diverse needs of children with disabilities and the different models of service delivery systems, there is a need for reorienting the existing pre-service programmes in general education from pre-school to university levels and to plan in-service and pre-service programmes in special education at all levels.

To implement the current concept of inclusive education, pre-school teachers should have in-service training on disabilities, and future training courses should include education of children with disabilities. In-service training programmes of two to three weeks' duration for general educators and special educators in all the disabilities and in specific areas of disability, are essential to effectively teach children with disabilities.

Pre-service programmes at degree and postgraduate levels are necessary to improve the quality of teacher training and to promote research and development activities in the field of special education.

All universities should have a department of special education to promote education of children with disabilities.

There should be separate training programmes for staff working in CBR programmes. The preparation of teachers for rural special education programmes should be planned differently, as the aim of these programmes would be to integrate disabled persons in their own environment and community.

Periodic evaluation of the training programmes and constant updating to meet the challenges of changing trends in special education should be part of the planning of teacher preparation.

The curriculum for each of the above programmes should be carefully developed by an expert group which includes practising special teachers. The feedback from the teachers is imperative in making the correct decisions about the content.

The discussions here reveal only some of the problems, which require much more study to help ensure quality in preparation of teachers for children with disabilities.

Teacher Training in Mental Retardation

In 1984, The Rehabilitation Council of India (RCI) was established. The RCI is a statutory body charged with the task of regulating and monitoring training programs for preparing professionals and personnel to serve individuals with disabilities. In 1993, the RCI established that all new professionals and personnel serving individuals with disabilities would be required to participate in training recognized by the RCI as well as register with the council. The RCI outlined training requirements for each disability area which regional centers must follow (Ministry of Welfare, 1998). This was the first time all personnel working with children and adults with special needs were required to participate in some formal training.

The National Institute for the Mentally Handicapped (NIMH) is under the auspices of RCI and attempts to develop and design appropriate models of care for individuals with mental retardation, as well as conduct and coordinate research in assessment, education, training and habilitation for this population (NIMH, 1998-99). The direct training of personnel to serve children and adults with mental retardation in the country is managed by NIMH. Both RCI and NIMH are agencies under the Government of India Society, Ministry of Welfare. The training of personnel in the area of mental retardation is coordinated by four regional centers of NIMH located in Calcutta, New Delphi, Mumbai, and Secunderabad.

NIMH administers three main programs: (1) a Bachelor's Degree in Mental Retardation (BMR), (2) a Diploma in Special Education, and (3) short training programs. Additionally, NIMH conducts 10-12 training programs through university departments, state governments, or nongovernmental voluntary organisations (NGOs).

Because India is such a large country, the number of training sessions offered through NIMH does not meet the needs of all that desire training. Consequently, the selection of participants is highly competitive. A small reimbursement is available for transportation to and from training and usually some accommodations are arranged for participants.

Bachelor's Degree in Mental Retardation. It is possible to receive a Bachelors Degree in Mental Retardation (BMR) from a university or NIMH. Both programs take about 3 years to complete. Admission requirements are determined by Osmania University, Hyderabad. The maximum age for admission is 25 years and candidates must have passed English in three qualifying examinations. Courses in Neurobiology, Psychology, Special Education, Speech-Language Pathology and Audiology, Physiotherapy and Occupational Therapy are offered.

Only about 20 students are admitted each year to the university programs. Students are selected based on merit from each of the four zones in the country. Their aggregate marks earned in the qualifying examination and the entrance examination conducted by NIMH in Secunderabad are used for selection. Due to a high level of unemployment and a general sense that Special Education may offer some employment stability in the future because of the Persons with Disabilities Act, hundreds of applications are received for each slot available. Postgraduate degrees in Special Education (Masters Degrees) are also being offered through the Rehabilitation Council of India in most areas of Special Education.

The university system in India is openly strained. Buildings are often in poor repair, campuses which were designed for 5,000 students may currently serve 60,000 students (Bearak, 1998). While only 3 percent of Indians ages 17-23 attend college, this still amounts to 7 million students seeking college training. Completion of a college degree is increasingly viewed as the admission ticket to the middle class for students from poorer backgrounds so more poor students are attending college than ever before. Some faculty report that a growing number of their students are first generation-learners which supports this trend (Bearak, 1998).

India allocates only 3.7 percent of its gross domestic product on education (Bearak, 1998). This amount exceeds most other nations in South Asia, but lags behind much of the developing world.

Diploma in Special Education (Mental Retardation). The diploma program is the most common training program for Special Education teachers in India. This program takes about one year. Participants chose to specialize in either Mental Retardation or Vocational Training and Employment for the Mentally Retarded. The program is conducted in about 31 training centers in the country (NIMH, 1998-99). It involves 1,000 hours of training, offered 5 days a week. The major content areas taught are: (a) Mental Retardation (nature and needs), (b) Special Education (curriculum and teaching), (c) Psychology, (d) Family and the Community, and (e) Speech Therapy, Physiotherapy and Occupational Therapy. The program is divided into lectures, known as theory, on subjects such as individualized programming, group teaching, use of teaching aids, art, crafts, music, yoga, behaviour modification, Physiotherapy, and Occupational and Speech-Language Therapy. Theory lectures tend to be taught in the afternoons. Participants are also given experience working in school settings, known as practicals.

The Diploma courses are limited to 20 participants. Most are sponsored by nongovernmental voluntary organisations (NGOs). NGOs in the past have been private schools for children with special needs. Participants are given a stipend to support themselves during the training, offered a hostel to live in and the cost of some travel. Participants spend 15 days training in a rural setting as well as 10 days on an educational tour of Special Education programs in India. As with all education in India, there is no cost for tuition. Again, there are many more applicants than openings. In 1999, over 500 applications were received for the 20 slots in the diploma program in the Calcutta NIMH Centre.

Participants must have a minimum schooling of Class 12 of high school that is roughly equivalent to a high school diploma. Applicants are selected based on recommendations, experience in the field, performance in an interview, and education. Applicants with college experience are given preference, as are those who are 35 years old and younger. About 20% of those accepted into the training are working currently in the field while about 5% tend to be parents of a child with a disability or have a sibling who is disabled.

Participants for the Diploma in Vocational Training and Employment (Mental Retardation) receive training in: (a) identifying and training appropriate work environments, (b) skills in the use of technology to develop the most productive work environments, (c) skills in managing clients with mental retardation in the work environment, and (d) skills in serving as administrators in vocational positions (NIMH, 1998-1999). Only two regional centers offer this type of program. Enrolment is limited to 15. Participants are required to have college training in engineering, vocational or science subjects or have a Bachelors in Special Education. A small training allowance is provided. The Diploma in Special Education is now considered the most basic training program for new teachers entering the field.

Short Term Training. About 30 short-term courses are offered annually through NIMH. These training sessions range from 2 days to 3 weeks for professionals already working in the field in mental retardation (inservice training) and for parents of children with mental retardation. Participants in short courses must be sponsored by their current employers to attend.

Short-term courses have a variety of topics. One course is a 3-week refresher training for professionals working in the field that is limited to 30 participants. Other courses are designed specifically for vocational professionals and teachers teaching in rural areas. One short-term program currently being offered across India is called Bridge Training. This is a one-month training course RCI requires for all teachers who began working in the field prior to 1993, but have no formal training. This describes the largest number of teachers working with the mentally retarded in India. RCI has declared it a national goal that all teachers serving children with special needs will have training, the least of which being the Bridge

Training by the year 2000. If a teacher working in the field does not receive and pass the training, it has been stated that the teacher can only be hired as a teaching assistant in the future.

Training Institutions such as Regional Colleges of Education, Institute of Advanced Study in Education, University Departments of Education

Elementary Teacher Education Programme leading to Diploma in Education (D.Ed.)

Infrastructure

- The institution must have at least 1500 sq. mts. land whereupon built-up area consisting of classrooms etc. shall not be less than 1000 sq. mts. Space in each instructional room shall be 10 sq.ft. per student. Built up Area for running other courses in combination with D.Ed programme shall be as under:-

Only D.Ed.	-1000 Sq mts.
B.Ed. plus D.Ed.	-2500 Sq.mts.
B.Ed. plus D.Ed. and M.Ed.	-3000 Sq.mts.

- There shall be provision for two classrooms, one multipurpose hall, one multipurpose laboratory, seminar/tutorial rooms, resource room for education of children with disability, separate rooms for the Principal, for the faculty members, for the office and for the administrative staff and a store. Appropriate space shall be provided for Music, Art, Drama, Work Experience activities. For every instructional room like class rooms, laboratory, library etc. space shall not be less than 10 sq.ft. per student. Multipurpose hall shall have the seating capacity for 150 persons.
- There shall be games facilities with a playground. Alternatively, the playground available with the attached school or local body may be utilized exclusively for fixed periods. Where there is scarcity of space as in metropolitan towns/hilly regions, facilities for small

court games, yoga and indoor games may be provided.

- Safeguard against fire hazard be provided in all parts of the building.
- The institutional campus, building, furniture etc. should be barrier free.
- Hostel for boys and girls separately and some residential quarters are desirable.

Instructional

(a) The institution shall have easy access to sufficient number (5-10) of recognized schools for practice teaching. The school should be within the radius of 10 kms. of recognized elementary schools for field work and practice teaching related activities of student teachers. A list of such schools shall be prepared. It is desirable that it has an attached elementary school of its own.

(b) There shall be a multipurpose educational laboratory with psychology and science sections, and a workshop attached to it.

(c) The science section shall have the apparatus required to demonstrate all the experiments as per the syllabus of elementary schools.

(d) The psychology section shall have facilities for observation of children, counselling & guidance, Personality and Interest Inventories.

(e) There shall be hardware and software facilities for language learning.

(f) There shall be an Educational Technology laboratory with hardware for projection and duplication and educational software, required for imparting Information Technology (IT) literacy, including TV, Camera etc.

(g) ROT (Received Only Terminal) and SIT (Satellite Interlinking Terminal) shall be desirable.

(h) There shall be a library equipped with minimum 2000 titles including text and reference books related to the prescribed course of study, educational encyclopedias, year books, electronic publications (CD Roms) and five educational journals on elementary education and related subjects. It should be augmented with addition of 200 titles annually. The library shall have photocopying facility and computers with internet facility for the use of faculty and student – teachers.

(i) There shall be an Art and Music section, equipped with art paper, boards, brushes, colours etc. for visual art, simple musical instruments such as harmonium, tabla, flute, mridanga, other local popular instruments, costumes and accessories for staging dance and drama performance, curtains and other accessories.

Amenities

- Functional and appropriate furniture in required number for instructional and other purposes.
- The institution shall provide *separate* common rooms for male and female teacher educators/students-teachers.
- Sufficient number of toilets, separate for male and female, shall be made available for staff and students.
- Arrangement may be made for parking of vehicles.
- Safe drinking water be provided in the institution.
- Effective arrangement be made for regular cleaning of campus, water and toilet facilities, repair and replacement of furniture and other equipment.

Secondary Teacher Education—Programme Leading to Bachelor of Education (B.Ed.) Degree

Facilities—Infrastructure

- The institution must have at least 2500 sq. mts. land whereupon built-up area consisting of classrooms etc. shall not be less than 1500 sq. mts. Space in each instructional room shall be 10 sq.ft. per student.

Built up Area for running other courses in combination with B.Ed programme shall be as under:-

Only B.Ed.	-	1500 Sq mts.
B.Ed. plus M.Ed.	-	2000 Sq.mts.
B.Ed. plus D.Ed.	-	2500 Sq.mts.
B.Ed. plus D.Ed. and M.Ed.	-	3000 Sq.mts.

- There shall be provision for not less than two classrooms, one multipurpose hall, three laboratories for conducting instructional activities for approved intake of 100 students, seminar/tutorial rooms, resource room for the education of children with disability, separate rooms for the Principal, for the faculty members, for the office and the administrative staff and a store. In every instructional room like classrooms, laboratories, library etc. space shall not be less than 10 sq.ft. per student. One classroom shall comfortably accommodate 50 student teachers. The Multipurpose Hall shall have a seating capacity for 150 persons. For additional intake proportional increase in the number of classrooms, tutorial rooms, etc.
- There shall be games facilities with a playground. Alternatively, the playground available with the attached school/college may be utilized and where there is scarcity of space as in the metropolitan towns/hilly regions, facilities for yoga, small court and indoor games may be provided.
- Safeguard against fire hazard be provided in all parts of the building.
- The institution campus, buildings, furniture etc. should be barrier free.
- Hostel for boys and girls separately and some residential quarters are desirable.

Instructional

(a) The institution shall have easy access to sufficient number of recognized secondary schools within reasonable distance for field work and practice teaching related activities of the student teachers. A list of such schools shall be prepared. It is desirable that the institution has an attached school under its control.

(b) There shall be a library-cum-reading room with seating capacity for at least 25% students equipped with minimum 1000 titles and 3000 books including text and reference books relevant to the course of study, educational encyclopedias, year books, electronic publications (CD Roms) and minimum five journals of teacher education and subscription to five others in related disciplines. The library holdings shall be augmented with addition of 200 titles annually. The library shall have photocopying facility and computer with internet facility for the use of faculty and student-teachers.

(c) There shall be a science laboratory. The laboratory shall have multiple sets of science apparatus required to perform and demonstrate the experiments prescribed in the syllabus for secondary/senior secondary classes. Chemicals, etc. should be provided in the required quantity.

(d) There shall be a Psychology Laboratory with apparatus for simple experiments related to educational psychology.

(e) There shall be hardware and software facilities for language learning.

(f) There shall be Educational Technology facilities with hardware and software including computers, TV, Camera.

(g) The ICT equipment like ROT (Received Only Terminal), SIT (Satellite Interlinking Terminal) etc. shall be desirable.

(h) There shall be a fully furnished work experience room.

Amenities

- Functional and appropriate furniture in required number for instructional and other purposes.

- The institution shall provide *separate* common rooms for male and female teacher educators/students-teachers.
- Sufficient number of toilets, separate for male and female, shall be made available for staff and students.
- Arrangement may be made for parking of vehicles.
- Safe drinking water be provided in the institution.
- Effective arrangement be made for regular cleaning of campus, water and toilet facilities, repair and replacement of furniture and other equipments.

Master of Education Programme Leading to Master of Education (M.Ed.) Degree

Facilities—Infrastructure

- The institution must have at least 2500 sq. mts. land whereupon built-up area consisting of classrooms etc. shall not be less than 2000 sq. mts inclusive of the space meant for B.Ed Classes. Space in each instructional room shall be 10 sq.ft. per student. Built up Area for running other courses in combination with M.Ed programme shall be as under:-

  B.Ed. plus M.Ed - 2000 Sq.mts

  B.Ed. plus D.Ed. and M.Ed. - 3000 Sq.mts.

- For an intake of 25 students, there shall be provision for at least one classroom, one hall/seminar room, laboratories for conducting instructional activities, separate rooms for the Professor/Head, for faculty members to accommodate seven to eight students, office for the administrative staff and a store.
- Safeguard against fire hazard be provided in all parts of the building.
- The institutional campus, buildings, furniture etc. should be barrier free.
- Hostel for boys and girls separately and some residential quarters are desirable.

Instructional

(a) There shall be a library-cum-reading room facility for at least 10 students and equipped with minimum 2000 titles including text and reference books related to all courses of study, educational encyclopedias, electronic publications (CD Roms) and minimum five professional research journals, internet connectivity. At least 100 quality books will be added in the library every year. The library shall have photocopying facility and computer with internet facility for the use of faculty and student teachers.

(b) There shall be a well-equipped educational technology and media laboratory, with hardware for projection and for duplication and software including TV, Camera.

(c) The ICT equipments like ROT (Received Only Terminal), SIT (Satellite Interlinking Terminal) required for imparting Information Technology (IT) literacy and for using digital resources in teacher education shall be desirable.

(d) There shall be a psychology laboratory with equipment for performing experiments as listed in the curriculum.

Amenities

- Functional and appropriate furniture in required number shall be provided for instructional and other purposes, including desks, chairs and tables, bookshelves, for students and teachers, in classrooms, halls, laboratories.
- The institution shall provide separate common rooms for male and female teacher educators/students-teachers.
- Sufficient number of toilets, separate for men and women, shall be provided for staff and students.
- Safe drinking water be provided in the institution.
- Arrangement shall be made for a canteen, telephone facility and parking of vehicles.

- Effective arrangements shall be made for regular cleaning of the campus, water and toilet facilities, necessary repairs and replenishment of furniture and other equipments.

Certificate in Physical Education Programme (C.P.Ed.)

Facilities—Infrastructure

- There shall be provision of two class rooms per unit intake, one multipurpose hall, one multipurpose laboratory, seminar/tutorial rooms, separate rooms for the principal, faculty members, office for the administrative staff and a store. For every instructional room like classrooms, laboratory, library etc. space shall not be less than 10 sq.ft. per student. Multi-Purpose Hall shall have the seating capacity for 150 persons.
- There shall be a multipurpose field for outdoor sports, at least 200 meter track and a hall for gymnastic and indoor games and sports. In hilly regions, where availability of open space is constrained, it can be shared with other institution.
- To provide these facilities, the Management/Institution shall at the time of making application, have in its possession a minimum of 5 acre of land/land and building either on ownership basis or on lease for as per the relevant regulations.
- Safeguard against fire hazard be provided in all parts of the building.
- The institutional campus, building, furniture etc. should be disabled-friendly.
- Hostel for boys and girls separately and some residential quarters are desirable.

Instructional

- The institution must have at least 5 acres of land which shall provide enough space for institutional building and for future expansion and open space for organizing games & sports. Built up area consisting of class rooms etc. shall not be less than 12000 sq. ft. This must be ensured even in Hilly Regions where the total land may be less than the required 5 acres.

Note: The existing recognized institutions will have to upgrade the infrastructural requirement as per present norms before 1st April, 2010.

There shall be a library equipped with minimum 2000 titles and reference books related to the prescribed courses of study, educational encyclopedias, year books, electronic publications (CD-ROMs) and at least five journals on physical education and related subjects.

The library shall have photocopying facility and Computer with Internet facility for the use of faculty and students teachers.

Laboratories

Education Technology Lab Equipment: Hardware for projection and duplication and educational Software required for imparting ICT literacy including the following:

Public Address System, Tape Recorder, T.V. Set, LCD Projector, One Epidiascope, Display Boards (three) and Movie Camera.

Anatomy, Physiology and Health Education Laboratory

- Human Skeleton -1
- A lever weighing machine -1
- An anthropometric Kit -1
- Growth charts and body system charts -10
- Desirable weight and height tables -2
- Skinfold calipers -2
- Spirometer -2
- Haemoglobino meter
- Sports-Psychology lab with some tests and apparatus

Sports Equipments

Athletic

- Hurdles -30
- Starting Clapper -2
- Measuring tape (steel) 15 Meter -1
- Measuring tape (steel) 30 Meter -1
- Measuring tape (steel) 50 Meter -1
- Wire for marking the track (100 Meter) -1
- Stop watches -8
- Starting block -8
- High jump stands -1 pair
- Cross Bar (High Jump) -6
- Discus-Men & Women -6 each
- Hammers 4 Kg., 5 Kg. -2 each
- Stop boards -2
- Mattress -6
- Stands for judges at finish -2
- Flag pole -20
- Javelin Men & Women (including two aluminum) -6
- Take off board -2

Games

- The basketball board and rings -1 (full set) balls-12
- Basket net -6 pairs
- Volleyball posts -4, balls-12
- Equipment for cricket, softball, - 2throw ball (Sets each)
- Table tennis 2 set table -5 dozen balls and 6-bat.
- Football goal posts with net -2 pairs, 12 balls
- Posts with flags -4 No.
- Hand ball posts -2 pairs, balls-6
- Net -2 pairs
- Badminton posts -4

- Badminton Rackets -24
- Badminton Shuttle Cock -10 Barrels
- Hockey goal posts with nets -1 pair
- Hockey sticks and balls -3 dozen,
- Kho-Kho Poles -2 set

Equipment for Indigenous Activities

- Lezium -50 No.
- Dumbbells -50 pairs
- Indian Clubs -50 pairs
- Flags, hoops rings and light apparatus for physical activities demonstration -50 each

Gymnastic Equipments

- Beat Board -2
- Parallel bars -1 Set
- Horizontal bar -1 Set
- Climbing ropes -6
- Mats -1 doz. coir+1 doz rubber
- Balance beams (adjustable sets) -1 Set
- Vaulting Table -1
- Weightlifting set/power lifting set -1

Cultural Activities: Suitable and adequate instruments, as and when needed for various activities shall be provided.

Miscellaneous

Other equipment required for major games, minor games, recreational games, relays and combative games.

Amenities

- Functional and appropriate furniture in required number for instructional and other purposes.
- The institution shall provide *separate* common rooms for male and female teacher educators/students-teachers.

- Sufficient number of toilets, separate for male and female, shall be made available for staff and students.
- Arrangement may be made for parking of vehicles.
- Safe drinking water be provided in the institution
- Effective arrangement be made for regular cleaning of campus, water and toilet facilities, repair and replacement of furniture and other equipments.

General

In case, one or more courses in teacher education are run by the same institution in the same building the facilities of multipurpose hall, playground, library and laboratory (with proportionate addition of books and equipments) and instructional space may be shared.

Teacher Education Scheme

1. Centrally sponsored scheme of Teacher Education was launched in 1987-88 with; inter alia, the following components:
   a. Establishment of District Institute of Education & Training (DIETs)-by upgradation of existing Elementary Teacher Education Institutions (ETEIs) wherever possible, and establishment of new DIET where necessary.
   b. Upgradation of selected Secondary Teacher Education Institutions (STETIs) into:
      i. Colleges of Teacher Education (CTEs)
      ii. Institutes of Advanced Study in Education (IASEs)
   c. Strengthening of State Council of Educational Research and Training (SCERTs)
2. The Scheme was revised in 2003 and the revised guidelines were issued in January, 2004. the main objectives of the Teacher Education Scheme are as follows:
   a. Speedy completion of DIET/CTE/IASE/SCERT projects sanctioned but not completed up to the end of the IX Plan period.

b. Making DIETs, IASEs sanctioned (and SCERTs strengthened) upto the IX Plan period, optimally functional and operational.

c. Sanction and implementation of fresh DIET/CTE/IASE/SCERT projects to the extent necessary.

d. Improvement in the quality of programmes to be undertaken by DIETs, etc. especially those of pre-service and in-service training, so as to enable them to effectively play their nodal role of improving quality of elementary and secondary education in their respective jurisdiction, as measured in terms of levels of learner achievements.

3. Criteria for setting up of DIETs/District Resource Centre (DRC) are:

a. One DIET for each district having a minimum of 2,500 teachers. If there is an existing Government ETEI in the district, it would be upgraded into a DIET. If no Government ETEI exists in the district, a new institution (DIET) will be established.

b. District Resource Centres in districts with less than 2,500 teachers. If a Government ETEI exists in the district, it would be upgraded into a DRC Otherwise, a new DRC would be established in which case it would not conduct pre-service course.

c. If in a district with more than 2,500 teachers, State Government whishes to establish a DRC in preference to a DIET, it would be able to do so.

4. In order to make proposals for the 11th Plan for Teacher Education, a sub-group under the chairmanship of Director, NCERT was set-up. Based on the recommendations of the sub-group, in addition to strengthening the existing provisions of the scheme, certain new schemes are proposed to be incorporated during 11th Plan:

o Augmenting teacher education capacity in SC/ST and minority areas (Block Institutes of Teacher Education)

- o Professional Development of in-service Elementary and Secondary Teachers.
  - – Training of untrained teachers and para-teachers.
  - – In-service training and subject knowledge upgradation of practicing teachers.
- o Professional development of teacher educators.
  - – Refresher courses.
  - – Fellow-ship programme.
- o Support to NGOs.
- o Special progamme for North-East.
- o Technology in Teacher Education
- o Integrating Elementary Teacher Education with Higher Education.

5. During the current financial year i.e. 2007-08, a provision of Rs. 500 crores has been made for the Teacher Education Scheme. Out of this, Rs. 50 crores has been earmarked for North Eastern Region.

Ideal Physical Facilities for Good Teacher Training Institutes and Colleges of Education

Pre-School Teacher Education Programme Leading to Certificate in Education (C.Ed.)

Infrastructure

- The institution must have at least 1000 sq. mts. land whereupon built-up area consisting of classrooms etc. shall not be less than 500 sq. mts. Space in each instructional room shall be 10 sq.ft. per student.
- There shall be provision for two classrooms, one large multipurpose hall, one spacious learning resource centre, seminar/tutorial rooms, resource room for education of the children with disability, separate rooms for the Principal, faculty members, office for the administrative staff and a store. Activities related to Music, Art, Drama, craft, material production and education technology may be conducted in multipurpose

hall. The size of instructional space shall not be less than 10 sq.ft. per student. Each classroom should be of such size as to comfortably accommodate 50 student-teachers. The Multi-Purpose Hall shall have the seating capacity for 150 persons.

- Reasonable outdoor space and also facilities for indoor games shall be provided for physical education, sports and athletics. There shall be games facilities with playground. Alternatively, the playground available with the attached school or local body may be utilized and where there is scarcity of space as in metropolitan towns/hilly regions, facilities for yoga, indoor games may be provided.
- Safeguard against fire hazard be provided in all parts of the building.
- The institutional campus, building, furniture etc. should be barrier free.
- Hostel for boys and girls separately and some residential quarters are desirable.

Instructional

- The institution shall have access to a cluster of nearby pre-school/ECE centers for field work and practice teaching related activities of student teachers. A list of such schools shall be prepared. It is desirable that the institution has its own attached Nursery school.
- The institution shall establish a composite Learning Resource Centre to provide a setting wherein teachers and students have access to a variety of materials and resources to support and enhance the teaching-learning process. These should include:
  - — Books, journals and magazines
  - — Children's books
  - — Audiovisual equipment – TV, VCR, tape recorder, slide projector
  - — Audiovisual aids, video – audio tapes, slides, films.

— Teaching aids – charts, pictures
— Developmental assessment check lists and measurement tools.
— Computer, Xerox machine.

Equipment and Materials for Different Activities

Teaching-Learning Materials and Aids

— The equipment and materials should be suitable and sufficient in quality and quantity for the variety of activities planned in the programme. These include the following:
— Educational kits, models, play materials, simple books on different topics (songs, games, activities, work pages), puppets, picture books, photographs, blow-ups, charts, maps, flash cards, handbooks, pictures, pictorial representations of developmental characteristics of children.

Equipment, Tools, Raw Material for Aids, Play Material and Arts and Crafts Activities

One set of wood working tools, one set of gardener's tools, raw materials and equipment required for toy making, doll making, tailoring, dress designing, puppetry, material for preparation of charts, models and other practical activities to be done by the student teacher – art material, waste material, stationery (chart paper, mount board etc.), tools like scissors, scales etc., cloth.

Audio Visual Equipment

As mentioned in 5.2.2, Hardware for projection and duplication and educational software facilities including TV, VCR, Audio Cassette Recorder, slide projector, blank audio video cassettes, video-audio tapes, slides, films, charts, pictures. ROT (Received Only Terminal) and SIT (Satellite Interlinking Terminal) would be desirable.

Music and Movement

Simple musical instruments such as Harmonium, Tabla, Flute, Manjira and other indigenous instruments.

Books, Journals and Magazines

A minimum of 1000 books on relevant subjects should be available during the first year of establishment of the institution and 100 standard books be added every year.

The collection of books should include children's encyclopedias, dictionaries, reference books, books on professional education, teachers' handbooks, books on and for children (including comics, stories, picture books/albums, poems). The institution should subscribe to at least three journals of which at least one should be on professional education.

Games and Sports

Adequate games and sports equipment for common indoor and outdoor games should be available.

Amenities

— Functional and appropriate furniture in required number for instructional and other purposes.

— The institution shall provide *separate* common rooms for male and female teacher educators/students-teachers.

— Sufficient number of toilets, separate for male and female, shall be made available for staff and students.

— Arrangement may be made for parking of vehicles.

— Safe drinking water be provided in the institution.

— Effective arrangement be made for regular cleaning of campus, water and toilet facilities, repair and replacement of furniture and other equipments.

General

If one or more courses in teacher education are run by the same institution in the same building, the facilities of playground, multipurpose hall, library and laboratory (with proportionate addition of books and equipments) and instructional space, can be shared.

UNIT-III

Selection of Student Teachers

Selection of Suitable Students for Teacher Training Programmes

Who are Looking for a Career Option in the Field of Teaching, must have some special qualities different from other professions.

As this field is so vast having areas of specialisations, different skills and type of training are required for different levels. Areas of specialisation include teaching at nursery schools, middle schools, high schools, colleges, universities, institutes, special schools etc. Each level calls for a different expertise. If you love to be with children, teaching at schools would be a good option, but if you want to be with young adults, it is better to look at the college or university level. Good teachers can bring out the best in every student.

They are the ones who make a difference in the lives of their students. Rousing students from their apathy and watching their curiosity grow is one of the biggest rewards of teaching.

The trick in being a popular teacher – the kind starry-eyed kids in school follow around with adoration writ large on their faces, and in college, seek out for advice, guidance and some simple hand-holding – is identifying yourself with the students. They are the most loved of teachers who climb down from the high perch of authority that their job automatically places them on, and see things from the students' perspective. And those who are aware of the power to shape lives that has been vested in them, and use it responsibly. Teaching is a highly noble profession, most suited one especially for women. Teachers are always a boon to society. Through their intelligence, patience and wisdom, they attempt to not only hone the learner's intellect and aptitude but also, create a well-rounded personality. Teaching has an influence in developing ones mind and character and also gives the satisfaction of having sparked the light of knowledge and dispelled the clouds of ignorance.

Personality Traits

This profession requires dedication, perseverance and patience. Knowledge of the subject one is teaching as well as a rich experience in co-curriculars; keenness to take on responsibility; tact; patience and the ability to get along with all kinds of people are essential. Main reason for opting this career could be interest in the subject, secure professional career and regular annual vacations. It can also be a second career for those who have retired from professional services.

You need to have a blend of mind, patience, confidence, liking for and an understanding of children which is a must. You must have organizing capacity, friendly and helpful nature to enter into this field. Teacher should have the ability to communicate well, to create a liking in young minds even in the case of most boring subjects. She/he should have a deep passion for the subject one handles. Must encourage in students the ability to analyse and think. A teacher must always remember that apart from teaching, it is he/she who shapes a child's character. Teacher has to be a friend, philosopher and guide to his wards.

Pre-primary and Elementary Teacher Education

Pre-primary teacher education is offered mainly by privately established schools generally recognised by the State Councils of Educational Research and Training, leading to certificates or diplomas in nursery teaching, early child care and education, and Montessori method. The courses are generally open to candidates who have passed secondary (Class 10) or (Class 10+2) examination.

The eligibility requirement for elementary teacher education programme is a pass in secondary or higher secondary examination. The District Institutes of Education and Training (DIETs) established as model institutions for preparing elementary teachers have prescribed senior secondary (Arts, Science, and Commerce) as the desired qualification requirement for admission to programmes offered by them. Different institutions have different nomenclatures of their awards, such as Basic Teaching Certificates (BTC), Junior Basic Training (JBT) Certificates, Elementary Teacher Education (ETE) Certificates, and DEd. Successful candidates are eligible for appointment as primary teachers for classes I-V.

Secondary Education Teachers

Education for secondary education teachers leading to the award of Bachelor of Education (B.Ed) degree is of one-year duration. Earlier the nomenclature was Bachelor of Training (BT). Admission requirement is a Bachelor's degree in any discipline. In some universities, the nomenclature of the award is Siksha Shastri. B.Ed course is offered by more than 120 universities. Dakshin Bharat Hindi Prachar Sabha (Chennai-600017) offers B.Ed courses in Hindi. B.Ed courses are also available through distance learning mode. Only recently, the NCTE had imposed rigorous norms on universities intending to offer it. This has been discussed in a subsequent section. The NCTE had proposed the B.Ed course should be of two year duration. This course has been introduced only in the four Regional Institutes of Education (earlier known as Regional Colleges of Education) at Ajmer, Bhopal, Bhubaneshwar and Mysore.

An alternative approach to prepare teachers for secondary stage was initiated in 1964 by the National Council of Educational Research and Training (NCERT) through the Regional Institutes of Education (RIEs). These four institutions used to offer integrated four-year course leading to the award of B.Sc. B.Ed., and B.A., B.Ed. degrees. The qualification requirement was a pass in higher secondary (10+2) examination (with science for B.Sc., B.Ed course). It was envisaged that four-year integrated programmes would gradually be adopted by all colleges. However, this did not materialise. The RIEs now offer only B.Sc., B.Ed. course of four-year duration. The entry requirement is a pass in 10+2 with PCM/CBZ. Several other universities have also started introducing such integrated programmes.

At the Master's degree level, more than 100 universities offer one-year course leading to the award of M.Ed. degree. Some universities (e.g., Rashtriya Sanskrit Vidyapeetha, Tirupati) named it Siksha Acharya. M.Ed. course is open to candidates possessing B.Ed. degrees. The course is of two-year duration. Introduction of M.Ed. courses in universities also needs the approval of the NCTE. In May 1999, the NCTE had asked them to apply for recognition of their M.Ed. courses.

Education, as a subject, is also offered both at the B.A (as one of the combinations) and the Master's degree level. M.A in Education is of two-year duration and is offered by education faculties of more than 25 universities. They are open to Bachelor's degree holders. Kalyani University (Kalyani-741235) and the Mysore University (Mysore-570005) offer M.A/M.Sc. (Education) and M.Sc. (Education) respectively which are open to B.Ed. degree holders. IGNOU offers a Ph.D (Education) course to distance mode.

Physical Education

Like teacher education, physical education is provided by separately established physical education colleges and university faculties of education. Lakshmibai National Institute of Physical Education (Gwalior-474002) is an exclusive university-level institution devoted to physical education and sports. It was the first institution to introduce the graduate and postgraduate courses in physical education. Two other reputed institutions in the field are Lakshmibai National College of Physical Education (Thiruvananthapuram-695581), and the Indira Gandhi Institute of Physical Education and Sports Science (New Delhi-110018).

Physical education is offered at three levels, viz., first degree level, as one of the combinations, Bachelor's Degree, and

Master's degree level. The Bachelor's degree course, leading to the award of Bachelor of Physical Education (BPEd or BPE), are offered by more than 45 universities. The duration of the course is three years and is open to candidates who have passed the 10+2 examination. Only seven universities have introduced courses in B.Ed (Physical Education) of one-year duration. Eligibility requirement is a Bachelor's degree in any branch.

At the Master's degree level, courses of both one-year and two-year duration are available. Of the 27 universities which have introduced the course, in 12 the duration is two years. Eligibility requirement for both is, however, BPEd (or BPE) degree. Five universities offer M.A (Physical Education) of two-year duration, while three others have M.Ed. (Physical Education) course. Annexure 3 gives a list of universities offering Master's degree courses.

Teachers for the Disabled

Education of teachers for teaching students with various disabilities began in the voluntary sector involved in imparting education to children with visual impairment. The first ever masters level degree (M.Ed) course in the area of visual disability started at Sri Rama Krishna Mission Vidyalaya College of Education (Coimbatore), an autonomous college affiliated to the Bharathiar University. In 1983, the National Council of Educational Research and Training (NCERT) initiated multi-category special education teacher preparation courses through the Regional Institutes of Education (then Regional Colleges of Education). However, they are no longer operational. The UGC has introduced a scheme for starting teacher preparation programmes for children with special needs.

The scheme called Teacher Preparation in Special Education (TEPSE) provides financial assistance to universities and colleges of education to start B.Ed. (Special Education) and M.Ed. (Special Education). With the establishment of the Rehabilitation Council of India (RCI) under the Rehabilitation Council Act, 1992 the programmes for teacher preparation have received great impetus. A large number of diploma courses of general nature as well as dealing with specific disabilities is now available. Degree level courses (B.Ed. and M.Ed.), either general or specific in nature, are also being introduced by universities. All the courses need the approval and recognition of the RCI. Annexure 4 gives a list of institutions which offer B.Ed (Special Education) and M.Ed. (Special Education) courses, general in nature.

Teacher Education in Specific Subjects

Preparing teachers for teaching in specific subject areas was first mooted by the NCERT. As stated earlier, the four Regional Institutes of Education introduced four-year programmes for preparing teacher for teaching arts and science subjects. At present, they offer only B.Sc. B.Ed. course. Several other universities have also introduced similar programmes. A small number of universities also offer B.Ed. and M.Ed. programmes of one-year duration in specific subjects.

The Central Institute of English and Foreign Languages (Hyderabad-500007) offers a number of programmes on Teaching of English as Second Language (TESL) at the Master's, pre-Doctoral, and Doctoral level. Regional Institute of English, South India (Bangalore-5600056) has also introduced PG Diploma in English Language Teaching through distance learning mode. The course is recognised by the NCTE. The University of Delhi (Delhi-110007) now offers a unique teacher education programme in elementary educaton leading to the award of BEIEd degree. It is an integrated course of four-year duration for which the entry requirement is a pass in 10+2 examination. At present, the course is available in six affiliated colleges.

The Regional Institutions of Education offer M.Ed (Elementary Education). Indira Gandhi National Open University (IGNOU) (New Delhi-110068) offers a Diploma in Primary Education specifically for teachers in North-Eastern States and Sikkim. A programme in distance learning mode it has three modules each of six month's duration. The course is open only to in-service primary and elementary school teachers with two years of teaching experience. IGNOU has also introduced a certificate programme in Teaching of Primary School Mathematics through distance learning mode. Courses in adult education are available only at the postgraduate diploma level.

Admission Tests

It's often the most simplest-sounding questions that are the trickiest ones to answer in an interview situation. But with some self reflection and insight into what interviewers are trying to find out, you should be able to answer any questions put to you with confidence.

Why Do You Want to be a Teacher?

Admissions tutors are looking for people who understand the breadth of the teaching role and why it appeals to them. Teaching isn't just about liking children or young people. A great deal of a teacher's time will be spent with other adults (for example teaching assistants, special needs co-ordinators and language supporters) and there are significant responsibilities that need to be taken on within the school setting, such as coordinator and leadership roles. You won't impress if your response is that you like children, all your family are teachers or that you like the sound of the long holidays!

What Worries You about Teaching?

An honest answer will probably stand you in good stead. However, if you appear to be terrified of pupils that will worry the assessors! It's true that all teachers work hard at behaviour management, but don't be over-influenced by the negative portrayal of schools on TV.

Another issue candidates raise is concern about the work/life balance. It is a legitimate response: even if you worked 24/7 in teaching there would still be things to do. I have also heard interviewees express uncertainty about managing other adults in the classroom. Basically, the question is designed to assess whether candidates have realistically thought through the different aspects of the teaching role.

Do You Think You will Make a Good Teacher?

You need to show that you appreciate which of your particular skills and attributes will equip you for the teaching profession. Be realistic – no-one will possess all the skills when they apply. It's much more important to show that you understand which qualities you will need to develop. Come into the interview prepared with hard evidence to demonstrate the experience and skills you have already amassed.

What would You Say to a Pupil who Says Learning (for example, your subject) is a Waste of Time?

Assessors want to see whether you understand why learning is not a waste of time and to explore your feelings about learning. If you are applying to become a secondary teacher, the interviewer will want to be convinced by your passion and enthusiasm for your subject. If you are applying for a primary course, you will be teaching a huge range of subjects: take some time to reflect upon which subjects you feel most passionate about and why before the interview.

Why have You Chosen this Age Range?

An assessor will want to feel certain that you know which age group is right for you and that you have thought your reasons through carefully. If you have an English degree and have chosen to teach at primary level, you may be asked why you wouldn't want to teach your subject at secondary level. There's no right or wrong answer here – it's about showing that you've made your decision for the right reasons. For example, a poor answer would be that you chose primary because you felt secondary school would be too hard – you need to give positive reasons for teaching a particular age grou

Sample Other Interview Questions for Teachers

1. Tell me about yourself.
2. What/who influenced you the most to become a teacher? Why did you choose education as your career?
3. How have your past experiences prepared you for teaching?

4. Why do you want to teach?
5. What do you enjoy most about working with young people?
6. What do you enjoy least about working with young people?
7. Tell me about your student teaching/internship experience(s). What kind of problems did you have and how did you resolve them?
8. What classroom management techniques did you use? How effective have they been for you?
9. How do you handle discipline problems? What is the most difficult aspect of discipline for you?
10. How would you handle a student who is a consistent behavioral problem?
11. How do you keep students on task?
12. How would you handle a student who refuses to work in your class or do what you ask?
13. A student is consistently late for class. How would you handle this situation?
14. Some students always finish their assignments early. How would you deal with the free time that they have?
15. What do you feel are the most important things students learn in your classroom?
16. Describe an ideal classroom.
17. Describe a teaching strategy you used to maximize the learning potential of all students.
18. Describe how you conduct a lesson. Describe the components of an effective lesson plan.
19. Do you believe in detailed lesson plans? How do you use lesson plans?
20. Define cooperative learning and give an example of how you have used it.
21. What curriculum materials have you developed?
22. How do you individualize your teaching?

23. Would you rather teach the slow learner or the advanced learner? Why?
24. How do you teach to low achievers?
25. How would you work with a mainstreamed learning disabled student?
26. How do you handle the different ability levels of students? How do you help a student who is having difficulty?
27. How do you work with students who perform below grade level?
28. How do you personally feel students learn?
29. How do you motivate students? What are several effective ways to motivate students toward active participation in the learning process?
30. How do you reinforce major ideas or concepts that you want students to learn?
31. How do you provide feedback to students about how they are doing?
32. How will you determine if students are learning? What evaluation techniques do you use?
33. How have/would you use paid/volunteer aides in your classroom?
34. How do you involve parents in the learning process?
35. What is your philosophy of teaching?
36. What attributes are common to good teaching?
37. What are the three most important strengths you possess that will make you a successful teacher?
38. Give me one or two examples of things that you discovered about yourself while student teaching that you would like to improve.
39. What kind of relationship do you have with your students?
40. How do you think your students would describe you?
41. What kind of learning environment do you try to create?

42. How do you reinforce self-esteem in students?
43. Describe your ability to listen and be responsive. Can you give me an example?
44. Are you the kind of person children and adults confide in?
45. How do you make students feel at ease around you, while still respecting you?
46. How do you show your students that you understand them and their frustrations?
47. Through your teaching, do you think students can be changed?
48. Is it appropriate to tell your class that you are angry with them?
49. What do you expect from your supervisor? What qualities would you like to have in your principal?
50. What issues in education are of greatest concern to you? Why?
51. What is the toughest aspect of teaching today? What are some of the greatest challenges of being an educator?
52. What is the most exciting initiative happening in your area of education today?
53. What books/journal articles have you read in the last six months/year?
54. Do you plan to continue your education/seek an advanced degree?
55. What do you want to accomplish in your profession?
56. Why should this district hire you?
57. What things about yourself would you like to bring out that have not been brought out in the interview?
58. What questions do you have that I may be able to answer?

Interview and Achievement Tests

An achievement test is a test of developed skill or knowledge. The most common type of achievement test is a standardized test developed to measure skills and knowledge learned in a given grade level, usually through planned instruction, such as training or classroom instruction. Achievement tests are often contrasted with tests that measure aptitude, a more general and stable cognitive trait.

Achievement test scores are often used in an educational system to determine what level of instruction for which a student is prepared. High achievement scores usually indicate a mastery of grade-level material, and the readiness for advanced instruction. Low achievement scores can indicate the need for remediation or repeating a course grade.

Under No Child Left Behind, achievement tests have taken on an additional role of assessing proficiency of students. Proficiency is defined as the amount of grade-appropriate knowledge and skills a student has acquired up to the point of testing. Better teaching practices are expected to increase the amount learned in a school year, and therefore to increase achievement scores, and yield more "proficient" students than before.

When writing achievement test items, writers usually begin with a list of content standards (either written by content specialists or based on state-created content standards) which specify exactly what students are expected to learn in a given school year. The goal of item writers is to create test items that measure the most important skills and knowledge attained in a given grade-level. The number and type of test items written is determined by the grade-level content standards. Content validity is determined by the representativeness of the items included on the final test.

Attitude Test

The normal and over-achievers have favourable attitude towards teaching but the under-achievers have unfavourable attitude towards teaching. The normal and over-achievers have satisfactory level of home environment but the under-achievers have average level of home environment. There is significant relationship between the B.Ed. students' attitude towards teaching profession and their home environment. Unfavourable attitude towards teaching and satisfactory home environment may be the reason for discrepancy between performance and proficiency of under achievers. Normal and over-achievers have favourable attitude towards teaching and extrovert type of personality. By providing proper motivation, the students can develop positive attitude and behaviour.

According to Richard M. Felder and Rebecca Brent (North Carolina State University) in the article How to Evaluate Teaching (2004) "Students are in better position than anyone else to judge certain aspects of teaching, such as how clear, interesting, respectful and fair a course instructor is, and they are the only ones who can say how an instructor has influenced their attitude towards the course subject. Their motivation to learn it and their self-confidence." McKeachie (1997) supported student evaluation of teachers' with considering it as the single most valid source of data on teaching. The University of British Columbia (UBC) had approved a policy on student evaluation of teaching while considering its importance.

In India N.S.S. Training College, Ottapalam (Run by Nair Service Society) in its Quality Policy practicing student evaluation of teacher by providing a questionnaire to the students. The Internal Quality Assurance Cell (Annammal College of Education for Women, Thutukudi) in its Annual Report 2006-07 highlighted their practice of student evaluation of teachers. T. Ramanna College, Aizawl (Mijoram) had also prepared the scheme of student evaluation of teachers as per recommendations of National Assessment and Accreditation Council (NAAC). University Grant Commission (UGC) also recommended the Autonomous colleges and Universities to adopt its scheme on student evaluation of teachers'.

These stapes taken by various government and non-government educational institutions proves that the teacher evaluation in any form become very much needed and become very important in present context. It motivates the teachers by treating them as professional in charge of their own professional growth and helpful to encourage teachers' professional growth and to improve teacher morale. The term teacher morale means a feeling, state of mind and a mental and emotional attitude. It means that the increased teacher morale indicates that teachers will enjoy teaching and students will enjoy learning. In this way it seems that teacher morale will become a pleasant effect of teacher evaluation.

Aptitude Test

Aptitude test is a measure of a person's natural ability or potential to learn a skill or set of skills. Abilities that are typically measured by aptitude tests include abstract, verbal, and numerical reasoning, because these give a rounded view of a person's general ability in relation to the workplace. Aptitude tests are a form of psychometric test and are administered by trained users.

The terms intelligence, ability, and aptitude are often used interchangeably to refer to behavior that is used to predict future learning or performance. However, subtle differences exist between the terms. The tests designed to measure these attributes differ in several significant ways.

What is an Aptitude Test?

Like intelligence tests, aptitude tests measure a student's overall performance across a broad range of mental capabilities. But aptitude tests also often include items which measure more specialized abilities—such as verbal and numerical skills—that predict scholastic performance in educational programs.

Compared to achievement tests, aptitude tests cover a broader area and look at a wider range of experiences. Achievement tests tend to measure recent learning and are closely tied to particular school subjects.

Aptitude tests tell us what a student brings to the task regardless of the specific curriculum that the student has already experienced. The difference between aptitude and achievement tests is sometimes a matter of degree. Some aptitude and achievement tests look a lot alike. In fact, the higher a student goes in levels of education, the more the content of aptitude tests resembles achievement tests. This is because the knowledge that a student has already accumulated is a good predictor of success at advanced levels.

What is The Value of Aptitude Testing?

Research data show that individually administered aptitude tests have the following qualities:

- They are excellent predictors of future scholastic achievement.
- They provide ways of comparing a child's performance with that of other children in the same situation.
- They provide a profile of strengths and weaknesses.
- They assess differences among individuals.
- They have uncovered hidden talents in some children, thus improving their educational opportunities.
- They are valuable tools for working with handicapped children.

In addition, group aptitude tests—usually given as part of a group achievement battery of tests—can be given quickly and inexpensively to large numbers of children. Children who obtain extreme scores can be easily identified to receive further specialized attention. Aptitude tests are valuable in making program and curricula decisions. They can also be used for grouping students as long as grouping is flexible.

How Can We Use Aptitude Test Results?

In general, aptitude test results have three major uses:

- *Instructional:* Teachers can use aptitude test results to adapt their curricula to match the level of their students, or to design assignments for students who differ widely. Aptitude test scores can also help teachers form realistic expectations of students. Knowing something about the aptitude level of students in a given class can help a teacher identify which students are not learning as much as could be predicted on the basis of aptitude scores. For instance, if a whole class were performing less well than would be predicted from aptitude test results, then curriculum, objectives, teaching methods, or student characteristics might be investigated.

- *Administrative:* Aptitude test scores can identify the general aptitude level of a high school, for example. This can be helpful in determining how much emphasis should be given to college preparatory programs. Aptitude tests can be used to help identify students to be accelerated or given extra attention, for grouping, and in predicting job training performance.
- *Guidance:* Guidance counselors use aptitude tests to help parents develop realistic expectations for their child's school performance and to help students understand their own strengths and weaknesses.

UNIT-IV

Organisation of Practice Teaching

Preparation of Trainees for Teaching—Model Lessons

These questions were handed out in a Teacher Training meeting that our Primary held. Answer these questions with a yes or no and then choose a few to improve on to help prepare yourself to be spiritually ready when you teach.

Are You Spiritually Prepared to Teach?

1. I pray to be filled with love for those I teach.
2. I pray for the children (or other students) I teach, both active and less active.
3. I ponder their needs as I prepare my lessons.
4. I strive to keep the commandments so the Holy Ghost will be my constant companion.
5. I study the scriptures on a regular basis.
6. I strive to live according to the gospel principles I teach my students, even if I do not completely understand them.
7. I am a positive example to the children (or students) I teach.
8. I seek the spirit while I study the scriptures.
9. I pray and sometimes fast for better understanding of the gospel principles.

10. I study my lesson with a prayer in my heart.
11. I know that my calling to teach is a calling from God.
12. I am striving to magnify my calling.

After the resurrected Savior had spent a day teaching the Nephites, He commanded them to take time to prepare for the teachings He would share the next day. He said, "Go ye unto your homes, and ponder upon the things which I have said, and ask the Father, in my name, that ye may understand, and prepare your minds for the morrow" (3 Nephi 17:3). You can apply this principle in your preparation as a teacher. As you take time to prepare thoughtfully and prayerfully, you will be blessed with greater understanding. You will be more receptive to the guidance of the Spirit.

Find Joy in Preparation-What Can I Learn?

Don't just focus on what you're teaching, think about what you can learn.

Start Your Preparation Early-Don't Procrastinate

Here are four tips to help you better prepare your lesson:

1. What should happen in the lives of those I teach as a result of this lesson?
   a. What should the children (or other students) feel while I'm teaching this lesson?
   b. What should they feel after the lesson?
   c. Note: Primary lessons provide the answers to the above two statements
2. Which specific principles should be taught?
   a. Often a lesson will contain more material than you can teach. Don't feel pressured to complete the entire lesson. Select the material best suited for your class first and if there is time left do the others.
   b. Remember that your lesson will not be the only time they will learn about the subject.
3. How should these principles be taught?

a. Get to know those you teach!

b. 40 different methods of teaching:

Activity verses- For little children, these verses are either said or sung while doing simple actions.

Application techniques- Ask students how they can apply to their own lives what they've learned.

Attention Activities- Should be brief and lead directly into the lesson.

Audiovisual Materials- Only Church appropriate materials should be used.

Brainstorming- The teacher presents a question or situation and gives the students a short amount of time to freely suggest solutions or ideas.

Buzz Sessions- Students are divided into small discussion groups, each assigned a topic or assignment.

Case Studies- True-to-life situations that prompt students to ponder or discuss what they would do in similar situations.

Chalk/Dry Erase Boards- Used to emphasize key facts, acknowledge students' ideas, clarify points, and make outlines or lists.

Choral Reading- Reading of verses or quotes as a group or class.

Comparison and Object Lessons- Using a physical object to represent a non-visual topic, i.e.: using soap to represent repentance or a seed for faith.

Demonstrations-

Dioramas- Miniature drawings (or other artwork) representing a story, usually done in a box (shoe box size) but can be done on a larger scale if necessary.

Discussions- Students can be asked ahead of time to discuss a certain topic either as a group or with the entire class.

Dramatizations- Acting out a scene from the scriptures, a story, or a time from our Church History.

Drawing Activities- Appropriate for children, this type of activity should be connected with the lesson.

Examples- Explaining hard-to-grasp concepts by using something the students can relate to. I.e.: A child rarely knows what one-tenth means. They understand better if there are 10 pennies in front of them and one is put into a tithing envelope.

Flannel Boards- Also for children, this method is a great way to help teach part of a lesson.

Games- Should relate to the lesson, but can be creative. Competition should not be the focus and there should not be losers, only winners.

Guest Speakers- Having someone to come to your class and share a personal experience or example.

*Handouts-*Perfect to help your students remember what they've learned after your lesson is over.

Lectures- Should be short and to the point to keep the attention of your students.

Likening- Directly applying to the lives of your students gospel principles, stories, and situations in the scriptures.

Maps- A great visual aid to help illustrate your lesson, many maps are available in both church and local libraries.

Memorization- Learning a scripture, quote, or verse by heart is great for more long term applications.

Music- Quickly brings the Spirit of the Lord into your classroom. Only Church appropriate music should be used.

Music With Narratives- Songs that teach about a principle can be followed by short text (read silently or aloud) or by another song.

Overhead Projectors- Can be used in multiple ways, including class participation and involvement in reading, answering questions, or taking quizzes.

Panel Discussions- Having at least two groups discuss a topic from different points of view.

Paper Stand-Up Figures- For children, these can be used to represent themselves or characters from the lesson.

Pictures- A visual aid that can be very affective if used in direct correlation with the lesson.

Puppets- All kinds of puppets (simple to more complex) can be made to tell a long story or part of history that might be boring if just narrated.

Reader's Theatres- Have students read a particular assignment and then explain the main points of what was read.

Recitations-Similar to Choral Readings but done on an individual level.

Role Playing-Scripts read with assigned characters and narrator(s) to help demonstrate part of the lesson.

Roller boxes- Illustrated stories on long sheets of paper which are wrapped around two sticks. The story is wrapped around one stick and is exposed (usually through a hole in a box) when wrapped around the other stick.

Scriptures- Should be used often, although can be simplified for young children.

Stations- Students are divided into groups and are taught a different point at each station.

Stories- Very effective to help apply gospel principles.

Visual Aids- Help maintain the attention of your students.

Work Sheets and Activity Sheets- Quizzes, puzzles, questions, and other type of work sheets can help students think of the points on a more personal level.

Love Them

It is so important to get to know those you teach. That's why we ask for faithful attendance and have activities outside of the Sunday setting.

"But ye will teach them to walk in the ways of truth and soberness; ye will teach them to love one another, and to serve one another." (Mosiah 4:15.) In order to teach our students to love one another, we must love them first. Teach with love, show your love, and let them know how important they are.

"Parents and teachers should see beyond the little girl in pigtails and should not be misled by the ragged little boy with a dirty face and holes in knees of his pants. True teachers and leaders see children as they may become. They see the valiant missionary who will one day share his testimony with the world and later become a righteous father who honours his priesthood." Boyd K. Packer, "Teach the Children", Ensign, May 1991.

For our Teacher Training I compiled most of this list using the ideas give in the manual, "Teaching, No Greater Call".

Preparing your classroom involves many different aspects. They are:

Cleanliness

- Pick up papers: Erase the chalk board
- Temperature: Not too hot or too cold (if possible)
- Lighting: Room should have adequate lighting
- Arrange chairs so the sun will not shine in anyone's eyes

Personal Touches

- Occasionally bring objects that improve the appearance of the room or relate to the lesson

Lesson Materials

- Have everything ready before hand (chalk, eraser, visual aids)
- Test electrical equipment to make sure it works properly

Seating

- So you can see each student and they can see you
- Students can see visual aids and/or chalkboard
- Smaller chairs should be used for smaller children, etc.
- Occasionally children may enjoy sitting on the floor

- If necessary designate seating to separate students who disturb each other (idea for younger classes: put students' names on paper attached to their chairs, or placed on the floor, before class).

Space

- Should have enough room for activities, games or crafts.

Criticism Lessons

Art criticism involves a specific way of looking at a work of art. You can make discernment about art without being a professional artist, all you need to do is learn to look (see) and think about what you are seeing. Learning how to criticize artwork properly will allow you to better understand works of art and why they have become important. The process of art criticism involves 4 actions. They are: describe, analyse, interpret and decide.

Some guidelines to help you are below:

Describe-what things are in the painting? Think of things like clothing, environment, etc.

Analyse-how are the elements of line, shape, form, texture, space and value used? How are the principles of unity pattern, rhythm, variety, balance, emphasis and proportion used?

Interpret-what is the artist trying to say to you? What is going on in the picture or artwork?

Decide-what do I think about this artwork? Do I like it? Why or why not?

How do I feel about whether the artist was successful in conveying an idea?

To better understand about deciding about how you feel about an artwork, it may help to take a look at the three common aesthetic theories below.

Is the artwork successful because:

Imitationalism / Realism-The artist rendered the images in a realistic manner. It is easy to discern the subject because of the realistic quality of the art.

Formalism / Composition-The artist was adept in using the elements and principles of design in the artwork. (This also refers to the placement, contrast, and interaction of all parts of the work.)

Emotionalism / Feelings-The artist did a good job of evoking an emotion or feeling from me.

Block Teaching

What is Block Teaching?

Block teaching is the re-organisation of the school year into approximately 12 'blocks' of 4 weeks each, instead of two semesters of 15 weeks each. There is no loss of curriculum time during block teaching. Changes to the curriculum are kept at a minimum.

Subjects are now taught in blocks of 4 weeks instead of over a 15-week semester. Students who used to take 6 – 7 subjects per semester will now take at most 2 subjects per block. That may not translate into a lighter workload but it gives the student an opportunity to focus on the 1 or 2 subjects at hand and give their best in the projects assigned. Compared to the semestral system, the student no longer needs to hand in 6-7 projects at a time.

It has been noticed that taking 6-7 subjects at a go and having to submit 6-7 projects within a tight time frame does take its toll on the quality of the work submitted. This is understandable as most students would be creatively stretched thin to produce good work for all the 6 to 7 subjects. In some instances, students may select certain projects to concentrate their energies on, unfortunately neglecting and possibly even failing the other subjects. This would affect their GPA standing and their progress in school.

With only 1 to 2 projects to manage in block teaching, students would be able to concentrate on these projects. They would be able to give more dedicated time to these 2 projects and their energies would not be as diffused as it otherwise would be. With good time management and planning skills, students are more likely to produce better quality work and do better in the long run.

Block Teaching Emulate Industry Conditions

Block teaching mimics the project management timeline in industry where designers work with short deadlines. The flow of work in block teaching allows students to ease themselves into the pace of work usually required in the professional arena, training them to think faster on their feet and conceptualise ideas more efficiently in a realistic time frame.

Design and art are interconnected. However, unlike the fine artist, designers are faced with deadlines in the professional world dictated by the tight turnaround time demanded of the industry. Block teaching gives students the opportunity to experience and hone their skills in an environment and project timeline as near as it can be to the real world. Adjusting to the needs of industry upon graduation and making that transition from school to work will be much easier and smoother for students under the block teaching system.

The current polytechnic vacation periods has a partial overlap with primary and secondary school vacation periods. Vacation blocks can now be planned to fit the usual school holiday vacations, thus enabling students who wish to spend time with their families to do so.

Scheduled

The time table is reconfigured such that students will now focus on these 1 or 2 subjects, attending class and seeing the lecturers in charge of these subjects, on a daily basis. Classes are now conducted over 4 main time slots in the school day: 0900–1200hrs, 1200-1500hrs, 1500-1800hrs and 1800-2100hrs. Block Teaching is organized such that the students would only attend classes between 0900-1800hrs or 1200-2100hrs.

Students are welcome to utilize any of the school's facilities from 0900-2100. Students could easily request for extension of opening hours through their lecturers. These requests should reach Manager/Admin latest by1600hrs on the day of need.

Most projects do not require "excessive" time to complete. However, students do get passionately involved when preparing their submissions. This could result in long hours, a common trend in top design schools. While the school encourages students to submit their best effort, students are also encouraged to take care of their health as fatigue can retard the creative process.

In the semestral system, a longer SIP / OSIP period of 16 weeks would be challenging because SIP and OSIP is normally conducted during the vacation periods. Block teaching allows the school to conduct SIP / OSIP continually throughout the year. The longer industry stint will give students a richer work experience and provide a better opportunity for learning. The continuous flow of interns into industry will facilitate involvement in exciting and significant projects.

Students can opt to take subjects during a planned vacation block, if necessary. In other words, they can 'choose' if they want to take the vacation or not, or study and work their way through it. So the pace of learning is entirely within the hands of the students. They choose if they would like to accelerate the learning process or if they need to 'catch up' to make up the CUs necessary for graduation.

In block teaching, there are no supplementary exams. Design courses are course-work based where students are continually assessed. If a student fails a subject, it would mean that the student did not have an adequate grasp of the subject. The student will take the subject again in another block. Students are allowed two (2) attempts to pass each subject. In the past students had to be in class at least 85% of the time. If class attendance falls below 85%, they faced being debarred from any assessment. With block teaching, debarment no longer applies. Students' attendance is an attitude issue and should not be linked to an academic outcome. But, Because block teaching is intensively taught, it would not be in the students' best interests to deliberately skip classes. Ultimately, the responsibility for learning falls on the student. Students are matured enough to make responsible choices for themselves and would be aware of the ramifications of not attending class. Attendance is still taken in class because lecturers do want to be on hand to help those who are managing a personal crisis or health situations.

Internship

India: many worlds within one country offering incredible beauty, diversity, culture, and opportunities of exploration, travel, discovery, and interning. Internship and travel to India is like paradise for those who know India and a surprise for those who do not know this amazing country. A country with a rich past (in some aspects older than recorded time), India is a country of contrasts and has many things that one can wish for.

India 's internship programs are highly organized and respected, offering benefits beyond just professional development. An internship in India presents a wonderful opportunity to be immerged within an amazing culture while simultaneously working in your area of interest. The internship experience in India supplies a number of hands-on experiences while also offering glimpses into the issues affecting developing countries.

The position provides opportunity to interns to take classes in Kindergartens, Pre-school, Elementary school, Middle school or High school, colleges etc. in renowned Indian institutions and acquire management experience in a professional environment. In addition, the teaching interns will have the opportunity to assist in academic works and participate in academic seminars and workshops.

The intern works with regular Teachers and assist them in supervising students, teaching classes, attending committee hearings, assessing student achievements, and completing other tasks as they occur. You will work from Monday to Friday. The internship is open to teachers/graduate or under graduate students who have genuine interest in teaching and up date their teaching skill. In return an internee can experience life in Indian culture and community and acquire sharing of knowledge, skill and learn different languages.. The duration of the internship will be 3 months to 1 year. Interns will be honoured with Certificates after successful completion of their international internship.

The internship is open to teachers/graduate or under graduate students who have genuine interest in teaching and up date their teaching skill.

Orientation, Language and Cultural Immersion

The internship in India experience starts with one week of language and cultural orientation. However, you can choose to take the orientation or go directly into an intern project.

You can earn academic credit for nearly every type of internship work in India. The best way to receive academic credit is through your college/university. Therefore, please contact your respective faculty/academic advisor about receiving college credit for your internship work. Your college/university may need additional information about the program prior to approval, as well as require you to submit a research paper or other requirements.

The teaching project covers teaching in several government schools in the country. In India, English is not included in primary, public school curriculums. Many poor children cannot afford private, English lessons-often continuing on to higher levels of education with little or poor knowledge of Basic English. Your role as an intern can help make a difference in these children's lives. This is a very good opportunity for interns with an educational background to learn the basic fundamentals of teaching a class and gain some experience in their desired profession. Interns are expected to be flexible and patient as well as possess a passion and love for teaching.

Intern's Responsibilities

In the teaching program, you either work as an independent teacher or as an assistant to an teacher. You will be teaching in government schools (most likely). If you don't get placement in a government school, the participant will then be teaching in either a semi-government or private school.. As an English teacher in India, interns will teach conversational English through by the books or educational materials designated by said schools. Interns may also organize games, art lessons, singing, dancing, as well as other creative, educational and extra-curricular activities. Interns may also assist children with homework as well as monitor academic progress. Schools may seek the assistance of interns with help in other, on-going academic activities or administrative duties.

Internship Project and Role of Supervisor

One of the most distinguished features of internships in India is the guidance of supervisor. There should be assigned a qualified supervisor to provide assistance for all interns throughout the duration of their chosen internship. Individuals filling the role of supervisor are usually either the director or chosen staff member of the project which interns choose.

During your time as an international intern, you will be assigned a number of duties which volunteers also perform. In the internship, you will select a particular area of your interest related to teaching and explore the issue further with the help of your assigned supervisor. Please note: the project supervisor DOES NOT develop internships as this is up to the intern to get as much or as little out of their projects. ALL participants should be proactive to ensure the ultimate success of their internships. Supervisors will provide at least five (5) hours each week to make certain that interns are adequately guided.

Teaching and SuperVision

Our beliefs about education greatly influence us as teachers and supervisors. Although many research studies have been done, none has found the solution to improving schools; human judgment about goals and purposes greatly affects our schools.

Supervision before Classroom Teaching and During Class Teaching

In the 1970's studies were done known as effective teaching research. This studies studied classrooms instead of schools as earlier studies have done. An effective teacher was described as one, who has a "can do" attitude, spends whatever time is needed for students, they have a professional attitude, and they expect their students to achieve. Classroom climate was also examined and a positive classroom was described as an academic work oriented atmosphere that was warm and supportive. There were found to be six functions of an effective classroom:

1. Review of earlier work
2. Presenting new content/skills
3. Student practice
4. Feedback and correction
5. Independent practice
6. Review.

Cautions Concerning Effective Teaching Research

Effective teaching research cannot always be generalized to all school populations. One of the problems with explicit teaching is not practical and cannot be used for all subject and content areas. At best we are teaching skills that benefit from direct instruction 40% of the time. Other researchers have observed teachers using effective teaching and their students had lower skills.

Effective and Good Schools: The Same?

One of the questions that must be deal with is "What is good?" We have to decide what we are looking for in a school. Once we know what we think a good is then we must decide how we become effective. Educators must know what their goals are for students before they can become effective.

Changing Views: New Emphasis on Constructivist Teaching and Learning

Constructivist teaching is the result of a variety of philosophers, psychologists, and educators. This theory believes that people create new knowledge as results of the interaction of their existing beliefs, knowledge, and values. Knowledge is constructed by the learner so it can be different for each person. Cognitive constructivism is focused on intellectual development while social constructivism states that knowledge is constructed based on the individual's interaction with their social context. A constructivist classroom is very different from a traditional classroom. The students have a larger role in a constructivist classroom. It is also more flexible with active and cooperative learning. Finally there is less testing and more authentic learning.

New Trends in Teacher Preparation

Teachers need to know what instruction they want to improve before they can actually begin to improve instruction. The supervisor's role is to help the teacher the teacher devise instructional strategies that can be used to improve instruction.

Beliefs about Education

Teacher and supervisor's beliefs about the purpose of education greatly influence the classroom and instructional improvement efforts.

Supervision Beliefs

Since most administrators are former teachers their background as a teacher influences their view of supervision.

Supervisory Platform as Related to Educational Philosophy

There are many different educational philosophies. Three major philosophies have a relationship with supervision.

Essentialism

This philosophy believes reality is absolute and unchanging. It dates back to the Greeks. This teaches the mind to think in a natural and logical way. There is a body of timeless knowledge and the supervisor must be the most knowledgeable. The teacher teaches truth. The supervisor is the expert and transmits knowledge to the teacher.

Experimentalism

This philosophy is based on pragmatism, progressivism and reconstructionism. They believe in the scientific method and in proving something as true. They also believe there is no absolute truth. Knowledge is always changing. Morality is seen as the behavior that promotes the group's great good. Teachers and students should not be content with knowledge they are constantly testing old hypotheses and trying new ones. The supervisor works democratically with teachers. They view schools as laboratories to test hypotheses.

Existentialism

This is the rejection of other philosophies and is a combination of essentialism and experimentalism. They believe in rational, scientific thinking to explore and frame knowledge. The individual is the source of reality and reality only exists within one's own existence. Human relations are very important and knowledge of one's self and allowing others the freedom to know themselves is very important. The supervisor allows the teacher to make their own choices. Teachers explore and learn on their own.

Checking Your Own Educational Philosophy and Supervisory Beliefs

Directive supervision is based on the belief that teaching consists of technical skills with known standards. In this model the supervisor job is to inform, direct, model and assess the competencies of the teachers. The supervisor is seen to have more responsibility that the teacher. Collaborative supervision is based on the belief that teaching is a problem solving activity. The supervisor's role is to guide the problem solving process. The supervisor and the teachers are seen as equals.

Non-directive supervision is based on the belief that learning is a private experience where students come up with their own solutions. The supervisor listens and is nonjudgmental and provides clarification for teachers. The supervisor is seen to have less decision making responsibility than the teacher.

Professional Development for Cooperating Teachers in India

There is a growing realization that professional development for teachers can be aided by strengthening and expanding "models of international exchange that build lasting cross-national partnerships among educational institutions with common interests and complementary objectives" (Riley 2000). One of the acknowledged areas of need is promoting greater sensibility to cultural differences (Dunn 1997; Zimpher and Ashburn 1992). Study-abroad programs increase openness to diversity and intercultural competence (Akande and Slawson 2000). Student teaching placements overseas will provide an opportunity for preservice teachers to explore and analyse their philosophy and methods of teaching in a new and different environment, enabling them to see themselves as professionals in a global context.

Opportunities for professional overseas experience for preservice teachers have been limited. International education has, until recently, focused on schools and general higher education. It is only in the past decade or so that teacher education has been given much attention. As an indication of the interest in teacher education, an international directory of teacher education institutions, the first of its kind, was published recently (International Council on Education for Teaching 1999). At the institutional level, the international perspective on teacher education has taken the form of student teaching-abroad programs in which student teachers spend either a part or the entire student teaching period in a country of their choice. Until recently, for student teachers from the United States, this has been limited to countries in Europe or Australia. Asia and Africa have not been of great interest particularly because of the language barrier student teachers may face in the classrooms.

The Role of Co-operating Schools and Teacher

Private schools in India are perceived as providing a better education and a higher caliber of teachers. More prestigious and catering mainly to a privileged section of society, they have a better profile than public schools, with higher results on examinations and high-quality teaching personnel (Kindgon and Dreze 1998; Surya 2000). Private school facilities are better than those that can be expected in most public schools; thus, innovations in education, whether they are systemic, instructional, or curricular, are more likely to take place in private institutions than in public schools (Gautama 1997). They are also selective in hiring and demand a high level of efficiency.

As a result, teachers are better trained, more dedicated, and more focused on the academic achievement of their students. Public school teachers, on the other hand, are perceived as lax in performing their regular teaching activities. It may be unrealistic, therefore, to expect them to take on other responsibilities with enthusiasm, especially when their own teacher education experiences may not have been inspiring or useful to them (Department of Education 1986).

COEs would therefore like private schools in India to host and supervise preservice teachers, because they may afford preservice teachers a more positive experience. However, teacher education in India is isolated from schools; neither public nor private school systems are closely involved in training future teachers (Central Advisory Board of Education 1992; Committee for Review of National Policy on Education 1990; Ramanathan 1998). Furthermore, private schools are wary of the quality of preservice students and do not participate widely in field experiences (Ramanathan 1999b).

Because fev' preservice teachers are placed in private schools, teachers in these schools have very little experience and are not significantly involved in the supervision or evaluation of student teachers. Neither the limited length of field experiences nor their responsibilities require them to be in close enough contact with preservice teachers to influence them significantly. University supervisors help student teachers with planning, observe the implementation, and are solely responsible for grading. Cooperating teachers are therefore peripheral to the experience (Ramanathan 1999a).

On the rare occasions cooperating teachers are expected to supervise student teachers, they have no guidelines to follow. Their own student teaching experience of three weeks does not compare with the minimum of 10 weeks of student teaching generally required in the United States. Their own supervision as student teachers also provided an unsuitable example (National Policy on Education 1986). Thus, the clinical model of supervision with a cycle of pre-observation conferencing, observation, and post-observation conferencing is unfamiliar to them (Ramanathan 1999b).

University supervisors are not a rich resource for cooperating teachers. Relations between them are superficial and sporadic (Ramanathan 1999a). Furthermore, higher education institutions in India are not research-oriented, being neither producers nor consumers of research (Raina 1997). It is difficult to change or modify the traditional supervisory practices of university supervisors to suit cooperating teachers.

Not surprisingly, COEs do not see it as incumbent on them to provide professional development for cooperating teachers in private schools. Sporadic attempts to do so have been unsuccessful for the same reasons as in the United States-lack of time or incentives for cooperating teachers. Efforts to make it a requirement at the district level have not met with success (Ramanathan 1998). Thus, cooperating teachers in India's private schools do not have a strong understanding of supervisory practices.

Therefore, if student teachers from the United States are to have the quality of mentoring in India they may expect from their cooperating teachers at home, mentors in India's private schools must have special training. This professional development must encompass the supervision and mentoring skills of their U.S. counterparts. In addition, they must learn to create a realistic environment for students to learn about teaching in a new culture. Finally, recognizing that this could be a learning opportunity for both mentor and mentee, cooperating teachers may question their own practices and beliefs in the light of student teachers' experiences. Apart from all the fresh teaching ideas student teachers will bring into the classroom, this unique situation provides cooperating teachers insights into their teaching context from a global perspective. Cooperating teachers must be alerted to this potential.

Microteaching

You know that the economic prosperity and good quality of any nation depends upon the development of human resources of that nation. The significant fact in the development of manpower resource refers to the competencies and the level on which these competencies are imparted. You also know that it largely depends on those who develop these competencies. Therefore, for this purpose we need highly competent teachers for imparting these competencies. It is essential that teachers imparting these competencies should have the capability to perform their task efficiently. For this, they need to acquire requisite competencies themselves.

In the present Unit we will attempt to understand as to what competencies are essential for becoming better teacher and how these competencies can be imparted.

Teaching: Definition

"Teaching means many different things, that teaching act varies from person to person and from situation to situation." (Bar, 1961)

"The behaviour or activities of persons as they go about doing whatever is required of teachers, particularly those activities which are concerned with the guidance or direction of learning of others." (Ryan, 1965)

"Teaching is the arrangement of contingencies of reinforcement under which students learn. They learn without teaching in their natural environment, but teachers arrange special contingencies which expedite learning and hastening the appearance of behaviour which would otherwise be acquired slowly or making scene of the appearance of behaviour which might otherwise never occur." (B.F. Skinner. 1968) "Teaching as an act of interpersonal influence aimed at changing the ways in which other persons can or will behave." (N.L. Gage, 1963)

What is a Teaching Skill?

Definition of teaching skill might be one of the following:

- A teaching skill is that behaviour of the teacher which facilitates pupils' learning directly or indirectly.

- A teaching skill includes all arts and behaviour of the teacher which maximizes pupils' learning.
- A teaching skill is that art of the teacher which makes communication between the teacher and pupils sufficiently.

Attempts have been made to list teaching skills. Allen and Ryan listed the following teaching skills at Stanford University in the U.S.A.

1. Stimulus Variation
2. Set induction
3. Closure
4. Teacher silence and non-verbal cues
5. Reinforcing pupil participation
6. Fluency in questioning
7. Probing questioning
8. Use of higher questions
9. Divergent questions
10. Recognizing and attending behaviour
11. Illustrating and use of examples
12. Lecturing
13. Planned repetition
14. Completeness of communication.

B.K. Passi has given the following list of Teaching Skills in his book "Becoming Better.

Teacher; Microteaching Approach"

1. Writing instructional objectives
2. Introducing a lesson
3. Fluency in questioning
4. Probing questioning
5. Explaining
6. Illustrating with examples

7. Stimulus variation
8. Silence and non-verbal cues
9. Reinforcement
10. Increasing pupil participation
11. Using black board
12. Achieving Closure
13. Recognizing attending behavior.

NCERT (National Council of Educational Research and Training) in its publication *Core Teaching Skills* (1982) has laid stress on the following teaching skills...

- writing instructional objectives
- Organizing the content
- Creating set for introducing the lesson
- introducing a lesson
- Structuring classroom questions
- Question delivery and its distribution
- Response management
- explaining
- illustrating with examples
- Using teaching aids
- Stimulus variation
- Pacing of the lesson
- Promoting pupil participation
- Use of blackboard
- Achieving closure of the lesson
- Giving assignments
- Evaluating the pupil's progress
- Diagnosing pupil learning difficulties and taking remedial measures
- Management of the class.

Core Teaching Skills

It is not possible to train all the pupil teachers in all these skills in any training programme because of the constraints of time and funds.

Therefore a set of teaching skills which cuts across the subject areas has been identified. They have been found very useful for every teacher. The set of these skills are known as CORE TEACHING SKILLS

Core Teaching Skills are:

1. Skill of Probing Questions
2. Skill of Explaining
3. Skill of Illustrating With Examples
4. Skill of Stimulus Variation
5. Skill of Reinforcement
6. Skill of Classroom Management
7. Skill of Using Blackboard
8. Skill of Introducing a lesson.

Core Teaching Skills and their Components

1. Probing Questions

   Components: Prompting, seeking further information, redirection, focusing, increasing critical awareness.

2. Explaining

   Components: Clarity, continuity, relevance to content using beginning and concluding statements, covering essential points.

3. Illustrating with examples

   Components: Simple, relevant and interesting examples appropriate media, use of inducts, deductive approach.

4. Stimulus variation

   Components: Body movements, gestures, change in speech pattern, change in interaction style, pausing, focusing, oral-visual switching.

5. Reinforcement

   Components: Use of praise words and statements, accepting and using pupils' idea, repeating and rephrasing, extra vertical cues, use of pleasant and approving gestures and expressions, writing pupils' answer on the black board.

6. Classroom Management

   Components: Call pupils bynames, Makenorms of classroom behaviour, attending behaviour reinforced, clarity of direction, check non-attending behaviour, keep pupils in Eye Span, check inappropriate behaviour immediately.

7. Use of blackboard

   Components: Legible, neat and adequate with reference to content covered.

Concept of Microteaching

Microteaching is a teacher training technique which helps the teacher trainee to master the teaching skills. It requires the teacher trainee

1. to teach a single concept of content
2. using a specified teaching skill
3. for a short time
4. to a very small member of pupils.

In this way the teacher trainee practices the teaching skill in terms of definable, observable, measurable and controllable form with repeated cycles till he attains mastery in the use of skill.

Meaning and Definition of Microteaching

Meaning

Micro teaching is a procedure in which a student teacher practices teaching with a reduce number of pupils in a reduced period of time with emphasis on a narrow and specific teaching skill.

Definition:

- "Microteaching is a scaled down teaching encounter in class size and time-D.W.Allen(1966)
- "Microteaching is defined as a system of controlled practice that makes it possible to concentrate on specified teaching behaviour and to practice teaching under controlled conditions."-D.W. Allen & A.W.Eve (1968)
- "Microteaching is a scaled down teaching encounter in which a teacher teaches a small unit to a group of five pupils for a small period of 5 to 20 minutes"-L.C. Singh (1977)

Objectives of Microteaching

- To enable teacher trainees to learn and assimilate new teaching skills under controlled conditions.
- To enable teacher trainees to master a number of teaching skills.
- To enable teacher trainees to gain confidence in teaching.

Characteristic of Microteaching

- Microteaching is a highly individualized training device
- Microteaching is an experiment in the field of teacher education which has been incorporated in the practice teaching schedule
- It is a student teaching skill training technique and not a teaching technique or method
- Microteaching is micro in the sense that it scale down the complexities of real teaching
- Practicing one skill at a time
- Reducing the class size to 5 – 10 pupil
- Reducing the duration of lesson to 5 – 10 minutes
- Limiting the content to a single concept
- immediate feedback helps in improving, fixing and motivating learning

- The student are providing immediate feedback in terms of peer group feedback, tape recorded/CCTV
- Microteaching advocates the choice and practice of one skill at a time.

Steps of Microteaching

The Microteaching programme involves the following steps:

Step I Particular skill to be practiced is explained to the teacher trainees in terms of the purpose and components of the skill with suitable examples.

Step II The teacher trainer gives the demonstration of the skill in Microteaching in simulated conditions to the teacher trainees.

Step III The teacher trainee plans a short lesson plan on the basis of the demonstrated skill for his/her practice.

Step IV The teacher trainee teaches the lesson to a small group of pupils. His lesson is supervised by the supervisor and peers.

Step V On the basis of the observation of a lesson, the supervisor gives feedback to the teacher trainee. The supervisor reinforces the instances of effective use of the skill and draws attention of the teacher trainee to the points where he could not do well.

Step VI In the light of the feed-back given by the supervisor, the teacher trainee replans the lesson plan in order to use the skill in more effective manner in the second trial.

Step VII The revised lesson is taught to another comparable group of pupils.

Step VIII The supervisor observes the re-teach lesson and gives re-feed back to the teacher trainee with convincing arguments and reasons.

Step IX The 'teach – re-teach' cycle may be repeated several times till adequate mastery level is achieved.

Diagramatic Representation of a Microteaching Cycle

Plan: This involves the selection of the topic and related content of such a nature in which the use of components of the skill under practice may be made easily and conveniently. The topic is analyzed into different activities of the teacher and the pupils. The activities are planned in such a logical sequence where maximum application of the components of a skill is possible.

Teach: This involves the attempts of the teacher trainee to use the components of the skill in suitable situations coming up in the process of teaching-learning as per his/her planning of activitieo.

If the situation is different and not as visualized(in the planning of tTe activities, the teacher should modify his/her behaviour ás per the demand of the situation in the Wlass. He should have the courage and confidence to handle the situation arising in the class effectively.

Feedback: This term refers to giving information to the teacher trainee about his performance. The information includes the points of strength as well as weakness relating to his/her performance. This helps the teacher trainee to improve upon his/her performance in the desired direction.

Re-plan: The teacher trainee replans his lesson incorporating the points of strength and removing the points not skillfully handled during teaching in the previous attempt either on the same topic or on another topic suiting to the teacher trainee for improvement.

Re-teach: This involves teaching to the same group of pupils if the topic is changed or to a different group of pupils if the topic is the same. This is done to remove boredom or monotony of the pupil. The teacher trainee teaches the class with renewed courage and confidence to perform better than the previous attempt.

Re-feedback: This is the most important component of Microteaching for behaviour modification of teacher trainee in the desired direction in each and every skill practice.

Time duration for the microteaching is;

- Teach: 6 Minutes.
- Feedback: 6 Minutes.
- Re-Plan:12 Minutes.
- Re-Teach: 6 Minutes.
- Re-Feedback: 6 Minutes.

Phases of Microteaching

There are three phases of the Microteaching procedure which you have studied in the previous section of this Unit. They are:

1. Knowledge Acquisition Phase.
2. Skill Acquisition Phase.
3. Transfer Phase of Microteaching.

1. *Knowledge Acquisition Phase (Pre-Active Phase)*

It includes the activities such as;

- Provide knowledge about teaching skills.
- Observe the demonstration of teaching skill.
- Analyse and discuss the demonstration of the teaching skill.

2. Skill Acquisition Phase (Inter-active Phase)

It includes the activities such as;

- Planning and preparation of micro lesson for a skill.
- Practicing the skill.
- Evaluation of the practiced skill (Feedback).
- Re-plan, Re-teach and re-feedback till the desired level of skill is achieved.

3. *Transfer Phase (Post –Active Phase)*

- Giving opportunity to use the mastered skill in normal class room teaching.
- Integrate the different skill practiced.

Link Practice (Integration of Teaching Skills)

When mastery has been attained in various skills, the teacher trainee is allowed to teach the skills together. This separate training programme to integrate various isolated skills is known as 'Link Practice'

- It helps the trainee to transfer effectively all the skills learnt in the micro teaching sessions.
- It helps to bridge the gap between training in isolated teaching skills and the real teaching situation faced by a student teacher.
- Desirable Number of Pupils: 15-20
- Preferable Duration: 20minutes.
- Desirable Number of Skills: 3-4 Skills
- Link practice or integration of skills can be done in two ways.

Integration in Parts

3 or 4 teaching skills are integrated and transferred them into a lesson of 15-20 minutes duration. And again 3 or 4 skills are integrated and are transferred all the skills to one lesson.

Integration as a Whole

Student teacher integrates all the individual teaching skills by taking them as a whole and transferred them into a real teaching situation.

Merits of Microteaching

- It helps to develop and master important teaching skills.
- It helps to accomplish specific teacher competencies.
- It caters the need of individual differences in the teacher training.
- It is more effective in modifying teacher behaviour.
- It is an individualized training technique.
- It employs real teaching situation for developing skills.
- It reduces the complexity of teaching process as it is a scaled down teaching.

- It helps to get deeper knowledge regarding the art of teaching.

Limitations of Microteaching

- It is skill oriented; Content not emphasized.
- A large number of trainees cannot be given the opportunity for re-teaching and re-planning.
- It is very time consuming technique.
- It requires special classroom setting.
- It covers only a few specific skills.
- It deviates from normal classroom teaching.
- It may raise administrative problem while arranging micro lessons.

Origin and Development of Microteaching

The idea of Microteaching originated for the first time at Stanford University in USA, when an Experimental Project on the identification of teaching skills was in progress under the guidance and supervision of the faculty members (Bush, Allen, McDonald Acheson and many others).

This project was aided by Ford Foundation and Kettering Foundation. The team of experts was assigned the development of testing and evaluation tools to measure the attainment of teaching skills. At this juncture Keath Acheson, a research worker was investigating the utility of video tape recorder in the development of technical teaching skills. This instrument could be used for recording the class interaction and the behaviours of the trainee vividly and accurately. This lead to the development of a systematic and accurate method of giving feedback to the teacher trainee. All the steps of Microteaching technique:

Teach '! Feedback '! Replan '! Reteach '! Refeedback were formulated. Thus the name of Microteaching was coined for this method of developing teaching skills in 1963. Since then this technique of teacher training has been widely used in almost all Colleges and Universities of Europe and Asia. In India, it is being used with great emphasis in all the teacher training programmes of developing teaching skills and competencies among teacher trainees.

Microteaching in India

- The department of Teacher education in the NCERT designed a project to study the effectiveness of Microteaching in 1975 in collaboration with the Centre of Advanced Study in Education (CASE) Baroda.
- Research and training programmes for teacher educators were also initiated in collaboration with the department of Education, University of Indore.
- Passi, Singh and Jangira developed instructional materials which were used to train teacher educators.

Flanders Interaction Analysis

Flanders Interaction Analysis is a system of classroom interaction analysis. The system in its original and modified forms have been used extensively in classroom observation studies (Wragg, 1999). It has also been used in the study of differences between expert and non-expert PBL tutors at University of Michigan Medical School (Davis et al 1992). It is a system for coding spontaneous verbal communication. The system has two primary uses, Firstly to provide evidence of difference in teaching patterns that distinguish one curriculum from another and secondly it can also provide data which may help to explain why differences in learning outcomes appeared or failed to appear. The system will be used for both purposes in the PEPBL study.

The Flanders Interaction Categories (FIAC) consist of 10 categories of communication which are said to be inclusive of all communication possibilities. There are seven categories used when the teacher is talking and two when the pupil is talking. Because the system is totally inclusive coding at a constant rate allows calculation of the proportion of time spent in one or more categories.

The major feature of the system is the analysis of patterns of initiative and response:

- To initiate = to make the first move, lead, begin, introduce idea or concept for the first time.
- To respond = to take action after an initiation, to counter, to amplify or react to ideas already expressed.

In the traditional teaching situation it is expected that the teacher will show more initiating behaviour than the pupils. It is hypothesized that in problem based learning (PBL) the balance between teacher and student initiating will be more toward the student.

Observational data suggest that there is a greater proportion of pupil talk in the PBL groups. Research using FIAC has suggested that the proportion of teacher statements that make use of, ideas and opinions expressed by the pupils (sometimes called 'indirectness') is directly related to average class scores on attitude scales and average achievement scores adjusted for initial ability. Thus if PBL does indeed result in higher levels of attainment and teacher behaviour in the PBL groups show greater measures of indirectness it could be argued that PBL works by forcing teachers to adopt teaching behaviour characterised by 'indirectness'.

Data Collection

In each of the four groups a total of five teaching sessions are observed in each year. The session tutors are informed a few days in advance that a particular session will be observed. In the first module the purposes of the observation include acting as a pilot for the principle investigator and to give the group the opportunity to experience the presence of the principle investigator during a teaching session.

For the two PBL groups, two further data collection points were randomly selected in each of modules two and three. The teaching sessions for modules two and three overlap in the SGL group and therefore these sessions were treated as sequential for the purpose of timing of data collection. Four further data collection points were randomly selected in each SGL group.

In all four groups the first session of module 2, the last session of module 3, and the two sessions on Advanced Life

Support were excluded from the possible times for observation. In the A24 SGL two sessions which are devoted to control & restraint techniques were also excluded.

The length of each teaching session is nominally pre determined. The PBL group teaching sessions are scheduled to last 3 hours and the SGL sessions a full day. During the session the principle investigator undertakes non-participant observation. This involves taking of concurrent field notes on the nature of student and tutor interaction.

During each session three 15-minute segments of classroom interaction are tape-recorded. The timings used are approximately the same in each group. The first section is taped between 15 & 30 minutes into the session, the second between 60 and 75 minutes, The third between 105 and 120 minutes.

The timing of the recordings are weighted towards the early part of the session because the experience of early observations has shown that sessions often do not go on for the scheduled amount of time. Taping does not always take place at exactly these times. The time shifts primarily for two reasons. Firstly because of a break in the session in which case the next recording is done 15 minutes after the session recommences. Secondly because the teacher gives the students an exercise to do which involves silent working alone or being divided into small groups. In either case the recording restarts once interaction between the class (as a whole in the case of small group work) is resumed.

The designers of the FIAC suggest that for a stable sample of teachers interaction patterns, approximately 6000 tallies collected from six to eight observations spaced according to a logical plan are required. They suggest that it is possible to collect less from an individual teacher if the concern is with a method or system of teaching (such as PBL). The taped data if collected as currently planned will generate a total of 550 minutes of teaching interaction over two years for each group. The coding system is that a code (tally) is allocated every 3 seconds.

On the basis of coding every three seconds the amount of taped data would provide 11000 tallies for each group or 22000 for the PBL curriculum and 22000 tallies for the SGL curriculum. It will not be possible to code and analyse this amount of data within the resource available to the project and it would appear unnecessary to do so. It is therefore proposed that 6 minutes of each 15-minute session will be coded. This will give a total of 18 minutes coding per teaching session observed, 180 minutes of coding per group or 360 minutes of coding for the PBL curriculum and 360 minutes of coding for the SGL curriculum. This would give a total of 3600 tallies per group or 7200 tallies for the PBL curriculum and 7200 tallies for the SGL curriculum. A different 6 minutes segment is randomly selected in each session.

Coding and Data Entry

The designers of the FIAC system recommend that a number of coding procedures are followed to improve the validity of the process. The principal investigator will undertake coding. The simplest form of analysis is to calculate the proportion of teacher talk, pupil talk, and silence.

The example in box 1 shows a hypothetical 60 seconds of verbal interaction coded using the FIAC categories (bold numbers).

Immediately above and below the line of code are the pairs of codes used for the purpose of analysing patterns of initiative and response. Pair one represents the teacher initializing by asking a question followed by a pupil response (4-8). The second pair consists of the same pupil response followed by the teacher's reaction, which is to use the pupil's idea (8-3).

The third pair shows the initial response by the teacher that is followed by the teacher giving more information (3-5). Data on the number of pairs in each category can be entered in a 10 × 10 matrix. The vertical column corresponds with the first number in the pair and the horizontal column the second. The datum entered into a cell is the frequency of interactions in that category. Analysis of the pairs can be used to detect the pattern of a lesson. For example, higher frequencies in the cells (3-3), (3-9),(9-3),(9-9) are said to be indicative of a more creative teaching pattern.

Analysis of Patterns of Interaction

The data generated can be used to calculate number of measures that describe and analyse what happens in a particular teaching session and/or can be used to make comparisons between different types of curricular. In so doing they can be also be used to develop and test hypothesis about how PBL 'works'. The calculation of these measures is summarised and each measure is discussed in more detail below.

Balance between Teacher Talk, Pupil Talk and Silence: This is simply the proportion of the total amount of interaction time that is taken up by the teacher, by pupils and in silence. Flanders argues that established norms are 80% teacher talk, 20% pupil talk, and 11-12% silence.. Observational data suggests that PBL will contain a higher % of pupil talk than the SGL curriculum. Whilst these measures of talk are useful a high proportion of pupil talk alone is not necessarily indicative of a creative student centred learning environment

Balance between Teacher and Pupil Initiation and Response: It is possible that the % of pupil and teacher talk may not be significantly different between the PBL and SGL curricular. Even if the balance is significantly different it is important to try and PEPBL Methodology working paper 6 m. newman, 04/2001 6 understand how and why this occurs. What may be important is the nature of the talk. Simple ratios can be calculated which analyse the data in terms of teacher initiative, teacher response and pupil initiative and these are described below. The Teachers Response Ratio (TRR) is an index of the teacher's tendency to react to the ideas and feelings of pupils. A high TRR indicates that the teacher is highly responsive to pupil talk. It is anticipated that PBL will have a higher TRR ratio. The Pupil Initiation Ratio (PIR) measures the proportion of pupil talk that is an act of initiation. Flanders argues that the average PIR = 34. A high PIR indicates that pupils show a lot of initiative in introducing their own ideas into the classroom discourse. It is expected that the PIR ratio will be higher in the PBL curriculum.

Teachers Reaction when Pupils Stop Talking: It is argued that the teachers reaction at a moment when a pupil stops talking is critical because each communication re-entry of the teacher sets the expectations of what will follow. It is also argued that patterns of teacher talk at this moment might also be more revealing as the spontaneous impulses of the teacher are more likely to emerge. The Teachers Immediate Response Ratio (TRR89) measures the tendency of the teacher to praise or integrate pupil ideas and feelings into the class discussion at the moment the pupil stops talking. It is calculated using data from the analysis of pairs. Given the tutorial role expected of teachers in the PBL system a high TRR89 may be expected. No difference between the two curricula in student attainment and/or % of pupil talk and/or PIR might be explained by a lower than expected TRR89. Similarly the TRR89 maybe useful to tease out any differences associated with the PBL system (?indicated by High % pupil talk and PIR) and those associated with the actions of the tutor (? High TRR89).

Teacher Directed Emphasis on Content: The cells in columns and rows four and five focus on teacher statements that are least likely to be involved with classroom management or processes. The Content Cross Ratio (CCR) indicates the degree to which discussion was directed to content by the teacher. It is suggested that there will be a clear difference in the CCR between PBL and SGL given the grater emphasis put on process in the PBL curriculum generally and on the teacher as afacilitator of classroom processes.

Sustained Expression in the Same Category: The Pupil Steady State Ratio (PSSR) is an index of the rapidity of teacher pupil interaction, which Flanders argues is more sensitive when the pupil talk is average or above average. It is expected that the PSSR will be higher in the PBL curriculum reflecting the higher level of pupil initiated talk. However observational data suggest that in some SGL sessions pupil talk maybe below average which may lead to higher than expected PSSR for these sessions.

Analysing the Transition from Teacher Centred to Student Centred Patterns of Interaction: It is also possible to analyse how the teacher manages the transition from teacher centred to student centred (i.e. creative inquiry) patterns of interaction.

For example Flanders argues that there are four possible ways for a teacher to move from the drill pattern to the creative pattern illustrated in figure two. Firstly using a 4-3 shift where the teacher voluntarily terminates their own idea and shifts to an idea previously expressed by students. Flanders argues that the most common mechanism is via an 8-3 transition, where the teacher makes use of ideas expressed by students, because this transition remains in control of the teacher. A 4-9 transition is most likely to occur when the teacher asks very broad based questions or PEPBL Methodology working paper 6 when the students ignore the teachers questions to instigate their own discussion. This requires teachers to have the ability to ask the type of question that provokes pupil talk. The students instigate an 8-9 transition as they shift from responding to the teacher's ideas and begin to express their own without interruption from the teacher.

Both the PBL and SGL curricula make the claim to use student centred approaches.

Observational data from the initial teaching sessions suggest that whilst both curricula and teachers are trying to bring this about they are doing so by different methods and with varying degrees of success. The measures already referred to will indicate to what degree this is achieved in both systems. Should it be demonstrated that PBL is successful in creating student centred patterns of interaction it will be possible to try and explain how this is achieved.

It could for example be the case that the PBL approach works by forcing the tutor and students into interaction patterns typical of creative enquiry by proscribing other forms of teacher communication e.g. lecturing. Put another way, PBL perhaps requires the teacher to focus their 'teaching activity' on the transition to and sustaining of, creative enquiry patterns. In which case it may be that there will be a very high preponderance of attempted (8-3) and (4-9) transitions earlier in the early PBL sessions and an increase in (8-9) transitions in later sessions.

Including Co-teaching in a Teacher Preparation Program: A Vital Addition

Co-teaching involves having a general and special education professional collaborate in the same classroom, working with a heterogeneous group of students. While this has become one of the more popular options for including students with disabilities into general education classes, few teacher preparation programs provide instruction in co-teaching. Far fewer actually model the technique for teacher trainees. Hence, it is not surprising that new teachers frequently feel ill-prepared to actually co-teach. This article describes a teacher preparation program in California that includes elementary, secondary, and special education students in a course co-taught by university and school-based instructors. The benefits and difficulties of co-teaching a university class are discussed and strategies for developing a successful co-teaching relationship are provided.

Co-teaching. By now, most educators have heard of it. Sometimes it's called collaborative or cooperative teaching, sometimes team teaching, sometimes teaming. No matter the name, as teachers obtain preliminary or clear credentials, or attend professional development seminars and conferences, the importance of co-teaching and collaboration between general and special educators continues to be emphasized. What exactly is co-teaching? Co-teaching, as defined by Cook and Friend (1995), is when "two or more professionals deliver substantive instruction to a diverse or blended group of students in a single physical space". In fact, according to the National Centre for Restructuring and Inclusion (1995), co-teaching is the most common service delivery model for teaching students with disabilities in the general education classroom. So, if co-teaching is so popular, what is the concern?

While co-teaching offers plenty of potential benefits for both students and faculty and is well documented in the literature (e.g., Friend & Cook, 2000; Hughes & Murawski, 2001; Walther-Thomas, 1997), the concern for most teachers lies in how co-teaching is implemented—or rather how it's not implemented (Murawski & Swanson, 2001). When two credentialed (or at least experienced) teachers are collaborating together in one classroom, great things can happen—few teachers will deny that. However, if those same teachers don't know how to work effectively together, or perhaps don't want to work together, that same situation can be disastrous for both students and teachers. The importance of demonstration as a technique for teaching a skill is well known and accepted amongst educators. For example, when introducing a new technique for teaching reading, most faculty describe the steps and rationale involved, model the technique and then, using guided practice procedures, have students practice the technique until competency is established. Why then do we expect our budding educators to learn about co-teaching without ever seeing it in practice?

Before any actual strategies for co-teaching can be utilized by teachers, it is critical to recognize that co-teaching (like many other special education initiatives) has been frequently presented to special education staff only (Murawski, in press). Teacher preparation courses at colleges and universities often "preach to the choir," expounding on the virtues of co-teaching to prospective special educators. However, it is important to note that general education teachers are less likely to have had this type of instruction and will therefore have a very different frame of reference than their special education colleagues. Thus, including both general and special educators in any efforts to teach and model co-teaching is imperative for real progress to be made.

Hudson and Glomb (1997) are among others (e.g., Cruz & Zaragoza, 1998; Dynak, Whitten, & Dynak, 1997; Hohenbrink, Johnston, & Westhoven, 1997) who have recognized that very few institutions of higher education (IHE's) actually implement co-teaching between faculty in their teacher preparation programs or even prepare their general and special educators to work collaboratively with one another. They note that "the discrepancies between teacher education and actual practice may result in special educators' and classroom teachers' coming to meetings that require collaboration with varied levels of expectation and preparation. These differences, in turn, can result in disparity, poor communication, and failure to attain child-related objectives" (Hudson & Glomb, 1997). Noting this discrepancy, the DELTA intern program at California State University, Northridge (CSUN) decided to take the steps needed to create a class that would model techniques espoused by teacher education faculty and prepare their students for future collaborative endeavours.

As part of a federal grant, the DELTA program combined elementary and secondary teacher trainees with special education teacher trainees in an "Introduction to Teaching" course as their first course in an intern credentialing program. In addition to this integration, it was decided that two instructors would co-teach the course. I teach the course at CSUN on co-teaching and collaboration, and do the bulk of my research in the area of co-teaching at the K-12 levels; thus, I immediately volunteered to be one of the instructors, hoping to be able to "practice what I preach." An effort was made to select a school-based instructor with strong ties to the community and the Los Angeles Unified School District (LAUSD) school district, in which all teacher trainees worked as emergency credentialed teachers. Barbara (a pseudonym) was an excellent selection. Barbara is a former secondary principal of a large high school, with extensive background in teaching reading. Barbara had taught other courses on a part-time basis with the university. As the university representive, I am an assistant professor in the department of special education, with an emphasis on mild-moderate disabilities. At the K-12 level, I have taught in both general and special education classes. Currently, I do the majority of my teaching, research and consultation on ways to successfully include students with mild/moderate disabilities (learning disabilities, emotional disturbance, mild mental retardation) into general education classes through the use of modifications, strategy instruction, and co-teaching between educators. Clearly, the prospect of teaching and modeling these skills to brand-new teacher trainees in both general and special education was exciting for me!

Throughout the course, Barbara and I met on a weekly basis for approximately two hours, using the time to discuss student progress, plan for future classes, and divide up responsibilities. We tried to include a variety of instructional techniques in the class, modeling different ways to structure assignments, grade papers, do groupwork, and teach new skills. We took turns teaching different parts of the course, with each of us being the "primary" instructor at some part during each three hour class session.

At times, we would implement the "one teach, one support" strategy (Cook & Friend, 1995), wherein one of us would be in front of the class, while the other circulated, passed out papers, answered individual questions, or checked individual work. At other times, we would "team teach" a lesson, with both of us feeling free to supplement and clarify what the other said, making sure we provided examples for elementary, secondary, and special education students. A nearby empty classroom also allowed us to occasionally break the class into groups, which we varied on a regular basis. Sometimes grouping was random, sometimes it was done by area, sometimes by the students' preference. As we taught our content in a manner meant to educate all students using a variety of techniques, grouping strategies, and learning modalities, our goal was to model for our students how they could then do the same with their students.

Our situation was relatively unique and yet, it shouldn't be. If we as educators believe that students will benefit by being included into heterogeneous classes and by being instructed by two professional educators who can collaborate to meet individual needs, why aren't we in turn implementing these techniques? Why aren't we modeling for our teacher trainees? Students frequently share with us the impact our collaboration has had on them; in fact, one student said "I learned more about co-teaching by watching you two do it than I did from anything I could read out of a book or in articles. Now I'm truly excited to try it!"

Was co-teaching easy? No. Anytime two or more individuals get together to work on something, there are bound to be differences. When teaching a course by myself, I am able to make last minute decisions, to plan late at night, to make changes without consulting anyone; these are things that are compromised when co-teaching. Barbara and I have different personalities and teaching styles and there were times when I wanted to teach something differently or spend more or less time on a particular topic. On the other hand, however, in working with Barbara, I found that I too learned a lot! Barbara had a wealth of information and experiences regarding the school district and its policies that led to specific examples to which the students could relate. She had taught this class previously to secondary education teachers and I was able to watch her and see how those teachers receive their training. From that, I was able to add information related to working with students who have special needs in those situations. I was able to take Barbara's lesson plans and suggest changes, additions, and modifications so that the elementary and special education interns would also benefit from instruction. I added research and citations from the literature to back up strategies we taught our students and, together, Barbara and I determined which content was crucial and which could be slated as "get to it if we have time." We shared grading, planning, and creating demonstration lessons, all of which easily made up for the excess time spent planning. In fact, it only took two brief sessions together at the end of the course for us to jointly grade the entire class's portfolios and final exam essays—a task that would have taken me a week if I were to attempt it alone!

Co-teaching is a viable option for any educator working with heterogeneous groups of students. Most IHE faculty would certainly agree that teacher preparation programs include very diverse groups of students. If we are truly dedicated to the idea of inclusion for students with disabilities at the K-12 level, it is imperative that we, as teacher trainers, implement and model co-teaching for our teacher trainees. The first step is to identify an appropriate class and an interested partner in the area of general education instruction. After that, however, it is more important to provide students with a positive model of co-teaching—and that takes work! Below are some strategies that co-teachers can employ to help ensure a successful relationship.

Strategies for Co-teaching

- Talk about your pet peeves early in the relationship
- Include signals that both instructors are equal partners by having both instructors' names on the board in the beginning of school and using "we" instead of "I". Do not allow students to feel that one instructor is responsible for general education students and one is responsible for special education students.
- Determine a regularly scheduled time each week for planning and reflection. If that cannot be a common planning time during office hours, consider regular lunch dates. Email is also a wonderful option for ongoing communication.
- Be open about your own strengths and weaknesses related to teaching, grading, organisational practices, planning, etc. Try to maximize each person's strengths by breaking up work by personal preferences.
- Talk to the students about this relationship and discuss the fact that, even if the instructors may have different opinions about something, students are never allowed to play "mother against father." Support one another in front of students—and then feel free to discuss the issues when you are in a private office until you come to a reasonable understanding, or until you agree to disagree.
- Use different instructional activities to model how teachers can avoid getting stuck in the same old-same old routine. Regroup students frequently, emphasizing the importance of having different students in different groups each time so that no one is stigmatized as being with a "special ed" group. By trying new things with your class, you will be modeling how teachers can do the same with their students.

- Encourage students to read Cook and Friend (1995) and Bauwens, Hourcade, and Friend (1989) for more strategies on how to regroup students into different models that can work with co-teaching. A helpful text on Collaboration (to include Co-teaching) is by Friend and Cook (2000).
- Every week, openly discuss what is going well and what is frustrating. If one instructor is taking over too frequently, it is important to address it early on. The more open the communication, the better the relationship and the more smoothly classes will run.
- Feel free to bring in other speakers. If students see that you are willing to accept others' opinions and expertise, as well as willing to collaborate with multiple people, they too will begin to consider doing the same with their classes.

Above all, be open to learning from one another. Provide one another positive reinforcement, on-going encouragement, and continued support. Teacher preparation faculty know that teaching adults can frequently be a daunting task; co-teaching allows you to have a partner with whom to discuss potential difficulties, take advantage of opportunities, and above all, celebrate successes.

UNIT-V

Dynamics of Teaching Strategies and Teaching Models of Teacher Education

Different Methods of Teaching

The following is a list of some of the methods of teaching

1. Read the description of each method, which will also be explained by your tutor.
2. Did you include the method in your list for activity 61?
3. Discuss each method in your groups.
4. In the table below fill in some of the advantages and problems of using each method. These may be advantages or problems to you as a teacher or to the students.
5. Decide on one topic or skill from your subject area for which each would be a good method.
   a. Demonstrations: Teacher showing a skill to the students while they watch.
   b. Practicals: All or some of the students practicing a skill which they have learnt or are learning.
   c. Experiments: These are related to practicals and are mainly used in science-related subjects, including Agriculture and Home Economics or Life Skills. Students are asked to do something, observe and record the results of what they do, and try to

explain these. Sometimes the teacher may do an experiment as a demonstration.

d. Lecturing: Teacher telling the students information or ideas while they listen.

e. Note-giving: Writing notes on the board for students to copy or giving handout for students to read.

f. Questioning: Teacher asking questions to individuals or whole class.

g. Discussion: Students talking to each other and sharing their ideas either in small groups or as a class. Teacher may or may not take part.

h. Brainstorming: Students asked to throw out as many ideas as possible in a short time either in groups or whole class. Usually someone writes the ideas down.

i. Seminars: One student asked to present a topic or teach a skill to the rest of the class. They must prepare this in advance.

j. Group work: Students work in groups on an activity. This may include making something; looking after a garden; or finding out about a particular topic. This may be for one lesson or for a group project lasting days or weeks.

k. Other methods: On the table below, add any other methods you thought of.

Interactive Teaching

There have been debates over time to establish whether teaching is a skill or an art. Some students believe in their teacher's performance as quite brilliant, others get motivated and excited with the presentation and teaching. For some others, their teachers bore them making the lesson dry, hard and leaving them more confused. All of these enthusiasms and opinions are eventually translated into students' academic achievement. However, what is pertinent in teaching and learning is the ability to apply skills to the art of teaching with an aim to motivate the learners. A blend of skills and art in teaching is also manifested in clearly structure lessons and manner of presentation. A teacher who can effectively do this is an active constructor of learning, who can, and should transmit knowledge, but should allow students voices to be heard as contributing members of class. This is typical in a discussion class. The teacher teaches, asks questions, and in doing so, he hears his voice. But he does not stop at that. In hearing his own voice, he begins to appreciate the need to hear the voices of those he teaches. This elicits a more participatory teaching, which can stimulate imaginative and conceptual thinking amongst students. In this case, students in tertiary institutions who had hitherto been used to the lecture teaching method, where they are, but, passive listeners.

The Interactive Nature of the Discussion Teaching Method

Most teachers of tertiary institutions tend to be more comfortable with the lecture method of teaching. As a teaching method, lecturing in tertiary institutions is a tradition. The level of students' maturity may be one of the reasons for using this method at that stage of learning. However in this article, the argument is for a more interactive teaching strategy that crosses all barriers and gulf peculiar with the lecture method. The focus here is the discussion method. It is a teaching strategy in which the teacher brings students face to face as they engage in verbal interchange of ideas. The teacher in his interactions with his learners performs a variety of roles. He is firstly a teacher whose business is to transmit knowledge, and in doing this he specifies the objectives of his lesson and examines the needs and background of the students for relevance of the topic and its suitability. Importantly too, in applying the discussion strategy to the teaching-learning process, the teacher plays the role of a manager, guide, initiator, referee and a summarizer.

The discussion teaching method is a design that provides opportunity for discussion between teacher and students, and students to students. It is a strategy that centres on shared conversations, discussions, and exchange of ideas in class. It gives opportunity for all to sit and listen, as well as talk and think, thus emphasizing the process of "coming to know" as valuable as "knowing the right answer". In other words, students in a discussion class are not passive listeners neither is the teacher a sole performer. Students are allowed to develop critical thinking ability, learn to evaluate ideas, concepts and principles, procedures and even programmes and policies on the basis of clearly set criteria. For instance, a student who participates in a discussion lesson learns to support his views rationally, based on facts, too. He appreciates the need to argue logically, define clearly—concepts and terms, and examine critically—rules, principles and constructs. Such a student learns to develop value processing skills in relation to changes that occur in his society.

Essentially too, the discussion strategy encourages cooperative team work between teacher and students and amongst students. It emphasizes the need for all to work cooperatively while developing societal relationships. Students see themselves as contributory members of the group, instead of separate and odd. According to Bennett (1995), such cooperative learning improves both academic achievement and students' interpersonal relationship. He goes on to argue that in most cases all students (including high, average and low achievers) tend to benefit from cooperative learning and team work. In the same vein, Johnson, Johnson and Holube (1988) have affirmed that such cooperative spirit in learning help students work together to complete a task successfully. This is also important in promoting students' independence.

Generally, in appraising the interactive nature of the discussion teaching method, that cooperative spirit of learning inherent is quite crucial. It emphasizes (students) individual and group accountability, with the teacher giving the feedback. Also, through such shared learning students develop shared responsibilities for leadership functions. Significantly too, interaction in the discussion strategy encourages rational arguments and logical reasoning. In doing this, the teacher helps to develop in his learners skills in conflict management and listening. Johnson and Johnson (1987) have also suggested that such interactions in the classroom that promote cooperative learning are successful strategy for reducing stereotyping and social rejection across disability, race and gender lines. In other words, all see themselves as members of a group as they participate in discussions, listen to each other, resolve differences, make suggestions and critically examine issues for the benefit of all. As students formulate their own views in the act of give and take, they also learn to resist the influences of their personal prejudices, commitments, stereotypes; likes and dislikes, at the same time continue to focus attention on the theme of problem at hand.

Besides its emphasis on a high level of interaction for possible cooperative learning, the discussion method is quite important in bringing about meaningful increase in students' achievement. Basically, teaching strategies stem from teacher's behaviour. This, in itself is further manifested in the teacher's effective use of academic learning time. Sadker and Sadker (1991) have argued that allocating adequate time to academic content is not enough. It is the teacher's ability to effectively use allocated time in classroom teaching that is the real key to student achievement. It is on this score that Berliner (1984) looks at academic time as three major parts. First is the allocated time. This, he describes as the amount of time a teacher schedules for a topic or subject. There is also the engaged time. This is actually that chunk of time in the whole of the engaged time that students spend in active involvement listening to lesson taught, participation in class discussions, question sessions, writing etc. Good and Brophy (1994) have asserted that the more the engaged time spent within the allocated time, the better students' achievement. Finally, there is the academic learning time which Berliner (1984) simply describes as "engaged time with a high success rate".

Looking at the above within the con text of the discussion teaching method, even though this teaching strategy may be seen as a complex activity, it is quite engaging. Thus, a good teacher can exploit that engaging nature of this method to the advantage of his student as well as his own teaching. Such a teacher could employ an interactive discussion strategy, where he, as manager, guide and initiator creates opportunities for his students to participate actively, not stand on the sideline as mere volunteers.

Ensuring Participation by all in the Discussion Teaching Strategy

Just as the topic for discussion is important in this teaching strategy, so is the seating plan and arrangement of participants clear definition of teacher's roles, precise determination of students' role, all with an aim to ensuring academic achievement. Generally, the emphasis on seating arrangement in the teaching-learning process, is the need for students to participate actively. Sommer (1967) has further identified direct visual contact between members of the participating group as the critical variable that leads to increase in communication and participation by students.

This has implication for increased learning achievement. In the same vein, in a discussion class, the sitting arrangement, the frequency and depth of eye contact are important variables that are determinants to students' level of participation and learning. It is in line with this that the teacher should pay attention to the type of communication network in which students are organised for a discussion class. Importantly, the communication pattern has its effect on the quality and frequency counts of student participation, and by implication, the quality of learning that occurs.

Generally, two major sitting patterns have been identified that can be adapted in a discussion class. They are the centralized sitting arrangement and the decentralized.

The centralized sitting network could take three forms namely the wheel configuration, the chain configuration and the Y-pattern. In the wheel configuration the interaction is such that the teacher takes the position of the hub of the wheel. The position is also privilege to any student who wants to be moderator or discussant. The position of teacher or moderator at the hub is to announce topics that would generate discussion among participants, ask for and receive signals from participants. It is also his duty to examine and present conclusions arrived at by all.

This sitting network can be quite ideal in discussion sessions if effectively managed by the teacher. He can achieve this by being more interactive and cooperative with his participants, thus, playing less a dominant role as the 'hub of the wheel' without which the wheel cannot turn. In effect, he is seen to play a dominant role when he receives signals, oral and nonverbal messages, offer solutions to problems, resolves conflicts and sends messages down the various channels of communications to participants. When he plays all such roles, he assumes a new posture as lecturer, thus employs the lecture method which is less interactive with students as passive participants.

Another centralized sitting network is the chain configuration. Here the teacher takes his place at the apex of the chain. In his position, inputs on discussions are fed back to him, he filters ideas, concepts and rules, and sends back to other participants at the periphery. He also sends back decisions arrived at, corrects obvious fallacies in arguments encountered, and proffers solutions to problems arrived at. Even though this sitting arrangement may make the teacher seem like one in charge, and a repository of knowledge, an interactive discussion method takes cognisance of the importance of shared conversation and discussion. Thus, whatever decisions are reached are indeed a joint effort of all participants. Such decisions are usually impersonal, objective, outcome reasoning and logical arguments.

Finally is the letter "Y" patterned sitting arrangement. Taking a centralized position with two or three channels of communication, the teacher plays a role of meeting the needs of all participants. He moderates opposing views, filters ideas, gathers information from al, offers solutions, comment on decision etc. He manages discussion in such a way that no line of communication is at disadvantage.

Generally, the teacher or moderator in any of the centralized sitting network may be seen to be in a vintage position and playing a dominant role. But in an interactive discussion classroom, the teacher's dominant role is limited to serve other participatory roles. He plays the initiator, manager, referee and summarizer. He can always hover from one of these roles to another. Significantly, the beauty of the interactive centralized sitting arrangement lies in the high degree of participation and agreement, centrality and opportunity for a blend in verbal and non-verbal exchanges.

The decentralized sitting arrangement is also very effective for a discussion teaching strategy. This sitting position is characterized by an all channel network sitting position.

In a sitting arrangement of this nature, no one individual, not even the teacher is in a position to dominate discussion. A topic is given and any student who is knowledgeable on it, or the teacher could direct or even dominate discussion. The effectiveness of this sitting arrangement is that students can freely participate. Ideas can be exchanged by all, using eye contacts to receive and send a variety of signals. Like the centralized communication network, the decentralized also aims at an interactive, discussion class session where all participate with greater academic success.

One Final Line on the Interactive Discussion Strategy

- The organisation of a discussion lesson is as important as the topic of discourse. The discussion lesson should be well organised to enable teacher analyse and evaluate issues raised.
- In a discussion lesson, the less the teacher talks, and with less interference too, the more students participate.
- The teacher in managing and directing a discussion session, should watch out for the logical drift of the discourse, and the relevance of points raised especially as it relates to set objectives.
- In the trend of discussion, it should be ensured that all participants are carried along. Pauses at intervals by the teacher or student moderator, give other participants time to be good listeners, think, digest thoughts and take down notes and salient points.
- Other ways of students' participation include an examination of teacher's subject content, in relation to

students' contributions, and evaluation of comments made.

- For a more active, participatory discussion class, the teacher should acquaint himself with the names of his students. This creates a more relaxed and friendly class.
- Time allotted to discussion class should be eventually spread. Teacher should be cautions not to rush any part of discussion, especially the last part. There is the tendency for teachers to rush through the last part of discussion. By so doing an otherwise beautiful summary could be destroyed, and vital information even distorted.
- A discussion class can be most complete, effective and interactive, if at the end of discussion, a separate session is set aside to summarise and evaluate content and topic discussed. This could be done in the same class session or separate period(s).
- Finally, the teacher or student should always prepare ahead, his content and topic. This enables him to be logical in his presentation and rational in his arguments, as he effortlessly drives home his points.

Conclusion

So far, an attempt has been made in explaining the concept of the discussion method of teaching. The interactive nature of this teaching strategy was also examined and appraised. To further express the level of participation by all, in this teaching method, a brief analysis of the sitting arrangement network was made.

Basically, the main intent in this article is to articulate the discussion teaching method as one that is interactive, cooperative and participation by all. It is also a teaching strategy that could stimulate imaginative and conceptual thinking amongst students. Importantly, it is anticipated that a method of this nature will be appreciated in tertiary institutions. It will be quite exciting especially for students who are hitherto used to the traditional lecture method which is sometimes quite less interactive.

Team Teaching

Team teaching involves a group of instructors working purposefully, regularly, and cooperatively to help a group of students of any age learn. Teachers together set goals for a course, design a syllabus, prepare individual lesson plans, teach students, and evaluate the results. They share insights, argue with one another, and perhaps even challenge students to decide which approach is better.

Teams can be single-discipline, interdisciplinary, or school-within-a-school teams that meet with a common set of students over an extended period of time. New teachers may be paired with veteran teachers. Innovations are encouraged, and modifications in class size, location, and time are permitted. Different personalities, voices, values, and approaches spark interest, keep attention, and prevent boredom.

The team-teaching approach allows for more interaction between teachers and students. Faculty evaluate students on their achievement of the learning goals; students evaluate faculty members on their teaching proficiency. Emphasis is on student and faculty growth, balancing initiative and shared responsibility, specialization and broadening horizons, the clear and interesting presentation of content and student development, democratic participation and common expectations, and cognitive, affective, and behavioral outcomes. This combination of analysis, synthesis, critical thinking, and practical applications can be done on all levels of education, from kindergarten through graduate school.

Working as a team, teachers model respect for differences, interdependence, and conflict-resolution skills. Team members together set the course goals and content, select common materials such as texts and films, and develop tests and final examinations for all students. They set the sequence of topics and supplemental materials. They also give their own interpretations of the materials and use their own teaching styles. The greater the agreement on common objectives and interests, the more likely that teaching will be interdependent and coordinated.

Teaching periods can be scheduled side by side or consecutively. For example, teachers of two similar classes may team up during the same or adjacent periods so that each teacher may focus on that phase of the course that he or she can best handle. Students can sometimes meet all together, sometimes in small groups supervised by individual teachers or teaching assistants, or they can work singly or together on projects in the library, laboratory, or fieldwork. Teachers can be at different sites, linked by video-conferencing, satellites, or the Internet.

Breaking out of the taken-for-granted single-subject, single-course, single-teacher pattern encourages other innovations and experiments. For example, students can be split along or across lines of sex, age, culture, or other interests, then recombined to stimulate reflection. Remedial programs and honours sections provide other attractive opportunities to make available appropriate and effective curricula for students with special needs or interests. They can address different study skills and learning techniques. Team teaching can also offset the danger of imposing ideas, values, and mindsets on minorities or less powerful ethnic groups. Teachers of different backgrounds can culturally enrich one another and students.

Advantages

Students do not all learn at the same rate. Periods of equal length are not appropriate for all learning situations. Educators are no longer dealing primarily with top-down transmission of the tried and true by the mature and experienced teacher to the young, immature, and inexperienced pupil in the single-subject classroom. Schools are moving toward the inclusion of another whole dimension of learning: the lateral transmission to every sentient member of society of what has just been discovered, invented, created, manufactured, or marketed. For this, team members with different areas of expertise are invaluable.

Of course, team teaching is not the only answer to all problems plaguing teachers, students, and administrators. It requires planning, skilled management, willingness to risk change and even failure, humility, open-mindedness, imagination, and creativity. But the results are worth it.

Teamwork improves the quality of teaching as various experts approach the same topic from different angles: theory and practice, past and present, different genders or ethnic backgrounds. Teacher strengths are combined and weaknesses are remedied. Poor teachers can be observed, critiqued, and improved by the other team members in a no threatening, supportive context. The evaluation done by a team of teachers will be more insightful and balanced than the introspection and self-evaluation of an individual teacher.

Working in teams spreads responsibility, encourages creativity, deepens friendships, and builds community among teachers. Teachers complement one another. They share insights, propose new approaches, and challenge assumptions. They learn new perspectives and insights, techniques and values from watching one another. Students enter into conversations between them as they debate, disagree with premises or conclusions, raise new questions, and point out consequences. Contrasting viewpoints encourage more active class participation and independent thinking from students, especially if there is team balance for gender, race, culture, and age. Team teaching is particularly effective with older and underprepared students when it moves beyond communicating facts to tap into their life experience.

The team cuts teaching burdens and boosts morale. The presence of another teacher reduces student-teacher personality problems. In an emergency one team member can attend to the problem while the class goes on. Sharing in decision-making bolsters self-confidence. As teachers see the quality of teaching and learning improve, their self-esteem and happiness grow. This aids in recruiting and keeping faculty.

Disadvantages

Team teaching is not always successful. Some teachers are rigid personality types or may be wedded to a single method. Some simply dislike the other teachers on the team. Some do not want to risk humiliation and discouragement at possible failures. Some fear they will be expected to do more work for the same salary. Others are unwilling to share the spotlight or their pet ideas or to lose total control.

Team teaching makes more demands on time and energy. Members must arrange mutually agreeable times for planning and evaluation. Discussions can be draining and group decisions take longer. Rethinking the courses to accommodate the team-teaching method is often inconvenient.

Opposition may also come from students, parents, and administrators who may resist change of any sort. Some students flourish in a highly structured environment that favors repetition. Some are confused by conflicting opinions. Too much variety may hinder habit formation.

Salaries may have to reflect the additional responsibilities undertaken by team members. Team leaders may need some form of bonus. Such costs could be met by enlarging some class sizes. Nonprofessional staff members could take over some responsibilities.

All things being considered, team teaching so enhances the quality of learning that it is sure to spread widely in the future.

Student Centered Methods such as Activity Method

Activities incorporated in lesson proved to be effective tools in an educational environment. We used activities to follow up lessons in several subject areas. For this project, we included activities that reinforced presentation, team-building skills during an Electronics class. We used simple objects and gadgets such as strings, papers and mobile phones to emphasize the concept to be delivered during the lesson. We observed the students participated with enthusiasm and even contributed to new activities, thus adding sparkle and liveliness to the learning atmosphere. Our project focused on ways to improve the self-confidence of students who are in the beginning developmental stages of learning. As we tried various strategies, we were required to examine existing practices, reexamine older practices, and experiment with novel methods to help our students grow.

Development

Plan: The teachers and students need to work in collaboration to make the teaching-learning process very interesting and engaging. Our experience on teaching various technical modules has taught us that student interaction and involvement are vital items in the transfer of knowledge from the teacher to the student. Most of the teaching is done in a traditional monologue session, where the teacher does the talking and the students are passive audience. Little is known to the teacher on the amount of knowledge consumed by the students. Unless the student seriously focuses on the key points delivered during the teaching, there is a definite reason for the knowledge to escape into thin air.

At this juncture, we feel it is appropriate to present a very practical statement by Confucius on how the human mind approaches the learning process:

I hear, and I forget.

I see, and I remember.

I do, and I understand. — Confucius

One of the best ways to understand something is to get ones hands on it and actually experiment with it. In electronics, this means putting small circuits together, powering them up, and seeing first hand what they do. We also experienced that when activities were given to the students, their involvement and interest were substantially observed. This is a true data collection on experimenting and observing the innovative teaching methods. Hence, we unanimously felt the need for a change in our mode of teaching and learning as activity-based teaching provides simple yet dynamic tools for an effective classroom teaching. We believe that activity-based teaching also taps into a source of energy and goodwill that would enable students to innovate and manage change.

Explore: The students whom we focused on in our project are from heterogeneous backgrounds. They seem to have low self-confidence in their abilities and skills. It was our task to change this and, by working with the students at school and the parents at home, we tried various strategies to accomplish this end. We observed and experienced some success, not only with the students we were focusing on, but also with many others in the classroom who were further motivated by the methods we used. Our project has produced new practices that meet the needs of many.

We experimented on various modes of teaching. After implementing each strategy, we conducted a survey to gather students' understanding on a certain topic. In one of our strategies involving activity-based teaching, a variety of interactive activities were designed to apply social constructivist principles. Students were seated at their desks in four groups. They were asked to increase or decrease the volumes of the ring tones of their mobile phones. They were given rubber bands and tuning forks and asked to observe the vibrations produced by them. They were told to draw their observations

Activity-based Teaching for Effective Learning

We observed that the learners participated actively to create their own knowledge rather than being passive knowledge consumers. At the end of this interactive session, both the teacher and the student had a feeling of achievement and contentment. Incorporating activities in the lesson provided a hope in tackling practical problems by using our own resources. We observed significant increase in the results in terms of increased understanding of the topic and improved interpersonal skills. This approach was well appreciated by both the students and the staff as the final result of teaching and learning was achieved.

Practice: We experimented with many teaching strategies and learnt that implementing activity based teaching had reaped positive results for the students and the teaching staff. This methodology involves commitment from the teachers and participation from the students. At the end of such an interactive session, both the teacher and the student felt a feeling of achievement and contentment. Activity-based teaching provides learners with hope in tackling practical problems by using their own resources. Hence, it is also a very useful tool in improving the existing conditions in our society. We used K-W-L strategy to assess the knowledge of our students at various stages of learning:

K stands for what the student already knows about the topic and its contents.

W stands for what the student would like to know on items related to the topic under discussion.

L stands for what the student learnt at the end of the lesson.

With animated slide presentations and relevant General Knowledge questions, we slowly directed the students to the topic under discussion. We demonstrated the concept by using common items such as tuning forks, rubber bands and mobile phones. We conducted roleplay on various stages of AM – Radio Receiver. Each student was given a role related to the stage of the receiver. After the role-play, various questions were directed randomly at the students. The students involved in the role-play as well as the student audience enthusiastically answered the questions and participated actively in the discussions.

Results of the Strategy

We distributed questionnaires and analyzed our observations while implementing the activity-based methodology in our teaching. Our research focused specifically on the topic of Amplitude Modulation and operations of various stages of a radio receiver set.

The research questions we examined were,

"What knowledge do students have about Amplitude Modulation and operations of important stages of a radio receiver?"

"How can our teaching enhance students' understanding?"

Pre-Assessment

Before administering activity-based teaching, we designed about six questions to gauge the level of understanding that students have on the topic of Amplitude Modulation and operations of various stages of a radio receiver set. We created a scale to rate each student's level of understanding based on the responses to the questions.

Post-Assessment

After teaching the lesson using activity-based methodology; we conducted a postassessment test, which consisted of the same questions that were on the pre-assessment. The main reason of post-assessment was to compare the results with those on preassessment and also to determine how Activity based teaching enhances students' understanding. post-assessment showed an increase of 16 students having some understanding of the topic.

The following criteria were used to observe student improvement:

Increased understanding of the topic

Improved Interpersonal skills

Willingness to participate in group activities.

Ability to relate the topic to real-life examples to traditional lecture methods) created, more interaction and better relationships is Developing a basis for deciding effective approaches to be used to improve the teaching–learning environment also benefits the school. The collaboration between the school, the teacher and the student is well established. Some of our students have the following feelings to share with all of us.

Lecture Cum Demonstration

Lecture Method

It is oldest teaching method given by philosophy of idealism. As used in education, the lecture method refers to the teaching procedure involved in clarification or explanation of the students of some major idea. This method lays emphasis on the penetration of contents. Teacher is more active and students are passive but he also uses question answers to keep them attentive in the class. It is used to motivate, clarify, expand and review the information. By changing Ms Voice, by impersonating characters, by shifting his posing, byusing simple devices, a teacher can deliver lessons effectively, while delivering his lecture; a teacher can indicate by her facial expressions, gestures and tones the exact slode of meaning that he wishes to convey. Thus we can say that when teacher takes the help of a lengthy-short explanation in order to clarify his ideas or some fact that explanation is termed as lecture or lecture method and after briefing about lecture method. Let's see what is a demonstration.

Demonstration Method: The dictionary meaning of the word "demonstration" is the outward showing of a feeling etc.; a description and explanation by experiment; so also logically to prove the truth; or a practical display of a piece of equipment to snow its display of a piece of equipment to show its capabilities. In short it is a proof provided by logic, argument etc.

To define "it is a physical display of the form, outline or a substance of object or events for the purpose of increasing knowledge of such objects or events.

Demonstration involves "showing what or showing how".

Demonstration is relatively uncomplicated process in that it does not require extensive verbal elaboration. Now it will be easy to define what is lecture cum demonstration method. To begin with, this method includes the merits of lecture method and demonstration method. The teacher performs the experiment in the class and goes on explaining what she does. It takes into account the active participation of the student and is thus not a lopsided process like the lecture method. The students see the actual apparatus and operations and help the teacher in demonstrating experiments and thereby they feel interested in learning. So also this mehod follows maxims from concrete to abstract Wherein the students observe the demonstration critically and try to draw inferences. Thus with help of lecture cum demonstration method their power of observation and reasoning are also exercised. So the important principle on which this method works is "Truth is that works."

Requirements of good Demonstration: The success of any demonstration following points should be kept in mind.

1. It should be planned and rehearsed by the teacher before hand.
2. The apparatus used for demonstration should be big enough to be seen by the whole class. If the class may be disciplined she may allow them to sit on the benches to enable them a better view.
3. Adequate lighting arrangements be made on demonstration table and a proper background table need to be provided.
4. All the pieces of apparatus be placed in order before starting the demonstration. The apparatus likely to be used should be placed in the left hand side of the table and it should be arranged in the same order in which it is likely to be used
5. Before actually starting the demonstration a clear statement about the purpose of demonstration be made to the students.
6. The teacher makes sure that the demonstration lecture method leads to active participation of the students in the process of teaching.
7. The demonstration should be quick and slick and should not appear to linger on unnecessarily.
8. The demonstration should be interesting so that it captures the attention of the students.
9. It would be better if the teacher demonstrates with materials or things the children handles in everyday life.
10. For active participation of students the teacher may call individual student in turn to help him in demonstration.
11. The teacher should write the summary of the principles arrived at because of demonstration on the blackboard. The black board can be also used for drawing the necessary diagrams.

These are some of the requirements of a good demonstrations.

Steps needed to conduct a Lecture-cum demonstration lesson.

1. Planning and preparation: A great care be taken by the teacher while planning and preparing his demonstration. He should keep the following points I mind while preparing his lesson.

   a. Subject matter.

   b. Questions to be asked.

   c. Apparatus required for the experiment

   To achieve the above stated objective the teacher should thoroughly go through the pages of the text book, relevant to the lesson. After this he should prepare his lesson plan in which he should essentially include the principles to be explained, a lot of experiments to be demonstrated and type of questions to be asked form the students. These questions be arranged in a systematic order to be followed in the class. Before actually demonstrating the experiment to a class, the experiment be rehearsed under the condition prevailing in the classroom. Inspite of this, some thing may go wrong at the actual lesson, so reserve apparatus is often useful the apparatus has to be arranged in a systematic manner on the demonstration table. Thus for the success of demonstration method a teacher has to prepare himself as thoroughly as possible.

2. Introduction of the lesson: As in every subject so also in the case of science the lesson should stat with proper motivation of the students. It is always considered more useful to introduce the lesson in a problematic way which would make the student's realise the importance of the topic. The usual way through which the teacher can introduce the lesson is by telling some personal experience or incident of a simple and interesting experiment. A good experiment carefully demonstrated is likely to leave an everlasting impression

on the mind of the young pupils and would set the students talking about it in the school.

3. Presentation: The method presenting the subject matter is very important. A good teacher should present his lesson in an interesting manner and not in an boring manner. To make the lesson interesting the teacher may not be very rigid too remain within the prescribed course rather he or she should make the lesson as much as broad based as possible. For widening the lesson the teacher may think of various useful application taught by him. He is also at the liberty to take examples and illustrations for allied branches of science like history, geography etc.

   Constant questions and answer should form a part of every demonstration lesson. Questions and cross question are essential for properly illuminating the principles discussed. Question should be arranged in such a way that their answers may form a complete teaching unit

4. Performance of experiment: A good observer has been described as a person who has learnt the use the senses of touch, sight, smell in an intelligent way. Through this method we want children to observe what happens in a experiment and to state it carefully. We also want them to make generalization without violating scientific spirit i.e. we should allow children from one experiment or observation. The following steps are generally accepted as valuable in conducting science experiment generally.

   a. Write the problem to be solved in simple words.
   b. To make a list of activities that has to be used to solve the problem.
   c. Gather material for conducting the experiment
   d. Work out a format of steps in the order of preocedure so that everyone knows what is to be done.
   e. Teacher should try the experiment before conduction.

f. Record the findings.

g. Assist students to make generalisation.

5. Black Board Summary: A summary of important results and principles should be written in the Blackboard. Use of blackboard should be also frequently used to draw sketches and diagrams. The entire procedure should be displayed to the students after the demonstration.

6. Supervision: Students are asked to take the complete notes of the black board summary including the sketches and diagrams drawn. Such a record will be quite helpful to the student while learning his lessons. Such a summary will prove beneficial only if it has been copied correctly from the black boards and to make sure that it is done so the teacher must check it frequently during this stage. Common Errors In Demonstration Lesson A summary of the common errors committed while delivering a demonstration lesson is given below:

   a) Apparatus may not be ready for use
   b) There may not be an apparent relation between the demonstration experiment and the topic under discussion.
   c) Black board summary not up to the mark
   d) Teacher may be in a hurry to arrive at a generalisation without allowing students to arrive at a generalisation from facts.
   e) Teacher may take to talking too much which will mar the enthusiasm of the students.
   f) Teacher may not have allowed sufficient time for recording of data.
   g) Teacher may fail to ask the right type of questions

Merits of Lecture cum Demonstration Method

a) It is an economical method as compared to a purely student centered method

b) It is a psychological method and students take active interest in the teaching learning process

c) It leads the students from concrete to abstract situations

d) It is suitable method if the apparatus to be handled is costly and sensitive. Such apparatus is likely to be handled and damaged by the students.

e) This method is safe if the experiment is dangerous.

f) In comparison to Heuristic, Project method it is time saving but purely Lecture method is too lengthy

g) It can be successfully used for all types of students

h) It improves the observational and reasoning sills of the students

Limitations of Lecture cum Demonstration Method

a) It provides no scope for "Learning by Doing" for the Students as students are only observing the Teacher performing.

b) Since Teacher performs the experiment at his/ her own pace many students may not be able to comprehend the concept being clarified.

c) Since this method is not child centred it makes no provision for individual differences, all types of students including slow learners and genius have to proceed with the same speed.

d) It fails to develop laboratory skills in the students.

e) It fails to impart training in scientific attitude. In this method students many a times fail to observe many finer details of the apparatus used because they observe it from a distance.

Project Method

Project method is a natural hearted, problem solving and purposeful activity carried to completion in a social environment this is the most concrete of all types of activity methods. It is the revolt against the traditional, bookish and passive environment of school. The project method of teaching is the practical outcome of the John Dewey's philosophy of pragmatism. Pragmatism has made a unique construction in the shape of project method enuciated by the Kilpatrick the follower of Dewey. In project method, study through workshop and source methods are also studied, concrete activity rather than academic work take the dominant place in the project method. The project method also transcends the subject barrier which is not done by other methods. In Project method the teacher instead of following the lecture method substitutes "the subject" with few outstanding problems and proceeds to solve the same by experiment method with the active cooperation of the students. The purpose of this method is to learn pupils into the trained investigators and prepare them for learning by living.

Importance of Project Method

1) The principle of purpose: A purposeful activity will stimulate and provide to the child to achieve the goal and to kindle interest in the activity and consequently accelerated the learning process.
2) The Principle of Activity: It is an activity oriented method. It enabler the pupil to plan independently and to carry out the project in the cooperation of the others.
3) The principle of freedom: The method provider free atmosphere to do activity since a project is a bit of real life that has been imported into school and freedom to choose activity according to the interests, need and capacities of the children give them a freedom of the free atmosphere.
4) The principle of Reality: This method implies learning by doing. It meand the learning by doing is real. It introduces real life situation in the curriculum and the students.
5) The principle of utility: Knowledge for knowledge sake doesn't appeal to a young child thus this method enable the pupil to learn skills which may help them in the later part of their life.
6) The principle of correlation: Knowledge is artificially fragmented otherwise it is holistic in nature correlation of subject is possible in project method.

Definitions of Project Method

- Ballard: "A project is a bit of real life that has been imported into the School".
- J. A. Stevenson: "A project is a problematic act carried to the completion in its Natural setting".
- Kilpatrick: "A project is a whole hearted purposeful activity proceeding in a social environment".
- W.W. Charters: "In the topical organisation principle are learned first while in the projects the problem are proposed which demands in the solution the development of principles by the learner as needed".

Different Types of Projects

- The producer type: Here the emphasis is directed towards the actual construction of a material object or article.
- The consumer type: Here the projective is to obtain either direct or vicarious experience such as reading and learning stories and also listening to a musical selection etc.
- The problem type: Here the chief purpose is to solve a problem involving the intellectual process such as determining the density of a certain liquid etc.
- The dill type: Where the objective is to attain a certain degree of skill in a reaction as learning a vocabulary.

Various Steps in Conducting Project

Creating the Situation: It is not right to force a project on the unwilling students. The students themselves should define state and choose their problems. Through mutual conversation the teacher helps in the making of a proposal by the students. The teacher would discover the taste, needs of the students and would provide situation wherein the students feel a spontaneous urge to carry out projects according to their felt needs. Selection of project: All the projects the children selects cannot be accepted and so only those projects which helps to meet the real needs of the students are selected. The teacher needs to participate and make the projects clearer to the students. For E.g. If teacher wants that there should be flower garden then he takes the student to a garden instead of ordering the students to plant a flower garden. The children thus are please to see the flowers and wonder why there are no flowers and the students select a project to have a flower garden. Thus in way teacher without ordering only by showing the situation can develop interest and select a project.

Planning: After the project is decided and accepted the teacher may develop an outline and ask the pupils to study it deeply at home. A class period may be devoted for this work. The teacher should draw attention of the students to the need of planning before undertaking the activity. The task of planning is difficult. Good planning leads to better result reach child should be encouraged to give his suggestions. Different proposal should be discussed and alternative consider the proposal. The best plan is agreed upon after a good deal of discussion, suggestions counter suggestion and rejections. The teacher needs to divided the work among the students according to their interest and ability and see that they move towards accomplishing the task.

Education of the Plan: In this the students start collecting the facts according to their own efficiency and the teacher nearly supervisor the task done by them. This is the stage at which the student perform many activities and learn many various useful experience. The children's are busy in collecting information, reading keeping accounts, calculating pries, visiting markets, museums etc For E.g.: Dramatizing the life of shivaji may be accepted as project in history. Where such a project is accepted the teacher may develop in broad outlines the life of shivaji and ask the pupils to study it thoroughly, children's should also be engaged in making maps of India showing the Mughal Empire. These maps may be utilized in the drama at the appropriate places.

Evaluating the Project: The work is to be reviewed where it is completed. Here the pupil criticizer his own task and he decides are accomplished objectives that he sets out to achieve are occoueplished or not. They express their ideas before the teacher with freedom about their drawback.

Recording: In this steps a complete record of all activities connected with the project must be maintained. In this all the pupils write in details about their all the five steps of the project with mention of consulted books aids, details of task etc. the project book should be well maintained. The project book should give the procedure of providing a situation and of choosing the project, duties assigned difficulties felt and experience gained etc.

Merits of the Project Method

1. The project strategy is based upon the laws of learning:
   a. Law of readiness: According to this law we learn most when our minds are already to receive. The project method prepares the mind of the students by providing them with suitable situation.
   b. Law of exercise: Learning to be effective must be practised. The project method affords many opportunities to the students to learn by doing.
   c. Law of effect: This law states that if learning is to be effective and fruitful it must be accompanied by satisfaction pleasure when they manipulate their own activities.
2. This method makes education effective because it is purposeful, meaning arouses curiosity etc. Learning becomes practical and intimately related with life. When meaningful purposeful activities are provided to the students get opportunities to acquaint themselves with the real problems of life. The students learn practical usefulness of different subject of the curriculum.
3. The pupil involves in real life problem practically. They are trained to face life in future since they work in natural conditions.
4. The project method gives unity of the curriculum. The subject do not remain isolated in this method, but instead they are co-related and thus students learn different learn different subjects in this method.

5. The pupil acquires knowledge which is useful for the present and future life in short time. The method providing sufficient opportunities to the students to work cooperatively for common purpose decision are arrived at democratic way.
6. This method imports training to the student to inculcate in there primary virtues like tolerance independence, open mindness, resourcefulness etc.
7. It cause an all round development of the pupils and attributes like self dependence and self confidence.
8. Dignity of labour is engendered through the project method. The students have to perform their activities on their own and thus they develop a taste for all kinds of work. They learn that there is nobleness working and doing things with their own.
9. The students work with great enthusiasm for the competition of their self chosen project. They do not feel tried as there is good deal of Varity in their work and the atmosphere is full of the freedom. As the children busy with their self chosen work they do not get opportunities to think of the anti social ways.

Limitation of Project Method

1. A project with limited scope cannot develop on all around personality secondly no project can teach all the subject and so some times teaching becomes haphazard and discontinuous.
2. Neglecting intellectual work: There is a widespread misconception that the project method glorifies hard work at the cost of intellectual work. The critics argue is that the children are kept busy in model making only.
3. In this brilliant students lead other students who are passive and follow blindly.
4. This method practice and the development of skill in various subjects. The students do not get adequate drill in arithmetic, reading spelling drawing etc.

5. Preparation of books suitable for the project work is by no means an easy task. Moreover material required for the implementation of a project is very costly. The method is not suitable for the ordinary schools.
6. Some student who is not inclined to take responsibility may remain in the back ground and do very little work.
7. The school teaching can become disorganized and irregular because the method needs freedom and flexibility.
8. For the successful working of this method, very learned efficient teachers are needed. The method impose heavy burden and responsibility upon the teacher.

Heuristic Method

In Heuristic method, the student be put in the place of an independent discoverer. Thus no help or guidance is provided by the teacher in this method.

In this method the teacher sets a problem for the students and then stands aside while they discover the answer. In words of Professor Armstrong, "Heuristic methods of teaching are methods which involve our placing students as far as possible in the altitude of the discoverer-methods which involve their finding out instead of being merely told about things".

The method requires the student to solve a number of problems experimentally. To almost every one — especially children — experiments and science are synonymous. Once an idea occurs to a scientist he immediately thinks in terms of ways of trying out his ideas to see if he is correct.

Trying to confirm or disprove some thing, or simply to test an idea, is the backbone of the experiment. Experiments start with questions in order to find answers, solve problems, clarify ideas or just to see what happens. Experimenting should be part of the elementary school science programme as an aid to helping children find solutions to science problems as well as for helping them to develop appreciation for one of the basic tools of science.

Procedure of the Method

The method requires the students to solve a number of problems experimentally. Each student is required to discover everything for himself and is to be told nothing. The students are led to discover facts with the help of experiments, apparatus and books. In this method the child behaves like a research scholar.

In the stage managed heuristic method, a problem sheet with minimum instructions is given to the student and he is required to perform the experiments concerning the problem in hand. He must follow the instructions, and enter in his notebook an account of what he has done and results arrived at. He must also put down his conclusion as to the bearing which the result has on the problem in hand. In this way he is led to reason from observation. Essentially therefore, the heuristic method is intended to provide a training in method. Knowledge is a secondary consideration altogether. The method is formative rather than informational. The procedures and skills in science problem solving can only be developed in class rooms where searching is encouraged, creative thinking is respected, and where it is safe to investigate, try out ideas.

Teachers Altitudes

One of the most important aspects of the problem solving approach to children's development in scientific thinking is the teacher's attitude. H's approach should be teaching science with a question mark instead of with an exclamation point. The acceptance of and the quest for unique solutions for the problem that the class is investigating should be a guiding principle in the teacher's approach to his programme of science. Teachers must develop sensitiveness to children and to the meanings of their behaviour Teachers should be ready to accept any suggestion for the solution of problems regardless of how irrelevant it may seem to him, for this is really the true spirit of scientific problem solving. By testing various ideas it can be shown to the child that perhaps his suggestion was not in accord with the information available It can then be shown that this failure gets as much closer to the correct solution by eliminating one possibility from many offered by the problem. In this method teacher should avoid the tempetation to tell the right answer to save time. The teacher should be convinced that road to scientific thinking takes time. Children should never be exposed to ridicule for their suggestions of possible answers otherwise they will show a strong tendency to stop suggestions. For success of this method a teacher should act like a guide and should provide only that much guidance as is rightly needed by the student. He should be sympathetic and courteous and should be capable enough to plan and devise problems for investigation by pupils. He should be capable of good supervision and be able to train the pupils in a way that he himself becomes dispensable.

Merits of Heuristic Method

This method of teaching science has the following merits:

(i) It develops the habit of enquiry and investigation among students.

(ii) It develops habit of self learning and self direction.

(iii) It develops scientific attitudes among students by making them truthful and honest for they learn how to arrive at decisions by actual experimentations.

(iv) It is psychologically sound system of learning as it is based on the maximum, "learning by doing"

(v) It develops in the student a habit of diligency.

(vi) In this method most of the work is done in school and so the teacher has no worry to assign on check home task.

(vii) It provides scope for individual attention to be paid by the establishing cordial relations between the teacher and the taught.

Limitations of Heuristic Method

Main limitations of this method are as under:

(i) It is a long and time consuming method and so it becomes difficult to cover the prescribed syllabus in time.

(ii) It pre-supposes a very small class and a gifted teacher and the method is too technical and scientific to be handled by an average teacher. The method expects of the teacher a great efficiency and hard, experience and training.

(iii) There is a tendency on the part of the teacher to emphasize those branches and parts of the subject which lend brandies of the subject which do not involve measurement and quantitative work and arc therefore not so suitable.

(iv) It is not suitable for beginners. In the early stages, the students needs enough guidance which if not given, may greatly disappoint them and it is possible that the child may develop a distaste for studies.

(v) In this method too much stress is placed on practical work which may lead a student to form a wrong idea of the nature of science as a whole. They grow up in the belief that science is some thing to be done in the laboratory, forgetting that laboratories were made for science and not science for laboratories.

(vi) The gradation of problems is a difficult task which requires sufficient skill and training. The succession of exercises is rarely planned to fit into a general scheme for building up the subject completely.

(vii) Some times experiments are performed merely for sake of doing them

(viii) Learning by this method, pupils leave school with little or no scientific appreciation of their physical environment. The romance of modern scientific discovery and invention remains out of picture for them and the humanizing influence of the subject has been kept away from them.

(ix) Evaluation of learning through heuristic method can be quite tedious.

(x) Presently enough teachers are not available for implementing learning by heuristic method.

Assignments

Assignments consist of both readings, problems and videos. The assigned reading provides you with the opportunity not only to obtain rule and process information. The problems provide you with the opportunity to develop your analytical and problem-solving skills. The assigned readings serve as a basis for solving problems. The problems will form the basis for classroom instruction.

Constructing Writing Assignments

Like writing essay exam questions, constructing effective writing assignments requires some thought and preparation on your part. First, you need to decide what your goals are in assigning writing. If you keep your goals in mind, you will find that constructing a writing assignment will be easier and the assignment is more likely to accomplish those goals.

Role: What role is the student to take in writing this paper? If the student is writing a book review, for example, he/she takes on the role of critic.

Audience: Who is the audience for this paper? What can students assume about the knowledge and background of their readers? Often students have difficulty writing because they conceive of their audience solely as their professor: "the instructor already knows all this, what can I say?" By imagining an audience to whom they can speak with authority, students can often write better, more interesting essays.

Format: In what format should this paper be written? Business memos, for example, typically open with standard headings and are very different from academic papers.

Task: What task is the student to accomplish? The task might be, for example, to summarize a text, to compare and contrast two theories, or to analyse an argument. Make sure your assignment clearly specifies this information, which is often referred to by the acronym RAFT (Role, Audience, Format, Task). The more clearly you indicate what you want in your assignment, the more likely it is that you will get it. When you assign writing, you need to decide and make explicit to students what standards you will use in evaluating you're their essays. Some areas of evaluation include accuracy or richness of content, organisation, and sentence-level correctness.

Making your criteria clear ahead of time eases your students' fears about the evaluation process to some extent. Moreover, students who know what standards against which their essays will be judged are more likely to try to meet those standards when they write. One way to make your standards clear to your students is a rubric which describes the characteristics of an "A" paper, a "B" paper, and so on. Sample rubrics are available from Campus Instructional Consulting.

Another good method is to grade a paper in front of the class. The paper you grade might be one written in the previous semester (with the student's name removed, of course). It is useful to perform this exercise with a paper which might receive an average grade rather than a superior one; the average paper that makes some interesting mistakes will teach students what to avoid, while a superior paper will only excite envy or hopelessness.

Regardless of the method you choose, you are welcome to consult with the Campus Writing Program, 855-4928. Its staff members will help you to construct rubrics or provide student papers to grade in class.

Responding to Student Writing

Writing is a tool for communication, and it is reasonable for you to expect coherent, lucid prose from your students. However, writing is also a mode of learning and a way for students to discover what they think about a subject. You should be willing to participate in this learning and discovery process as well as grade the product (Adapted with permission from Farris, 1985).

The quality of student writing is often far below acceptable standards. Many instructors try to ignore the problem by insisting that writing skills are not part of their assigned subject area. This attitude results in further problems for both instructors and their students. If you demand good writing, make your expectations known and offer help to those who need it (or refer students to Writing Tutorial Services, Ballantine Hall 206). Students will try to meet your demands; make your standards worth meeting.

Not all instructor comments on student papers are equal. Instructors often find it useful to involve themselves in students' writing (and learning) processes, rather than simply "correcting" the final products by having them submit first drafts which are given constructive criticism on content, organisation, and presentation. One-to-one conferences after the student has read the critique and perhaps begun a second draft are invaluable. The second draft is graded and usually demonstrates improvement on all fronts, especially in the depth of analysis and support for an argument so often found lacking in one-draft student papers.

Comments on a first draft are typically different from those given on a final draft. On a first draft, comments usually address whole-paper level concerns. Is there a clear thesis that appropriately addresses the assignment? Is the evidence appropriate and convincing? Is the organisation clear? It is often a good idea at this stage to phrase you comments as questions you as a reader would like the writer to address. In addition, if you connect your comments to specific phrases or sentences in the student's text and avoid vague directives such as "be specific" or "expand," the student will have a clearer idea of how to revise the text. In the early stages of the writing process there is little point in addressing sentence-level problems, as during revision many of those sentences may disappear. Comments on a final draft have a different purpose—to justify a grade, to point to sections that are particularly effective or ineffective, or to address sentence-level concerns, for example.

As you read student essays and diagnose writing problems, you may notice patterns. A paper full of long, convoluted sentences, for example, may indicate that the student is struggling with very complex concepts. Ideally, in your comments you may be able to help the student find ways to discuss those concepts without adding to their complexity. If the essay contains glaring grammatical or mechanical errors, it may be because the student is unfamiliar with the discipline or topic. Even experienced writers may let grammar lapse when they are writing on a topic or in a discipline new to them. If your students are inexperienced writers, you may read many papers in which the thesis is stated in the conclusion rather than at the beginning. In these cases, the student may have begun to write before thinking through the argument to be presented; writing a draft at this preliminary stage becomes a process of discovering the argument. Such a student can benefit substantially from some carefully phrased comments and an opportunity to revise (Adapted by permission from L. Kurz, personal communication, 1996).

Peer feedback groups in which students read each other their first drafts for critique are also useful. These groups work best when students observe a fairly strict protocol: generally each student reads the draft twice. The first time group members listen only; on the second reading they write comments on their photocopy and/or fill out a form designed to address problems specific to the assignment. Then one at a time, the group members offer their comments to the writer. One advantage to the peer feedback method is that you are not the only audience for the students' writing. They hear suggestions for improving their drafts from others before you read the papers.

Avoid the trap of editing papers for students. The point is to get the students to be able to edit their own papers; tell them there is a grammatical problem in a line, but don't fix it for them. Written comments, especially about grammar and mechanics, do very little to improve the student's next effort. Also, getting back a paper covered in red ink can devastate students' morale and confidence in their writing ability.

Richard Haswell, in "Minimal Marking" (1983), advocates responding to surface error, grammar, and mechanics problems, by indicating the presence of such an error "only with a check in the margin by the line in which it occurs." One check per error, so two checks in the margin means two errors in the line. He marks these problems, records the number of them, and returns the essay to the student. He requires the student to correct checked errors and resubmit the essay for evaluation. No grade is recorded until this stage.

Haswell claims that much less of his time is spent on surface error, allowing more attention to substance. This also reduces the reverse "halo effect" where the irritation caused by explaining and correcting surface errors causes an instructor to devalue the student's content. Haswell also claims that he saves more time by not correcting surface errors than he loses in looking at each paper twice. (Adapted with permission from Kurz, 1996, Kalish 1993, and Farris, 1985).

Tutorial

An instructional lesson that leads the user through key features and functions of things such as software applications, hardware devices, processes, system designs, and programming languages. The tutorial typically is set up as a series of steps that progress through levels of difficulty and understanding. For this reason, the tutorial is best followed in its logical sequence in order to understand all of the elements of what the user is trying to learn

Teaching and learning styles are, by their very nature, changing and in recent years there has been a noticeable move from lecture-based activities towards more student-centred activities. Case studies are an increasingly popular form of teaching and have an important role in developing skills and knowledge in students.

This guide explores the use of the case-based approach to support engineering education and, more specifically, their role in Materials Science related Higher Education courses. This will include looking at the 'traditional' Materials Science and Engineering courses as well as the more multidisciplinary courses (e.g. Biomedical Materials Science, Sports and Materials Science etc.).

This guide highlights the good practice we have identified, and also discusses our experiences (both good and bad) of the adoption and implementation of this type of learning activity. We hope that by explaining our rationale for the adoption of case studies, and by discussing their development and structure, you will be encouraged to consider your own teaching methods and whether this approach, or aspects of it, is appropriate to you. At the end of the guide are 5 examples of case studies that illustrate some of the different topics discussed below.

Meaning and Assumptions of Teaching Models

Meaning of Teaching Models (Models of Teaching)

View of Paul Eggan and Others: "Teaching models re prescriptive teaching strategies designed to accomplish particular teaching goals."

View of Joyce and Weil: They have given three meanings of teaching models:

(i) "Teaching models are just instructional designs. They describe the process of specifying and producing particular environmental situations which cause the student to interact in such a way that specific change occurs in his behavior." (1972)

(ii) Teaching model is a "pattern or plan which can be used to shape a curriculum or course, to select instructional materials and to guide a teacher's actions." (1972) Models are designed to attain specific goals. When a teacher identifies a goal, selects a particular strategy designed to attain that goal, we can say that he is using model approach.

(iii) "A model of teaching consists of guidelines for designing educational activities and environments. It specifies ways of teaching and learning that are intended to attain certain kinds of goals."

View of N.K. Jangira: "A model of teaching is a set of inter-related components arranged in a sequence which provides guidelines to realize specific goal. It helps in designing instructional activities and environmental facilities, carrying out of these activities and realization of the stipulated objectives." (1983)

H. C. Wyld, "To confirm in behavior, action and to direct one's action according to some particular design or ideal."

Families of Teaching Models

- Information Social Personal Behavior
- Processing Interaction Development Modification
- Models Models Models Models
- Concept Jurisprudential Inquiry
- Attainment Model Model

Fundamental Elements of a Teaching Model:

1. Focus
2. Syntax
3. Social system
4. Principles of reaction
5. Support system
6. Application.

Concept Attainment Model

Emerged out of the study of thinking process in human beings. It is based on the assertion that a human being is endowed with the capacity to discriminate and to categorize things in groups. This model is used for teaching concepts to the students. It enables them to understand fully the similarities and relationship among various things of the environment.

Concept Attainment Model in terms of Elements:

Focus: The main focus of the model is to develop inductive reasoning of the students. Bruner and his associates orient their work for the description of a process by which the students discriminate the attribute of the things, persons, events and place them into categories. The students are also taught about the concept which is of great use to them in order to live successfully in different life situations.

Syntax: Structure of the model has the following four phases.

* Presentation of data
* Analysis of hypothesis

- Formation of hypothesis
- Teacher reaction
- Rejection or confirmation of hypothesis

* Closure

* Practice

Principle of Reaction: Immediate check of wrong answers and acceptance of right answers is a must.

Social System: The teaching situation is moderately structured. The teacher has to control all actions of the classroom, but reasonable freedom is given for discussion within different phases of teaching.

Support System: The lessons require concepts which can be arranged so that concept may be drawn from the material.

Application: Concept attainment model is very useful in teaching the concepts through inductive reasoning.

Effects of C.A.M.

Jurisprudential Inquiry Model

Assumptions:

- Social values legitimately conflict with one another.
- Negotiations of Difference can help to resolve complex and controversial issues.
- A skilful citizen is like a competent judge. He/She listens to the evidence, analyzes the legal positions taken by both sides, weighs these positions and the evidence assess the meaning provisions of the law and finally make the best possible decision.
- To play the role; three types of competencies are required:

(1) Familiarity with values

(2) Skills for clarifying and resolving issues

(3) Knowledge of contemporary political and public issues.

Syntax

Phase One: Orientation to the case

- Teacher introduces materials
- Teacher review facts

Phase Two: Identify the issues

- Students synthesize facts into policy issues
- Students select one policy issue for discussion
- Students identify values and value conflicts
- Students recognize underlying factual and definitional questions

Phase Three: Taking Positions

- Students articulate a position
- Students state basis of position in terms of social value and consequences of decisions

Phase Four: Exploring the Stance(s), Patterns of Argumentation

- Establish the point at which the value is violated
- Provide the desirable or undesirable consequences
- Clarify one value conflict with analogies
- Set priorities. Assert priority of one value over another

Phase Five: Refining and Qualifying the Position

- Students state positions and reasons for positions and examine number of similar situations
- Students quality positions

Phase Six: Testing Factual Assumptions behind Qualified Positions

- Identify factual assumptions and determine if they are relevant
- Determine the predicted consequences and examine their factual validity (will they actually occur)

Principles of Reaction

(1) Maintain a vigorous intellectual climate

(2) Respect all views and avoid direct evaluation of student opinions

(3) See that issues are thoroughly explored

(4) Probe for relevance, consistency, specificity, generality, definitional clarity and contunity.

(5) Avoid taking a stand

(6) Maintain dialectical style.

Support System

Sourced documents that focus on a problem situation.

Teaching Models by Taba, Turner

Definition

The Taba teaching strategy model (our name) was defined in the sixties by Hilda Taba and aims to help designing courses down to lessons in areas where students are supposed to learn how to think.

Background Assumptions

According to Joyce and Weil (2000:131), Taba built her approach around three assumptions:

1. Thinking can be taught (through engaging students in practice, in particular inductive reasoning).
2. Thinking is an active transaction between the individual and data. This relies on earlier theories, e.g. Bruner's concept attainment, an important component of concept learning
3. Processes of thought evolve by a sequence that is "lawful", somewhat in the sense of mastery learning.

Taba identified three inductive thinking skills:

- concept formation (concept learning)

- interpretation of data
- application of principles

The Model

According to Joyce and Weil (2000), think inductively, Handbook to Elementary Social Studies we made a provisional summary of the model (have to get the original at some point- Daniel K. Schneider).

Concept Formation

This stage includes three major steps: listing items (exemplars of concepts), group similar items together, label these (with a concept name).

- Phase 1: Identifying and listing
  - o What do you know about.... ?
  - o For lessons in your own classroom, you might ask the following: What did you see? What did you hear? What do you know about...?
- Phase 2: Grouping according to common attributes
  - o Do any of these go together? Why?
- Phase 3: Categorizing (labelling of the categories above)
  - o How would you name these groups?

Interpretation of Data

This stage includes interpreting, inferring, and generalization and leads to concept attainment (i.e. students develop deductive capabilities).

- Phase 4: Identifying critical relationships (differentiation)
  - o What do you notice about the data ? What did you see ?
- Phase 5: Exploring relationships (cause-effect)
  - o Why did this or that happen? What do you think this means?
  - o Do you notice any connections within the records or across the data?

- Phase 6: Making inferences
  - o What makes you think about this?
  - o What can you conclude?

Note: At some point phases 1/2/3 can be repeated or revised.

Application of Principles

- Phase 7: Predicting consequences
  - o What if?
- Phase 8: Explaining and/or supporting predictions
  - o Why do you think this or that would happen?
  - o Based on the data, would these conditions be logical?
- Phase 9: Testing and generalization
  - o What would it take to make this generally true ?

UNIT-VI

Teacher and School Organisation

Objectives of Professional Development

Ovewrview: Few could argue with the view that more is expected from today's educators than ever before. Federal mandates, state accountability plans, and greater local accountability all point to the fact that continuous school improvement is not optional but required. How do educators improve their ability to retool teaching, update curricula, integrate new research methodologies into instruction, meet the growing list of the sociopolitical needs of students, and raise test scores? The most frequent answer is professional development. Yet significant challenges impede the ability of professional development to make a difference in improving student learning: rigid, antiquated scheduling; limited funding; and, in too many schools, an inadequate and ineffective follow-up and evaluation process.

Also related to the issue is the need to examine two different aspects of professional development: functions and structures. The *functions* of professional development are the types and outcomes of teacher learning opportunities. Functions focus on the "what" of professional development—such as study groups, train the trainer, action research, and one-shot training sessions. The function of a study group, for example, is for five or six teachers and administrators to exchange ideas, plan lessons, give feedback, and discuss school policy. An increasing amount of research is being conducted on professional development functions, their effectiveness, and their impact on student learning and achievement.

The *structures* of professional development are the procedures used by the educational leaders who plan professional development for their district or school. Structures must be in place in order for effective, high-quality functions to occur. Structures focus on the "how"—making time, location, and funding sources available for faculty development. Little research has been done on the effectiveness of the various structures that have been designed by creative administrators and teachers in their efforts to make time for professional development. For example, which professional development meeting times—early morning, after school, inservice days, Saturdays, or summer—yield the greatest gains in improved student learning and achievement?

Structures often are considered obstacles to the implementation of the functions of professional development. Administrators and teachers cite lack of time, money, and even space as reasons for not being able to implement a research-based professional development plan.

Professional Prospects for Teachers

It requires organisation to place highly qualified teachers in every classroom. To achieve this goal, policies concerning time for professional development must change. In *What Matters Most: Teaching for America's Future*, the National Commission on Teaching investment relationship between teacher knowledge and skills and student achievement: "Teacher expertise is the most important factor in student achievement".

How much professional development time is *enough* to meet today's high expectations for teachers and students? Although there is no clear answer to this question, the need for time is real. As per recommendations at least 25 percent of an educator's time be devoted to professional learning. Such time is essential for mastering and incorporating new practices into classroom instruction. Darling-Hammond (1999) contends that it is unrealistic to expect teachers to learn how to incorporate complicated practices into their instructional design after only a few hours of training. Canady and Rettig (1995) suggest that schools schedule at least five, and preferably 10, days of workshops when implementing major instructional changes.

In USA the National Education Commission on Time and Learning (1994) also uncovered some premises known by educators to be false. One that relates to structure is "the myth that schools can be transformed without giving teachers the time they need to retool themselves and reorganize their work". In its discussion of obstacles to continuous school improvement, the commission stated, "Both learners and teachers need more time—not to do more of the same, but to use all time in new, different, and better ways. The key to liberating learning lies in unlocking time".

The media is quick to use the international assessments—such as the Trends in International Mathematics and Science Study (TIMSS) and the Programme for International Student Assessment (PISA)—to compare U.S. test scores to those of other nations. Yet little is shared with the American public about how much time is scheduled for collaboration, training, and planning in many other nations. U.S. teachers spend more than 1,000 hours teaching per year while Asian and European teachers spend 600 to 800 hours teaching per year (Darling-Hammond, 1999; McRobbie, 2000). Missing from U.S. teachers' schedules is the time to acquire new pieces of knowledge; develop new skills; collaborate, coordinate, and plan with others; create and align curriculum to standards; observe other teachers; and self-reflect and evaluate.

According to Black (2003), policymakers must address the need for additional funding to remedy the lack of time for quality professional development in order for today's educational system to make continuous improvement. Yet the creation of different professional development structures will not in and of itself guarantee improved test scores. Very little will change in a school's classrooms without a data-driven, coordinated, focused plan; multiple-year support (job-embedded coaching, reflection, and feedback); and administrative follow-up and accountability planning (Aronson, Zimmerman, & Carlos, 1998; Richardson, 2002).

The implementation of new instructional strategies increases and improves through accompanied observation and feedback (Boudah, Logan, & Greenwood, 2001; Vaughn, Hughes, Klingner, & Schumm, 1998). Observation of master teachers using desired instructional methodologies and peer-to-peer feedback—whether in the form of critical friends, cognitive coaching, or a less formal program—are effective for improved faculty performance. Because both observation and feedback require teachers to leave their classrooms, most districts support this form of professional development through the use of substitute teachers. Teachers restructure their instructional day to allow as many visits or demonstrations as possible while substitutes move from room to room.

All these topics and concerns are equally important to policymakers, educational leaders, and teachers. And, as these groups address these matters, they ask important questions: What are others doing to create time for faculty and staff professional development? When do teachers find the time to think aloud together, to create, to change, to integrate new knowledge and methodologies? Among the emerging answers are the following strategies.

Steps to tackle Teacher Absenteeism

Teacher absenteeism is one of the major areas of concern for educational administrators and planners. This has a direct bearing on enrolment, retention and quality of learning. The Shiksha Karmi Project which was launched in Rajasthan with assistance from SIDA in the year 1987 to revitalise and expand primary education in remote and backward villages has been successful in tackling the problem of teachers absenteeism by providing specially selected local youth, who work as para teachers, with vigorous training and continuous support. Community participation has been elicited on a large scale for project activities.

The basic assumptions, concept, and strategies of SKP stand validated. Shiksha Karmis have earned the respect and recognition of the village community and their peers. The SK Schools are running regularly, enrolment and retention has increased substantially and educational attainments of the children have shown significant improvement. The success of this project has already prompted other States to send their teams to Rajasthan and see if it could be replicated in their States to tackle the problem of teacher absenteeism. Shiksha Karmi Project is a fine example of international cooperation in the field of basic education and Swedish International Development Agency is bearing 50% of the expenditure on the project. The balance 50% is being borne by the

Government of Rajasthan. During the IX Plan period it is proposed to explore the possibility of launching similar projects in other educationally backward States with the help of international aid agencies, central assistance and contributions by State Governments. A, provision of Rs.50 crore is being made for this purpose.

Training of Teachers in Specialised Areas

With increasing specialisation there is a need and demand for training of teachers in specialised areas such as pre-school education, vocational education, physical education, special education for disabled children, mathematics teaching, environmental studies, etc. In order to make upper primary education effective in terms of quality, it is necessary to move from the class room teachers system (which is quite appropriate at the primary stage) to the subject teacher system especially in curriculum area like Science, Mathematics, English (they, are applicable), Physical Education, Art Education, and work experience. Instituting a specialisation course in primary education and primary teacher education in selected faculties of education in the universities and in certain selected colleges of education. It is proposed that selected DIETs, IASEs & CTEs may be supported for undertaking teacher training in specialised areas indicated above. Central assistance may be provided for this purpose by NCTE during IX Plan.

Education for the Disabled Children

According to the Programme of Action, 1992 there are about 12.59 million children in the age group of 5-18 years for which necessary arrangements have to be made if the targets of universalisation of elementary education (UEE) has to be achieved. There has been a large expansion in the integrated education of disabled children in the common schools as well as in the special school system in the recent years. These efforts have to be intensified after the recent enactment of the Persons With Disabilities (Equal Opportunities, Protection of Rights and Full Participation) Act, 1995 which provides for compulsory access to schools to every disabled child. In order to provide teachers who are fully equipped to meet the educational needs of these children, the nation has to provide Sufficient facilities for training of such teachers. Present facilities for pre-service and in-service training in the country are not adequate POA (1986) and POA (1992) have therefore emphasised that the task of training of special teachers should be undertaken by various agencies immediately. It is therefore proposed to promote one year B.Ed (spl. education) in selected university departments of education with specialisation in visual disability, speech and hearing disability, multi-category disabilities and integrated education of disabled. One institution in each region of the country may be chosen to specialise in each of these four Categories. Thus in all 16 institutions may be covered under this programme. The identified institutions which are willing to take up such programmes may be given assistance for additional staff, equipment, Curriculum and materials development and contingencies. The estimated expenditure during IX Plan on this component may be about Rs. 10 crores.

Programme of Support for Construction of Teachers' Houses in Remote Areas

As mentioned in para 13, the NPE and POA envisage several steps to improve pay and service conditions of teachers. One of the most important of these pertains to solving the problem of housing of teachers. Lack of proper housing is one of the main reasons for teacher absenteeism in remote rural areas which, in turn, leads to a virtual breakdown of the educational delivery system. A CABE Sub-committee has also gone into the issue of providing housing facilities for women teachers, and its recommendations have been endorsed by the CABE. Pursuant to the recommendations of the above sub-committee, a fully Centrally-assisted programme may be taken up during IX Plan period for construction of Houses for elementary school teachers, Using institutional

finance. Modalities of the Scheme could be worked out by involving State Governments and financial institutions. Simultaneously State Governments would be Urged to increase the quantum of House Building Advance available for teachers to enable a larger number of teachers to construct their own houses during their career. An amount of Rs.250 crore is proposed as the Central share for operationalisation of the above scheme during the plan period.

Role of Voluntary Agencies in Teacher Education

Several Non Government Organisations (NGOs) are involved in designing and delivering innovative and experimental programmes of primary teacher education in different parts of the country.

Externally assisted projects in basic education which include DPEP, Lok Jumbish and Shiksha Karmi Projects have also given new direction to teacher training by introducing decentralised training at block and cluster levels; emphasising child-centred, contextually relevant and joyful learning processes, and incorporating minimum levels of learning in text-books and teacher training. The UNICEF sponsored teacher-empowerment projects in Madhya Pradesh, Rajasthan, Maharashtra and Uttar Pradesh have improved school environment, teacher morale and teaching practices in interior rural primary schools. These projects have also made useful inputs in training trainers and emphasising the importance of 'Shikshak Dharma'.

Some of the successful programmes need to be upscaled and replicated on a wider scale through dissemination, exchange of ideas and experiences and support to NGOs during the Ninth Five Year Plan. For this purpose salient features of experimental and innovative teacher education programme may be summarised as follows:

- Recurrent and rigorous academic training of teachers in a residential situation.
- Emphasis on inputs to facilitate realisation of 'Shikshak Dharma' i.e. the higher moral purpose of teaching as a profession as, a means to bring about attitudinal changes and improve the prevailing work culture.
- Utilisation of educational facilities, including premises of senior, secondary and secondary schools, at block and cluster levels to develop resource centres for professional upgradation of teachers nearer their place of work.
- Careful identification, selection and training of master trainers for imparting high quality and intensive training to primary school teachers.
- Social orientation and sensitisation of teachers to problems of rural schools, disadvantaged sections of society, girls and the) local communities.
- Active participation of teachers in design and development of teacher training programmes, low-cost teaching aids; earring materials, etc.
- Recognition of multigrade and multi-level learning situations in rural schools as challenges to be specially addressed in professional preparation of teachers.
- Emphasis on improving class room teaching practise in tandem with curriculum and materials.
- Evolving training programmes which are participative, trainee friendly and use self/learning training materials.
- Generating community, support and resources to improve the school environment and consequently teachers morale and self-esteem.
- Placing emphasis on improving knowledge and skills of teachers in Science and Mathematics.

- Development of innovative and contextually relevant materials for guiding teachers, supplementing textbooks and enriching the learning process.
- Creation of mechanisms for continuous review, feedback and upgradation of teacher performance.

During the Ninth Plan efforts would be made to strengthen the partnership between government and non-government organisations for promotion and delivery of contextually relevant, innovative and experimental programmes for teacher education. It is expected that this would have a positive impact on teacher morale, motivation and performance. It is envisaged that in backward pockets and tribal areas, where qualified and trained teachers especially women, are not available, services of NGOs could be utilised to provide education and training in a residential situation to local youth to enable them to serve as para-teachers.

The Madhya Pradesh Government has launched an entirely new elementary education package from July, 1996 called the 'Sikhna Shikhana' Practice' package, which is activity based, embedded in local culture and environment and joyful.

The package has emerged out of a major policy decision by the State Government and intense field work at the grass-root level by governmental and non-governmental agencies working in partnership.

The major policy decision taken by the Technical Resource Support Group, set up as an apex body by the State Government, has been to invite voluntary groups and other educational institutions to undertake creating teaching learning material, teacher training methods, monitoring methods through field trialling. SCERT, instead of being a norm setting agency, has also been one of the trialling agencies. The effort of the agencies are shared through constant interaction and then amalgamated into a package which is the 'Sikhna Sikhana' package. The contents, teacher training methodology and monitoring system are integrated as also the resource material that the children use in transacting the contents. The major partner involved in this process has been the NGO Eklavya which is working in elementary education in Madhya Pradesh for over 15 years. This is an excellent example of how universalisation with quality improvement can be brought about through partnership between the government and NGOs. The initial phase of the programme covers 16 districts which are both DPEP and non-DPEP districts, Creation of NGO supported Technical Resource Support Groups in other States on similar lines would be encouraged and Supported in the Ninth Plan. An allocation of Rs.50 crore is proposed during Ixth Plan for Supporting NGOs, effort in Teacher Education.

Meaning and Programme of In-service Training

Realising the need for Inservice education of educational personnel teachers, teacher educators, administrators and supervisors and Panchayat Raj functionaries on a continuing basis, it is imperative to develop a network of institutions with a specific mandate to provide training to all educational personnel in the country atleast once in five years supplemented by refresher programmes of shorter duration every year. A, large number of institutions like SCERTs, IASEs, CTEs and DIETs have already been set tip with this objective in view. This training network which has evolved during the Seventh and Eighth Five Year Plans needs to be consolidated and further augmented to achieve the target of covering Fill educational personnel, as stated above.

NCTE, NCERT, NIEPA shall be responsible for formulation, implementation, coordination and monitoring of scheme of inservice education of teacher educators, teachers, educational planners and administrators. These institutions shall also be required to provide academic resource support to inservice teacher education institutions by developing exemplary training packages and guidelines and methodologies for monitoring and evaluating quality of training. At the state level, SCERTs would be responsible for providing academic resource support to District Institutes of Education and Training (DIETs) with regard to training of elementary school teachers. SCERTs may also coordinate inservice training of secondary school teachers to be provided by CTEs and IASEs. SCERTs may also take up training of heads of Secondary and Senior secondary schools in their respective States. The CTEs shall be responsible for providing training to senior:secondary teachers and elementary teacher educators. The demarcation of responsibilities on these lines shall help to avoid duplication of effort on the part of different institutions.

Strengthening Teacher Education Division

The implementation of the programme proposed to be undertaken in IX Plan to achieve the objectives outlined in this document Would need augmentation of manpower and facilities available in the Teacher Education Division. There is, therefore, an imperative need to adequately strengthen the Teacher Education Division in terms of manpower and availability of requisite infrastructure for efficient functioning of the Division. It is proposed to make an allocation of Rs. 2.50 crore for the Plan period.

Role of States

For all States, teachers' salaries constitute the largest share of the education budget. Teachers are the principal instruments through which the States fulfil their constitutional obligations of universalising the elementary education. Thus improving teachers' performance is a crucial challenge before States today. In the following Paragraph we would attempt to define the role of States in reducing the mismatch between demand and supply of trained manpower as well improving the status and motivation of teachers to enable them to attain their rightful place in the modern society.

Mismatch Between Demand and Supply

As explained in para 30 to 32 of this document the mismatch between demand and supply of trained manpower in the States has a direct bearing on the morale of the teaching community, besides putting a strain on the State exchequer as the money being spent on pre-service teacher-education exceeds the requirements of the State educational system. Proper manpower planning is the only answer to this vexed problem and for this States would have to make a realistic assessment of their requirements of trained manpower and match this with tie capacity of their teacher training institutions. Wherever they find excess built up capacity for pre-service teacher training, efforts should be made! to utilise it for the purpose of inservice training of teachers, an area where almost all States have been found to be deficient during the VIII Plan. States would be encouraged during the IX Plan to utilise the expertise being developed by NGTE in the area of manpower planning to tackle this long pending problem effectively.

Untrained Teachers

As could be seen from the figures of untrained teachers in States indicated in Annexures VIII-IX of this document about 10% of our primary teachers lack basic training in education, Viewed in the backdrop, of excess teacher training capacity in several States,, the position becomes dichotomous. During the IX Plan, State with a huge backlog of untrained teachers would be expected to come up with specific schemes for imparting training to these teachers on a crash programme basis with the assistance of national institutions such as NOS, IGNOU, NCERT and N.C.T.E. The Diploma programme developed for teachers of the North-Eastern region by, IGNOU and NCERT is an illustration of this approach. The National Action Plan for primary teacher training through distance education seeks to address this problem.

Stutus and Motivation of Teachers

Teachers today are concerned about their working conditions, their emoluments and their social and professional status. States would have to pay greater attention to these aspects as lack of Suitable working conditions and appropriate environment for good teacher performance could be the most serious challenge in improving educational outcomes.

Qualifications

Most States have now prescribed 12 years schooling as the minimum requirements for general education of elementary school teachers. A few States, however, still have entry qualifications equivalent to 10 years of schooling. If teachers are recruited with low academic qualifications their status and performance is likely to be adversely affected. To make up for deficiencies in general education during pro-service training results in insufficient allocation of time for training in pedagogical skills and practice teaching. Also teacher training is more expensive for the State than general education. All teachers at the elementary level should have +2 educational qualification to enable them to meet the growing challenge of explosion of knowledge in a rapidly changing world. In the IX Plan, States which do not have 12 years of schooling as qualification for elementary teachers would be persuaded and, if necessary, supported to achieve this objective.

Service Conditions of Teachers

Pay and Allowances

It is expected that the 5th Central Pay Commission and the State Pay Commissions would take into account the onerous social and professional responsibilities of teachers in determining their pay and service conditions. It should be ensured that teachers salaries, allowances and retirements benefits are comparable to those of other public services with similar qualifications and responsibilities. In an era of liberalisation and globalisation of India's economy, which has created several attractive and highly paid avenues of employment, the need for attracting and retaining the best talent in the teaching profession cannot be over-emphasised. In this context, proper recognition and compensation for the difficult and challenging conditions in which a majority of India's rural teachers work for long years would appear to be overdue.

Redressal of Teachers' Grievances

Insufficient attention to regular and prompt settlement of service related and retirement claims of teachers has dented their morale considerably. The massive litigation in this regard is an additional burden on the teachers as well as the administration. State Governments would be expected to make sincere and concerted effort to redress the situation during IX

Plan. Some of the measures which should be taken are as follows:-

- Formulation and adoption of efficient and rational policies for recruitment and deployment of teachers. It would be appropriate for States to adopt the recommendations of the CABE Committee on Transfers and Postings of Teachers.
- Creation of quasi-judicial and administrative mechanisms to redress service-related grievances of teachers and reduce litigation.
- Initiation of programmes such as 11 Point Programme of Rajasthan and Pension Adalats of Indian Railways for settlement of service and retirement benefits of teachers.
- Recurrent programmes of residential teacher training to improve their morale and motivation.

Improvement of Working Environment

It is necessary to make sufficient investments for, improving the infrastructure facilities and environment of government schools. Effective implementation of schemes such as Operation Blackboard and Jawahar Rojgar Yojana could make a useful contribution in this respect.

Incentives and recognition for teachers who are successful in mobilising community resources for this purpose ought to be institutionalised, Teachers may be given support and encouragement through a more sensitive and responsive supervisory system which should not be over-burdened with the responsibility for a large number of schools.

The issue of increasing burden of non-educational, administrative and development work on teachers should be tackled seriously as it has a negative effect on the quality of learning and effectiveness; of schools. It should be possible for a national consensus to emerge for engaging teachers only in work relating to elections, census and literacy, besides their primary task of teaching.

Rewards

The prevailing system of reward and recognition of teachers appears to be inadequate to provide them with necessary motivation. Efforts would be made to expand avenues for rewarding selfless and dedicated performance by teachers through joint initiatives of government and the community.

Accountability

It cannot be denied that, there is widespread dissatisfaction in the society at large regarding lack of accountability, indiscipline and absenteeism among teachers. To some extent a centralised and unresponsive administrative system is responsible for this state of affairs. Renewed efforts would, therefore, be necessary on the part of 'State Governments to involve teachers' associations, Panchayat Raj Institutions and the local community in improving teacher performance, accountability and attendance.

Principles and Types of Time Table—Budgeting

Thoughtful Planning Produces Valuable Time

Traditional Strategies: Early dismissal and fewer student-attendance days are traditional mechanisms for increasing the time for teacher training and dialogue.

- Banked Time. Some districts or buildings add time to their instructional day, banking the time for early releases or full-day trainings. Community Consolidated School District 146, a K–8 district in Tinley Park, Illinois, for example, banks 20 minutes a day to create nine school improvement days. These days are used by building leadership for a wide range of needs—faculty meetings, writing of school improvement goals, and professional development.
- Extended Day. To gain professional development time, Guskey (1998) recommends adding hours to the day—either before or after school or during an extended lunch period. This situation causes minimal academic disruption but can be difficult for teachers who have

to put in more than a full day of work, have personal responsibilities at home, or have coaching or other extracurricular responsibilities before or after school.

Online Opportunities for Professional Development

Increasingly, organisations and associations are offering online professional development to faculty. An added benefit to using technology in this manner is the fact that professional development has been shown to be effective when technology is focused on higher-level learning (Holmes, 2000).

- Anytime/Anywhere Professional Development. These opportunities cover all disciplines. Training comes in different media formats—including videotapes; online, course-based, distance learning; and various combinations of media. Among the benefits of such professional development are access to content-area teachers located all over the country and greater comfort levels for sharing ideas and thoughts electronically rather than face-to-face. Common experiences and interests provide a possible networked community, as well as the opportunity for ongoing interactions and sharing between members long after the course or training has been completed (Koufman-Frederick, Lillie, Pattison-Gordon, Watt, & Carter, 1999; Serim, 1995).

The Public Broadcasting Service (PBS) TeacherLine professional development courses are one example of such opportunities. According to a PBS promotional e-mail (personal communication, June 1, 2004), some 96 percent of participating teachers reported that TeacherLine courses met or exceeded their expectations.

During the summer of 2004, PBS offered 30 online courses on a national basis, and some member stations offered additional local courses. Facilitated by experienced educators, the six-week online courses are designed for PK–12 classroom teachers in reading and language arts, mathematics, and technology integration. In addition to offering participants new content knowledge, instructional strategies, and lesson plans, the courses also allow teachers to "share knowledge, wisdom, and expertise... [in] a supportive and collaborative online environment" (PBS, personal communication, June 1, 2004).

- Online Support for Trainers. Online seminars also provide support for in-district trainers. Some school districts are willing to spend large sums of money to have in-district faculty or staff trained as trainers—a strategy that has long been shown to be effective. What has been missing, however, is the ongoing technical and emotional support these individuals need to effectively meet the challenges of training and supporting teacher development. In-district trainers need opportunities for continued development and for deepening their knowledge and skills, as well as objective feedback from others (Feger, Woleck, & Hickman, 2004). Administrators should encourage trainers to establish strong, networked relationships during the training and should support the maintenance of those contacts after the trainer begins training with staff.

Goals:

- High-quality professional development is a priority for the school or district.
- Professional development is an integral part of the overall school improvement plan.
- Professional development is based on frameworks that model research and evidence-based decision making.
- For accountability purposes, the effectiveness of professional development is linked with improved student learning and achievement.
- Quality time is allocated for the planning, preparation, and implementation of all professional development activities.
- Various professional development strategies are available and provide effective options for individuals and groups of teachers.

- Students, parents, and community members have a clear understanding of the goals and planned outcomes of professional development time used.

Action Options: Stakeholders can take the following steps to ensure that adequate time is found for effective professional development:

School Board

- Require all buildings in the district to have a professional development planning committee that examines the research and aligns professional development to the NCERT Standards for Staff Development, the school improvement plan, the data-driven needs of the faculty, and student achievement needs.
- Require follow-up reports on the impact of the resources allocated to professional development.

School Administrators

- Ensure that professional development is systemic, research-based, job-embedded, ongoing, and supported by follow-up.
- Give professional development the necessary resources (time, budgetary, administrative follow-up, and emotional support) for effective implementation.
- Establish professional development frameworks that model research and evidence-based decision making.
- Use data to drive all decisions related to the selection of topics, emphasis, and need for professional development.
- Ensure that all planning uses data to support follow-up and student impact from the professional development.
- Inform students, parents, and community members of the school improvement plan and the need for professional development time.

Teachers

- Understand that adequate time for high-quality professional development is essential to professional growth and improved student learning.
- Engage wholeheartedly in professional development activities.
- Remain flexible regarding various strategies for finding time for professional development.

UNIT-VII

Research in Teacher Education

Areas of Research in Teacher Education—Institutional Context, Curriculum Context and Practicing School Context

Teacher education today is an integral part of any educational system. Teaching, being both a skill and an art, was found amenable to transmission in the early years of the 19th century. If, for ages, teacher education, per se, was a caste or family affair, it could not afford to remain so after education became a mass movement. Mass literacy goals as well as the emergence of technology transformed the very character of teacher training and its philosophy. The National Policy on Education, 1986, reflects precisely this change in its concept and practice. Now, teacher education is no longer limited to primary or secondary levels of teachers but extends far beyond. The creation of the Academic Staff College under the aegis of the UGC is a case in point. No wonder then that teacher education has emerged as an important area of educational research.

In the four surveys so far, taken together, 410 studies have been identified as belonging to the area of teacher education. Researchers working in this area have brought into their study a wide spectrum of variables. If one has studied selection procedures, another has developed curriculum for teacher education programmes and a third has tried to find out the effect of innovative instructional procedures on teacher effectiveness. This is largely due to the fact that teacher education is a long, complicated series of operations. Each operation, in itself, is an extremely complex set of steps. All these interact almost simultaneously. The institution, the process of admission, training climate, administrative setup, the student-teacher, the personal characteristics of teachers, practice schools-these factors, and quite a few more, are constantly at work in the real setting.

To conduct research in any area in a wholly systematized manner, so as to place it in a gestalt perspective is beyond the ability of any single researcher operating in isolation. This can be said even more specifically about researches in this field. Currently these researches are pursued in isolation with little or no contact with each other; the researchers are isolated in their attempts to transform teacher education. In this situation, it is necessary for the reviewer to superimpose a classificatory system which can help in identifying clusters of variables. A cluster of variables, thus identified, may be called an area of research. Though every cluster of variables will have something or other to do with the remaining clusters, it may be said that they do not completely overlap and hence each has an identity of its own.

Reviews of studies in the area of teacher education have been attempted by Lulla and Singh (1974), Mehrotra (1979), Das and Jangira (1983), Bhatnagar (1980), and Pillay (1987). A synoptic overview of the nature of these reviews would help one to take stock of the researches completed in the area. Lulla and Singh (1974), in their trand report in, 'A Survey of Research in Education' (Buch, 1974), classified teacher education research into six areas, namely, selection criteria; abilities and qualities of the teacher; pre-service and inservice training of teachers; workload, job satisfaction and difficulties experienced by the teachers; procedures and practices of teacher education in India; and personality variables of teachers, In his trend report in the Second Survey of Research in Education, Mehrotra (1979) did the classification differently. Here the varia-bles were clustered under contextual, input, process and output categories. In the

Third Survey, Jangira (1986) adopted a systems model of classifying (as per Sage, 1974) variables under context-presage-process-product categories. Usage of the terms, context-presage-process-product, instead of input-process-output, has certain advantages for classification of studies. One is that it does not have a bias towards instructional system from which input-process-product suffers. Secondly, the context-presage-process-product approach views teacher education from a systems point of view, taking into consideration the effect of other subsystems (external or internal) on the working of the subsystems of teacher education. Thirdly, it is a more elaborate approach that looks into the effects of internal and external constraints on the stystem and the resistance of the system to them that is, it sees the working of the system in the context of other systems/subsystems.

The present trend report is based on the studies abstracted in the three earlier surveys (Buch 1974, Buch 1979 and Buch 1986) and also 150 additional studies identified for the area in this volume. All these 410 studies done at Ph.D. and project levels have been taken together for identifying emerging trends. No separate classification has been thus worked out for the additional studies separately. This had been done with view to avoiding overlapping and to present a comprehensive view of trends in the area over a substantial period. The studies have been viewed from three points of view-their nature, methodology of research, and a systems approach to teacher education.

Nature of Studies

There are 276 studies at Ph.D. level, and 134 at project level. Out of the Ph.D. studies, 245 are in education, 26 in psychology and six in other disciplines. The most explored area in teacher education is pre-service education, having 248 studies, while 110 studies have been done in in-service education. There are 36 studies that have tried to probe both pre-service and in-service education.

It may be noted that up to 1950 no work had been done in this area. Even up to 1960, the very little work that was done which was restricted to education of primary, secondary and technical teachers. In the years, 1961-70, there was a slight change and the researchers began to work in areas of pre-primary and higher teacher education also. After 1980, there has been a spurt in researches in the area, of teacher education and 183 studies pertaining to different levels of teacher education were conducted. In a span of four years (1984-87), 100 studies were conducted in teacher education at all levels. Again, the explored area was sec-ondary teacher education. The most favoured area with researchers has been secondary teacher education and the most neglected one, pre-primary teacher education. This trend suggests that researchers need to explore areas of teacher education, other than secondary education, also.

A close scrutiny of the projects reveals that the NCERT has been a pioneer agency that took up 62 per cent of the projects completed in. teacher education. This institution also laid more stress on projects in secondary teacher education and much less on pre-primary and primary teacher education. Other institutes that have followed the NCERT in completing a number of projects in teacher education are the SCERTs. Out of these, the SCERTs of Rajasthan and Andhra Pradesh are more prominent. Their areas of concern have been elementary and secondary teacher education. Technical Teachers Education Institutions took up projects on teacher education of polytechnic teachers. The least explored area of teacher education at the project-level has been teacher education for college and university teachers. The university departments of education need to explore this field.

Methodology

Another way of classifying the studies could be by the methodology followed by the researchers. Different researchers followed different research procedures according to the nature of the problem selected by them. The major purpose of most of the studies has been determination of the status of the variables. Next in the rank comes prediction of the variables. Determination of the causes occupies third position. Cross-cultural studies constitute 40 per cent and longitudinal studies six per cent of the total. Among the different methods of research followed, nearly 49 per cent can be classified as survey studies, 26 per cent as experimental, eight per cent as case studies, nine per cent as historical, and six per cent as exploratory studies. There are only two studies that had a review of the literature in teachers education as their major objective. In most of the studies, students of different courses and teachers formed the controlled factors studied under higher education. In secondary teacher education, the controlled factors were student teachers, teacher educators, students, parents of students, supervisors and learning material. In primary teacher education, elementary classes, teachers of primary schools, and curriculum of primary teacher education programmes are the controlled factors. Researchers have paid little attention to developmental and evaluation studies. There is a need to go in for such studies so as to provide guidelines for future teacher-education programmes.

Sample

The researchers have selected their samples mainly from locations where they were pursuing their research, though not in the case of cross-cultural and comparative studies. Depending upon the location of the university, institution, investigator, purpose of the study and so on, samples have been drawn from different parts of the country. The population, for different types of sample, has been educational institutions, teachers, students, student-teachers, teacher-educators, supervisors, pupils, headmasters or principals, administrators, etc. The size of the sample varied according to the nature of the population. In the case of pupils; sample size in some cases has been as large as 3000, and in case of administrators as low as five. In general, sample size varied from ten to 1000, according to the nature of the subjects/participants in the studies. The methodology of drawing the sample happens to be simple randomization, multi-stage randomization, stratified sampling, random stratified, clustered, etc., depending upon the nature of the related population and the purpose of the study. The variations in samples, the size and methodology of sampling, have been very wide. Because of this variability in sample size, characteristics of the sample and methodology employed for selecting the sample, generalizations cannot be easily drawn from the findings of the studies.

Tools Employed

The questionnaire and the observation scale are the commonest among the tools used by the, researchers. Other tools included personal data sheets, interview schedules, check lists and institutional records. In the case of questionnaires, 16 PF has been the most widely used for measuring personality and, in the case of observation scales, the Baroda General Teaching Competence Scale has been put to maximum use by researchers. Most of them have used available standardized tools in their studies. They have also developed their own tools and standardized them. These have been mainly concerned with questionnaire, observation schedule, interview schedule, etc. In the process of standardization of the tools, they followed the usual prescribed procedures like item analysis, finding out reliability and validity. In some cases, they have gone in for establishing norms also.

Statistical Techniques Employed

During the analysis of data, researchers have made use of raw scores and only rarely converted them into standard scores. Depending upon the methodology used in the study, the researchers have made use of correlation, factor analysis, regression and prediction, analysis of variance, analysis of covariance, t-test, chi-square, sign test, etc. along with measures of central tendency and dispersion. The most favoured statistical tools have been parametric tests. Non-parametric tests did not find much favour with investigators. The experimental studies have made use of pre-experimental and experimental designs. Among the most experimental designs have been simple pre-test, post-test designs with one treatment and one control group. Factor analytical studies have aimed at identifying factors implicit in the structure of relationship between different variables pertaining to different individuals. Regression studies have aimed at establishing multiple regression equations and multiple correlations between predictors like personality traits, teaching skills and criteria like teaching competence, examination marks in theory and practice teaching, etc.

Systems Approach to Teacher Education

Keeping in view the advantages of a systems approach, the present trend report is based on studies identified in the area of teacher education and done at both Ph.D. and project levels. Teacher education has been viewed here from a systems approach point of view and the studies have been categorized as context-presage-process-product studies. Because of overlapping and also because of the researchers studying variables belonging to different categories, this trend report is presented under different combinations of these categories. The major headings of the trend report are context studies, presage studies, context-presage studies, presage-process studies, context-product studies, and process-product studies.

The Context.Studies: This area of research in teacher education covers studies on institutional characteristics, student-teacher characteristics, teacher characteristics, and classroom context. The institutional-characteristics-related variables are the climate obtaining in teacher-education institutions, administrative set-up, etc. Under student-teacher characteristics, studies pertain to one or more variables, viz., student-teacher formative experiences, their academic qualifications, abilities, personality factors, intelligence, etc. The studies concerned with teacher characteristics have variables like personality traits, self-concept, job expectation, role expectancy, role performance, etc. Classroom context studies include certain classroom variables such as classroom climate, size of the classroom and curriculum at teacher training and practising school level. The trend of the context studies is presented here according to this classification.

Institutional Context: In this category are clustered those studies that have traced the growth of teacher education in their respective geographical regions, viz. states, districts, etc. Other types of studies surveyed the institutions with respect to their admission procedure, number of student-teachers enrolled, facilities available, etc. Such studies have their value on two counts. One is that they help in understanding the present problems in teacher education programmes and the other is that they indicate the extent of achievement and scope of improvement.

Institutional Context

Developmental Perspective: There are 67 studies of the growth of teacher education programme at the national level, regional level and state level. There are 24 studies of teacher education in historical perspective in India and other countries like Bangladesh and Thailand. The researchers have also studied growth of teacher education in different fields, e.g., technical teacher education, English teaching, and education of women teachers. There are 26 such studies. The other set of 17 studies includes those that have evaluated teacher-education institutions from the point of view of innovations carried out, teaching strategies adopted, etc. Mishra (1986) studied the growth of teacher education for women with respect to the history of women's education, institutions involved and number of student-teachers in the institutions. Dash (1985) studied the development of teacher education programmes in Orissa. Hemambujam (1983) made a study of teacher education programme at secondary level in Tamil Nadu. The researchers also made a study of development and organisation of in-service teacher-education programmes. Pathak (1985) traced the growth of in-service teacher education programmes in India. Butala (1987) made a study of in-service programmes conducted by secondary teacher training colleges of Gujarat State with respect to number of programmes conducted. Arya (1986) studied the tension education activities organized by the Northern Teachers Colleges in Thailand. All these inquiries have either historically or through the survey method studied the growth of teacher education institutions. Gogate (1985) went a step further and made a case study of teacher education in Marathwada at different levels. The study revealed that there was a teacher-education programme for elementary and secondary teachers in the region but none for university and college teachers. But this may not be true for all regions. There are some universities in India that have introduced teacher-education programmes for college teachers. Kadwadkar (1984) made a study of this aspect and traced the growth of professional courses for college teachers in India.

Another set of studies has surveyed the existing teacher-education programme with respect to admissions, teaching staff and facilities available. These have their relevance because they expose the gap between what exists at present and what is required. It is only on this basis that planning of an effective teacher-education-programme can be done at different levels of education and at different stages, viz., pre-service and in-service.

The NCERT has conducted a number of surveys of institutions of teacher education as part of general surveys of elementary and secondary education programmes. This effort has been supplemented by the SCERTs at state level. There are 84 such studies, out of which 48 are at Ph.D. level and 36 at institutional level. The regional SCERT (1966) made a survey of the primary teachers training programme in the State of Rajasthan. The survey was conducted with respect to qualifications for admission, teaching staff available, syllabus, arrangement of practice teaching, difficulties faced, and stipends for student-teachers. Seetharamu and Sharda (1984) and Seetharamu and Usha (1986) made a status study of institutions of primary and secondary teacher education respectively of Bangalore city with respect to admission procedure, physical facilities and financial status. Indradevi (1985) studied the clientele of teacher education programmes (both at M.Ed. and B.Ed. level) run through the non-formal system of education. Kumar et al (1986) tried to find out motivating factors due to which teachers joined the summer-school-cum-correspondence courses of the NCERT for the B.Ed. degree. The factors were found to be compulsions rather than interests. The regional SCERT (1981) evaluated the in-service training programme for primary teachers in teacher-training institutions in Andhra Pradesh with respect to staff, books and teaching strategies adopted. In another study, the SCERT (1980) surveyed inservice training of secondary teachers in science teaching centres attached to colleges of education in Andhra Pradesh. All these surveys painted a dismal picture of teacher education so far as the qualitative aspect was concerned. Dearth of required physical facilities and adequate financial provisions were the major findings. Similar revelations were made when the researchers carried out studies with respect to the teacher-education programme in specific disciplines. Gangaiah (1986) evaluated English-teacher education in Andhra Pradesh both at the pre-service and in-service stage. It was found that proficiency, in English of trainees was not taken care of and the training programmes were not need-based.

There are studies that survey teacher education programmes with respect to-their objectives and innovations carried out. Shaw (1986) surveyed the management of a teacher-education programme with respect to its objectives, criteria of allocation of methods of teaching to student-teachers and innovative practices carried out.

Mohanty (1984) studied teaching programmes in the colleges of education of Orissa. Raj (1984) made a survey of teaching programmes in secondary teacher education colleges of the northern region of India with respect to supervisory practices and current duties of those in charge of practice teaching. All these studies sought to look into the inner functional variables.

There were also studies aimed at investigating the peripheral functional variables of institutions, viz., how persons living on the outer precincts of the institution viewed it and got benefit from it. Babu et al (1986) evaluated the Regional College of Education (Mysore) from the point of view of awareness of the people about the courses offered by it.

The objectives of these studies have primarily been collection of information and making suggestions for improvement. But researchers have not been doing justice to the second objective in most cases. There is a need that such studies be conducted with in-depth analysis, insight and intensive logical thinking so that valid lessons are learnt for organizing teacher-education programmes in the country.

Institutional Context

Comparative Aspect: There are 29 comparative studies of existing teacher education programmes. These have compared different teacher-education programmes with respect to the facilities available, courses of study, demonstration or practice teaching schools, clientele,. etc. They make a contribution to teacher education as they point out possible improvements that can be made in the existing set-up. In this way, guidelines for planned reform and development of teacher-education programmes tan be made, keeping in mind the working of different models of teacher-education.

There are nine studies that compare the features of Indian teacher-education programmes with that of developed and developing countries. Researchers like Ghosh (1977) compared Indian teacher-education programmes with those of developed countries like the USA and UK. He came to the conclusion that, apart from differences in teacher education systems between developed and developing countries, the teachers in all these cases came from middle-class groups. Further, the courses and curricula of study in all these models of teacher education needed revision. These studies show that all is not gold everywhere. The criticism against such studies is that they compare the systems irrespective of needs, requirements and environment prevailing in, different countries.

Researchers have also compared different teacher-education models in India. Kalla (1984) studied Gandhi Shiksha Bhavan College with respect to innovations carried out and its deviation from the Bombay University model. Yadav (1980) compared teacher-education institutions of different states and their organisational set-up, viz., colleges of Haryana, the Central Institute of Education, Delhi and the Regional College of Education, Ajmer. He found that facilities, courses of study, socioeconomic status, and clientele (student-teachers) differed in all three cases. Roy (1985) compared the teacher-education programme for English teachers of two institutions-the CIEFL (Hyderabad) and Patna University. He pointed out some structural flaws in the English-teacher preparation programme of Patna University. All these studies have one common observation, that is, teacher-education programmes are better in those institutions which have some missionary spirit and autonomous status in designing and managing their courses and programmes, thus making a case for autonomous status for teacher-education institutions. The National Education Policy (1986) has suggested the establishment of such autonomous college. This opens up a new dimension of teacher-education for researchers to ponder over and study.

Institutional Environment Context

Institutional environment is often assumed to be positively related with teacher-education programmes. There are 14 studies that can be included in this set of variables. Most of them have looked into organisational climate, administrative set-up, etc. Their contribution towards teacher education programmes is the creation of awareness about the operational functioning of teachers-education institutions and highlight the scope for change and adoption of innovations. The studies quoted in the previous surveys have shown that teacher-education institutions in most cases (especially the privately managed ones) work under conditions of insecurity because of the nature of staff recruitment. A study conducted by the SCERT (1981) for evaluating in-service teacher-education institutions in Andhra

Pradesh from the administrative point of view pointed out that the teachers had to undertake a lot of paperwork in order to attend a training programme. There are other studies that have identified different types of organisational climate obtaining in various colleges of education. A cursory look at all these studies shows that many of them are just peripheral to the main concern of management of teacher-education institutions. It is necessary that researchers explore institutional environment from various angles, viz., role conflict of different functionaries, analysis of educational laws and acts concerned with teacher education, institutional viability in terms of number of admissions and goals of teacher-education, and evaluation of management practices adopted by different institutions with respect to economic, psychological and sociological factors.

Curriculum Context: Another set of context variables includes studies related to teacher education curriculum. The curriculum, in specific, is a medium that translates socio-educational philosophies into teaching procedures and teaching outcomes. So also, these studies provide an insight into the kind of curriculum that is needed for having a teacher education programme that will cater to the needs of teachers in particular and education of children in general. There are 38 studies that have evaluated fundamental courses at different levels. Out of these, 23 have limited themselves to courses at the B.Ed. level. The courses have been mostly evaluated by seeking the opinion of teachers, teacher-educators, heads of schools and other personnel connected with teacher-education programmes. Other researchers have developed their own curricula and tried them in their teacher-education institutions in order' to. test these for expected outcomes.

Arora (1986) evaluated the B.Ed. teacher-education curriculum of the-universities of Punjab, Haryana and Chandigarh, keeping in view the needs of science teachers in schools. Pradhananga (1986) examined the syllabi of elementary teacher-education institutions of Nepal with respect to instructional programme and coordination between different components of theory and practice teaching. He elicited the views of administrators, experts, headmasters, teachers and student-teachers. Most studies of this kind, following a similar procedure, did not find the curriculum suited to the needs of the schools teaching programmes. They found a great gap between theory and practice teaching. Some studies done in the sixties and seventies did not find theory related to practice teaching at all. Almost all studies in curriculum context suggested changes in the curriculum in general and theory courses in particular. Some researchers went a step further and developed their own curricula for student-teachers and tried the same in teacher-education institutions. Mian (1983) developed a programme of curriculum content and methodology in the areas of science and agriculture for teacher-training colleges of Bangladesh. He studied its workability on the basis of the opinions of teachers, instructors and college alumni.

A close look at the studies done in the field of curriculum reveals that almost all of them have concluded that the present curricula of teacher-education at different levels do not meet felt needs. These studies have also tried to suggest a new curriculum but their suggestions have also been limited to the same framework as that in which the old or present curriculum existed. Further, these studies evaluated the curriculum from the point of view of different personnel attached to the teacher-education system. Rarely have studies gone in for evaluation of curriculum from the consumers' point of view, that is, teacher-effectiveness, student-teachers' interest,-solving school problems, workability in existing school conditions, etc. The researchers need to explore such vital issues of curriculum relating to theory and practice and that also at different levels, primary, secondary and higher. Further, researches are needed to develop new curriculum programmes after removing current drawbacks and try the same in the institutions to find out their effectiveness. The effectiveness of a curriculum has not only to be seen from the point of view of others, but rather from the angle of desired behavioural changes that it can bring about in the student-teachers. To carry out such experiments, one obvious handicap with the researchers seems to be the rigid process of functioning of the universities. But those colleges and university departments that have autonomy in the construction and adoption of curricular courses need to go in for such research studies.

Practising School Context: Another important aspect that affects the teacher-education programme is the practising school. These schools serve as links between laboratory conditions (teacher-education institutions) and real conditions (schools or colleges). Researches in this area provide awareness as to how close a training setting approxi-mates the workplace and how transfer of teaching skill can be facilitated in the student-teachers.

There are five studies (already reported in the previous surveys) which have examined practising schools from the point of view of facilities provided in the teacher-education institution, their availability to student-teachers at the time of the practising session, the perception of principals of colleges of education, teacher-educators, student-teachers, headmasters, etc. The practising school, though an important part of the teacher-education programme, has not attracted the attention of researchers. One obvious reason for this is that practising schools have not been an integral part of teacher-education institutions in India and their separate entity does not allow researchers to take up this area of research. But, there is a need to probe this area not only from the cooperation point of view but also from the angle of sources of expert feedback and apprenticeship training.

Context Studies-Student-Teacher Characteristics: The characteristics of student-teachers and their formative experiences are another set of context variables. There are 89 studies that have taken student-teachers' cognitive and non-cognitive variables into accounts. Such studies are probably conducted with a hunch that characteristics are conducive to adoption of a particular profession and teaching is no exception. The researchers, taking up these studies investigated self-concept, creativity, personality traits, adjustment, social maturity, etc. of the student-teachers. They tried to answer the question, 'Are there inherent characteristics in an individual that play their role in shaping him for the job? Whether this question is answered or not is one thing, but these types of studies are helpful in long-term planning for intake in the teacher-education programme.

Pillai (1985) tried to identify factors that influenced graduates in choosing teaching as a career. Some researchers have also tried to find out the motivating factor that impelled students to join teaching courses. Kumar (1986) studied the motivation factor behind students joining the B.Ed. correspondence courses. The potent factor was found to be personal likes and dislikes. Upadhyay (1984), along with motivation, compared attitude and values among student-teachers belonging to different universities of Uttar Pradesh. The study revealed that geographical set-up and institutional structure did not relate to characteristics of student-teachers. Rai (1983) took up a study of self-concept of prospective teachers.

Ls'verne (1985) compared high, medium and low creative student-teachers in terms of personality components. Donga (1987) studied adjustment differences among different student-teacher groups according to sex, marital status, age, educational qualifications, SES and residential accommodation. Tripathi (1983) studied personality traits of student-teachers as related to creativity, SES and sex. Pandeya (1983) prepared personality profiles of student-teachers belonging to groups based on sex and SES.

Savaluk (1983) and Pattramon (1986) studied social maturity of B.Ed. students of Thailand in relation to sex, level of study and social and family adjustment. Sirirassamee (1983) compared adjustment problems of different groups of student-teachers. The groups were based on sex, years of study, teaching subject and student control ideology. Malik (1978) studied the relationship of real and ideal self-concept of teacher trainees with personality dimensions and attitude towards teaching profession. Rao (1986) studied inter-relationship of values, adjustment, and teaching attitude of student-teachers at different levels of socioeconomic status. All these studies have mainly concentrated on investigating characteristics of studentteachers belonging to different groups based on sex, socioeconomic status, educational qualifications and subject of teaching offered. Further, the investigators were mainly concerned with student-teachers of secondary level. There are only 14 studies of student-teachers of primary level. But there are no studies which investigate such characteristics of prospective teachers in higher education, though some universities have such teacher-education programmes. Probably, teacher-education courses at the higher education level have not been extensive enough to attract the attention of investigators.

A peculiar feature of these studies is that they have approached the student-teacher not as a student of education, or a student under training in teaching skills, but as a person who is acquiring the traits of a teacher. The investigators need to see the student-teacher from a different angle and study the characteristics that are conducive to attaining particular teaching skills and promote learning. The study of reading habits, study hours, learning needs, etc. of student-teachers will be helpful for teacher-education programmes in a developing country like India.

Context Studies: Teacher Characteristics

Another set of context studies is concerned with teacher characteristics. There are 178 studies that have investigated the characteristics of teachers in pre-primary (9), primary (41), secondary (84), higher (26) and technical (18) education. These studies have their relevance in the field of teacher education on three counts. First, they try to answer the question, 'Who is a good teacher?' Secondly, these studies specify the conditions under which the teacher is working. Thirdly, such studies provide guidelines for arranging in-service courses for teachers.

Thakur (1976) tried to identify the characteristics of a good teacher. There were 19 such studies but the definition or concept of a good teacher differed in all these studies. Some researchers have studied the 'good teacher' from the perception of other members related to school or college life, including students. The other studies have taken account of teachers' teaching with respect to its bearing on achievement of students. Gupta (1977) studied effectiveness of teachers through the effect of teachers' classroom behaviour on pupil creativity. Prakasham (1986) studied teaching competence arising out of school organisational climate. Shobha (1985) studied the ability of teachers to predict students' performance in the examination. Apart from finding out the effect of the teacher on pupils, researchers like Srisucondharatna (1985) studied teachers as a factor affecting modernization. He studied personality characteristics of teachers in the process of modernization. Other studies on characteristics of teachers have covered a variety of variables operational problems of secondary and primary school teachers (Kumar, 1985; Singh, 1975), utilization of time in different activities (Kudesia, 1986), learning needs (Kudesia, 1984), teacher morale (Vichao, 1983; Kanchana, 1985; Narula, 1986), attitudes and values (Saran, 1975; Wera, 1982; and Gupta, 1986), personality characteristics (Kaul, 1977;

Hossain, 1983; Som, 1984; Puranik, 1985), self-concept (Rai, 1983; Chadda, 1985), job satisfaction and job involvement (Mistry, 1985; Abdulsamad, 1986; Ahmad, 1986; Dixit, 1986), job satisfaction and professional honesty (Srivastava, 1986), role conflict (Mehta, 1985), role expectation and role performance (George, 1982), innovative proneness (Shukla, 1984), caste prejudices (Saxena, 1975), attitude towards environmental education (Gupta, 1986), sociometric structure of teachers in schools (Kaur, 1985). Through the study of such variables, the investigators projected the picture of a teacher.

Investigators also studied subject-specific and sex-specific characteristics of teachers. Balwinder (1986) studied job satisfaction of home-science teachers with respect to personal and professional characteristics. Bhamwari (1986) studied role perspective of women teachers in relation to marital status, age, educational background, etc. Saita (1984) studied role conflict ex-perienced by women teachers of Thailand. There are at least 20 such studies that have investigated characteristics of women teachers. One conclusion that can be drawn from such studies is that sex-specific characteristics do not make for differences in the job of teaching. Researchers like Kumar (1982) went deep into the subject and made a job analysis of secondary school teachers and identified different jobs done by the teachers. Banerji (1984) investigated the grievances of college and university teachers.

Apart from the characteristics of teachers, researchers also studied thinking patterns and ideologies of teachers working in schools. Sharique (1984) studied the educational viewpoint of secondary school teachers about aims, methods, pupil control, policy of promotion, etc. Mishra (1986) made a study of teachers with respect to degree of overall meaning in life and sources of meaning in personal and professional life. Such studies are an encouraging trend in research in teacher education. They will provide qualitative analysis for input variables in the shape of characteristics of teachers for teacher education programmes especially at the inservice stage.

The other set of studies connected with teacher characteristics are of the conditions under which the teachers work.. These are mainly surveys of schools and colleges. The reports of five surveys conducted at the national level have already made their appearance in the three earlier surveys of educational research (Buch 1974, 1979, 1986). Along with these, a review of a few more surveys will help in understanding problems linked with teacher education. Sharma (1976) surveyed the schools of backward areas of Rajasthan with respect to teacher-pupil ratio, number of teachers teaching science, and needs of teachers in the backward areas. In another survey, Sharma (1981) tried to find out the number of untrained teachers in the primary schools of Rajasthan. Gogate (1984) surveyed the educational qualifications of teachers to find out whether the subject they had offered at their first degree level was the same as that which they were teaching at the secondary level. At the higher education level, Singh (1984) investigated the procedure of recruitment of teachers in universities and colleges. Banerji (1984) studied the grievances of college and university teachers. Naqvi (1984) surveyed the basic factors that were related to mobility, inbreeding and retention of teachers at university and college level. All these surveys have one thing in common: they all tell us that prevailing conditions are not conducive to teachers teaching according to expectations.

All these studies have been concerned with areas like selection, occupational choice, social origin and status of teachers, intellectual abilities, personality characteristics, values, attitudes, teachers role, need, problems, working conditions, etc. One can observe that these studies concentrate on non-cognitive variables and only a few have studied cognitive variables. Another feature of these studies is that they have studied the characteristics of teachers mainly at secondary level, and only a few have studied characteristics of teachers working at pre-primary, primary, higher and technical educational levels. Researchers need to pay attention to these not-so-explored areas. Also, there is a need to investigate the training needs of the teachers working in different geographical and educational environments. Such studies can be of great help in planning in-service teacher education programmes in view of the fact that teacher education has to be a continuous process and changes are currently taking place in school curriculum.

Presage Studies

This area covers variables related to teacher educators' characteristics, such as the formative experience of the teacher-educator, his education, professional experience, training, personality factors, intelligence, attitude and his training skills. These studies have their importance as they help in management and manpower planning in teacher-education programmes. But this area has not attracted the attention of researchers. Only 12 studies can be counted to fall in this set. Valand (1983) studied innovative proneness of teacher-educators of primary teacher-training colleges of Gujarat. Innovative proneness was identified through teacher-educators' attitude towards specific innovations. It was found that innovative proneness varied with respect to age, experience, sex and professional, and academic qualifications. Pramua (1987) investigated the attitude of teacher-educators towards non-formal education in Thailand. The attitude was found to be related with sex, level of creativity and teaching experience. The other studies reported in earlier surveys only investigated non-cognitive variables. Studies are required in the cognitive aspect of teacher-educators. Above all the professional aspect of the teacher-educator needs to be studied with deeper insight. The job of teacher-educator is different from that of the school-teacher. Therefore, the studies have to be done with respect to job analysis, role performance, job satisfaction, etc. of the teacher-educator.

Context-Presage Studies

In this set are categorized those studies that have related context variables of institutional environment with the presage variables of characteristics of teacher-educators. Only four studies fall in this area, out of which only one is reported in this survey. Chaichana (1981) studied the relationship of organisational climate with teacher-educators' morale in the teachers colleges of Thailand. A sample of 530 teacher-educators from 36 teachers colleges of Thailand was taken. Teachers colleges were identified as having open and closed climate. The study revealed that the morale of teacher-educators was high in teachers colleges having open climate as compared to those having closed climate. With such a small number of studies it is difficult to comment. More studies are required in this area so as to restructure teacher-education programmes in India. Keeping in view the varied institutional responsibilities of teacher-educators in India, the researchers need to conduct studies which compare and relate teacher-educators' behaviour and responsibility with different types of institutions.

Presage-Process Studies

Studies of the relationship between presage variables and process variables are grouped in this set. The presage studies are linked with the characteristics of teacher-educators. The process studies consist of classroom transaction and mediating processes that lead to learning such as attending, practising, task persistence, active learning time, student-teacher's engagement with learning task, teacher-educator's supervisory behaviour, etc. The studies that link the presage and process variables have their importance for drawing up guidelines for evaluating practice-teaching programmes and adopting innovations.

But this area has not been able to attract the attention of researchers and only four studies could be categorized for this set. In these studies, the investigators have studied the characteristics of teacher-educators as related to their supervisory behaviour. Tripathi (1984) studied the relationship between personality traits of teacher-educators with their supervisory practices at the B.Ed. stage. He found that personality traits of teacher-educators were related to their mode of supervision. Teprongtong (1984) studied the difference in role performed and role expected of teacher-educators as supervisors in the eyes of student-teachers. Apart from a supervisory role, the teacher-educator plays other roles also in teacher education as a specialist in education and task-oriented jobs. Such roles need to be probed with respect to characteristics of teacher-educators.

Context-Product Studies

In this set, studies have related teacher/student-teacher characteristics and institutional characteristics (context variables) with the outcomes of teacher education programmes (product variables). Product variables can be categorized in two types-one that describes immediate outcomes of teacher-education programmes and the other that looks into long-term outcomes.

The immediate outcome variables are those that pertain to teacher/student-teacher outcome as reflected in achievement, attitude, teaching skills, etc. The long-term outcome variables used in the studies pertain to professional skills, teaching success or teaching effectiveness. The definition or concept of teaching success or teaching effectiveness has been used differently by various researchers, rather it has been dependent upon the tools used by them. Such studies make a contribution to teacher education as they try to answer the question, 'What pre-conditions are required to become a successful/effective teacher?' This area is one of the most explored areas in teacher education. There are 56 studies that can be categorized for this set. These can be further divided into two sections; one of studies relating teacher/student-teacher characteristics with teaching effectiveness; and another of studies that relate institutional environment with teaching effectiveness. Twenty-two studies have related institutional context variables with product variables. Joshi (1985) studied expressed attitude of teachers in relation to Christian and non-Christian managed institutions. He found a change in the role behaviour of teachers belonging to different managements.

There is a large number of studies reported in earlier surveys that have been concerned with the effect of organisational climate and institutional environment on teacher's teaching, adjustment and his classroom behaviour. Other studies have taken into account the Institutional environment with respect to organisational climate and social cohesiveness in the teacher-education institution and found its impact on achievement of student-teachers in theory and practice teaching, their attitude, adjustment, etc. Such, studies tested the hunch that the organisational climate of an institution was positively related with academic and other intellectual attainments of the participants.

In a second section can be included studies which related context variables or teacher/student-teacher characteristics with the product variables of teaching success or teaching effectiveness. There are 34 such studies. Gopalacharyulu (1984) studied the relationship of personality, attitude towards teaching and socioeconomic status with the achievement of student-teachers in B.Ed. Patil (1984) studied the relationship of sex, academic qualifications and intelligence of B.Ed. students with their achievement in theory. Radha (1984) compared personality characteristics of the science studentteachers who achieved high and low scores in the B.Ed. All these studies pointed out that characteristics like personal adjustment, attitude towards professional work, scientific temper, etc. were related to performance in the B.Ed. and could predict teaching performance. Some researchers went a step further and related characteristics of teachers/student-teachers with their attainment of teaching skills. Katiyar (1982) and Dubey (1986) studied personality traits of studentteachers having high and low attainment scores on various teaching skills. Their studies revealed differences in personality traits of high and low achievers. The extent of variation in the product variables used in all these studies is so high that it is difficult to make inferences. Further, the researchers limited the product variables to classroom functioning of the teacher. The skills and behaviour of the teacher required to deal with the outside classroom situation have not been studied by researchers. There is a need that non-intellectual and psychomotor learning outcomes of the teachers be studied with respect to their characteristics and institutional environment.

Process-Product Studies

The process-product studies included the process variables related to the functioning of teacher-education programme and product variables like teacher effectiveness, general teaching competence, attitude towards teaching, adjustment, maturity of student-teachers, creative abilities, knowledge and comprehension skills, social awareness, etc. These studies have much to contribute towards teacher-education programmes as these spell out ways of process of teacher education. In these studies, two categories can be distinguished. The first is those that took up the existing teacher-education programmes and studied their effects on teaching competence. The second concentrated on some innovation in the teacher training system and used it in the form of an instructional design system. The researchers followed a series of steps like framing objectives, learning experiences, planned training procedures, systematic observation of classroom transactions and a feedback to the learner. Such studies used various innovations like microteaching, classroom interaction training system and training in models of teaching.

Studies in Innovative Teacher Training Practices

Most of the studies in this category are impact studies as these ascribed the change in product variables to the ongoing teacher-education programme. They investigated the product variables when the student-teachers entered the existing system and later when they were just about to leave the college. Mehta (1985) and Pillai (1985) studied the impact with respect to change in attitude towards teaching, motivating factor for choosing teaching, and change in values.

Banga (1983) studied the impact of a teacher-training programme in physical education on physical fitness, personality characteristics, adjustment and maturity of student teachers. Kudesia (1986) studied the effect of a technical teachers training programme on teaching skills. All these researches concluded that a change in student-teachers' behaviour took place because of training. In a similar context, some researchers compared trained and untrained teachers on various product variables and found trained teachers different from their untrained counterparts. Bhide (1987) compared them on self-concept. Researchers like Das (1979) went a step further and compared trained and untrained teachers of primary level on their ability to solve the problem of wastage and stagnation. However, results revealed that training of teachers did not contribute to checking wastage and stagnation.

Some researchers compared the products of two different operational schemes of teacher education. Singh (1985) compared teaching competence, role performance, and attitude towards teaching of teachers trained through a one-year B.Ed. course and a four-year integrated teacher-education course run in the regional colleges of education. The teachers of the two courses were not found to be different. Gogate (1983) went a step further and studied the effect of a training programme not only on teachers but also on teacher education and extension education workers. The training programme was organized for the education of socially and economically backward children. A change was found in the awareness of the subjects involved in the training programme about the methods of teaching required for the target group. However, a close look at all these studies shows that the impact of present teacher-education programmes has been investigated only at the peripheral level. A deeper analysis is needed so as to study the impact of training at social, economic and cultural levels, The researchers need to study the impact of training with respect to teachers' contribution to society as a factor of social and cultural change.

Studies in Innovative Teacher Training Practices

The second set of studies used some innovations in operational teacher education programmes. The innovations used had. been concerned with various aspects of teacher-education programmes. Researchers like Bhatt (1966) studied the effect of the Kapason training scheme where student-teachers, apart from usual practice teaching and theory, were also trained in organizing creative activities in arts and craft. The training was found to be effective. Adinarayan (1983) trained student-teachers in stating objectives, analysis of the context and techniques of evaluation. The experimental group was found to be better on inquiry and investigatory skills. All such studies introduced specific innovations in the operational teacher-education programme and investigated its effectiveness. There are other studies that used innovations concerned with the theory or practice teaching part of the teacher-education programme. The innovations in the theory part had been development and use of self-learning material and the use of mass media, whereas in the case of practice teaching part, the innovations were behaviour modification techniques, microteaching and training in models of teaching. Most of these studies are experimental in nature and employ experimental design as per their objectives to judge the effectiveness of the innovations with respect to teaching competence.

(i) Studies in Use of Learning Material: The innovations of teaching through instructional strategies motivated researchers to develop self-learning material and study its effectiveness in the field of teacher education also. Sangaun (1984) developed programmed learning material, Jayalakshmi (1985) developed instructional material and Bhatt (1982) developed software material to be presented in simulation or programmed learning style. All of them took up the subject of educational psychology for developing instructional material. They studied the effectiveness of the material with respect to trainees' achievement and attitude at different levels of sex, SES, intelligence and English reading comprehension. Lambhate (1987) developed instructional material for teachers teaching science with relevant rural aids, graphics and models. These studies made use of the Skinnerian approach for the development of instructional material. Researchers like Sheth (1984) developed a self-instructional multimedia package for developing teaching skills among teachers. Some researchers went a step further and developed instructional material for remediation of deficiencies. Swamy, N. (1984) developed a diagnostic test and learning material for remediation of deficiencies in secondary school physics for student-teachers. Mukherjee (1983) identified reading disabilities of teachers in English language and developed remedial self-instructional material for the same. Researchers like Datar (1984) developed question banks in educational psychology. However, there is a need to develop self-instructional material in structured form from the different theory papers of teacher-education programmes. Researchers also need to develop instructional material for remediation of deficiencies in language, sciences and social sciences for teachers/ student-teachers especially at primary level, the reason being that, at primary level, the teachers are less educated and require more subject clarity.

(ii) Studies in Use of Mass Media: With the advent of television and radio programmes in India and the stress of national bodies like the UGC and NCERT on the use of television in teacher-education programmes, researchers have been tempted to make studies in this direction. Mohanty et al., (1976) surveyed the reaction of teachers to educational TV programmes for in-service primary teachers. In yet another study, the same researchers assessed the popularity of radio programmes among the participants in an in-service teacher education programmes. These studies were primarily conducted with the objective of providing feedback to the media managers for their teacher education programme. Now, when there is increased use of media like television and radio in education in India, it is desirable that studies be conducted in different regions of the country to evaluate television and radio programmes in teacher education. The researchers also need to plan studies to assess the improvement in teaching competency of teachers because of use of mass media in teacher-education programmes.

(iii) Studies in Microteaching: In practice teaching, one of the innovations that has attracted the attention of researchers is microteaching. The research in this field in the beginning aimed mainly at finding out effectiveness of microteaching with respect to improvement in teaching competence. But after its effectiveness was established and it was made a part of teacher-education programmes in many universities in India, the researchers conducted studies in improvement in components of various teaching skills, strategies for integration of different teaching skills, effect of different types of feedback and sources of feedback, development of multimedia packages for training in teaching skills. Such a trend in research studies is helpful in adopting the innovations in different sets of conditions.

There are 49 studies in all in the field of microteaching out of which 22 are reported in this survey. Yogendrakumar et al. (1980), Naik (1984) and Thakkar (1985) went in for establishing effectiveness of microteaching with respect to improvement in teaching competence of student teachers. Researchers like Sharma (1980), Lalitha (1981), Sharma (1982), Bawa (1984), Bhatia (1984), Chathley (1984), Dave (1987), and Ekbote (1987), studied the effect of different strategies of integration of skills on teaching competence of student teachers. It can be concluded from their findings that planned integration of skills is helpful in improving teaching competence. Some researchers compared various strategies of feedback used during the process of microteaching. Syag (1983) and Prabhune et al. (1984) compared three strategies of feedback, viz., self (audio-feedback), peer and supervi-sory feedback. They found peer-feedback to be most effective in improving competence in teaching skills. One feature common to all these researches is that they use teaching competence as a criterion to measure attainment of skills. But these studies are unable to answer the question, 'What minimum level of competence needs to be achieved when a teaching skill is said to be attained?' In this direction, Joshi (1984) made a venture and developed a performance criteria for testing efficacy of student-teachers in attaining teaching skills. Further, product variables considered in the studies were not only general teaching competence but also pupil attainment, pupil liking, peer assessment, headmaster's perception, attitude of student-teachers and teacher educators towards microteaching (Sidhu, 1983; Khan, 1985; Kalyanpurkar, 1986; and Oak, 1986).

Almost all these studies are experimental and employed pretest, post-test control group design. Among these, Sidhu (1983) and Syag (1983) went a step ahead and conducted longitudinal studies. They studied the carry-over effect of microteaching on different product variables just after training, six months after training and two years after training. They came out with the conclusion that microteaching training retained its effect over time. More studies of this kind are required to arrive at generalizations. Further studies in microteaching are required to specify skills that are required for teaching different subjects at different levels, viz., 'elementary, secondary and higher education. In this direction, Pratap (1982) made a venture and studied skills required for teaching modem mathematics at secondary level. More studies in this direction will help for planning the teaching of different subjects.

The researches done in the field of microteaching are still at a preliminary stage. More imaginative and analytical studies are required so as to answer various questions like 'What specific skills are required for teaching different subjects? How many microteaching cycles are required to attain competence? What exactly should be the length of a lesson plan? What are the skill-relevant behavioural changes that take place during attainment of skill?' Apart from finding answers to these questions, the researchers need to study the microteaching skills with respect to their proportion being used in the classroom rather than limiting themselves to a few most used skills in the classroom.

(iv) Studies in Techniques of Behaviour Modification: Still another training system that stresses specification of behavioural objectives, reinforcement of desired behaviours and rapid feedback of the effects of such reinforcement is the system of teacher behaviour modification. In this volume there is a separate chapter on teacher behaviour but in the present chapter only those studies have been considered that are connected with training of teachers in modification of their classroom behaviour. Shukla (1985) studied the effect of transaction training on different indices of teaching. Bhalwankar (1984) developed a scale suited to the Indian set-up for observing and training teachers in classroom behaviour indices. Dogra (1986) studied the effect of the content analysis system of classroom communication behaviour pattern. Gupta (1983) studied the effect of training in behaviour modification in simulation. The intent of these studies was to get teachers maximize the frequency of such indices that affected the pattern of learning in the pupils. They tested the proposition that using a particular system of recording teacher behaviour, and feeding the same back to the teachers, will get them to engage in more and more desired behaviour towards their pupils. The studies reported in this survey are a step in advance of those reported in previous surveys as these did not simply use the Flanders Interaction Analysis System to observe and train teachers/student-teachers interaction analysis; rather, they used interaction categories united to the subject taught by the teacher. But the question that remains still unanswered is, 'How can the behaviour of the teacher be modified through training be maintained over a long period of time? 'The researchers need to conduct studies in this direction so as to establish the lasting limits of learnt behaviour in teachers.

(v) Studies in Training in Teaching Models: The standard training models used in teacher education have been classroom interaction analysis and microteaching. These models are predominantly behaviouristic in nature. These have been used as training models, irrespective of the subject being taught and objective being achieved. However, the researchers have started trying out several alternative models for training in teaching of information, social interaction, behaviour modification, personal abilities, etc. Such a system of training includes elements like theoretical orientation, observation and demonstration, peer practice and feedback, and coaching in a real classroom situation. Passi et al. (1986) took up a study at the national level with a view to establishing the effect of these four elements on teaching competence in one particular model of teaching. In a similar study, Passi et al. (1986) studied the effect of training in models of teaching on the competence of student-teachers and their willingness to use the same in their classrooms. It was found that training had a positive effect on the product variables of competence and willingness. Such studies represent a welcome trend in two ways. One is that they are a departure from a purely behaviouristic orientation in teacher education, and secondly they help in recognizing the fact that there are different models of teacher education with respect to different aspects of teaching.

Studies in training of teachers in models of teaching need to be designed to find out how far training in particular teaching model improves the conceptual level of the trainees, their teaching style, adoption of various skills and transfer and reutilization of the same in different situations. The researchers need to find out specifically the number of demonstrations, practice sessions and coaching exposures that would help the student-teacher master a particular teaching model. Further studies also need to be done with respect to methods and types of feedback that could bring the desired level of competence in a student-teacher within minimum exposure time.

Training in Teaching Models

A cursory look at the number of researches conducted in the last three decades reveals that more and more studies are being conducted in the area of teacher education. The quantitative leap, however, cannot be taken to imply that the area is being exhaustively explored; rather it is difficult to claim that the researchers took cognisance of the gaps pointed out in the trend reports of the earlier surveys. Lack of coordination and planned effort on the part of researchers has made the gaps more conspicuous. Further, the emphasis given to teacher education programmes in the National Education Policy (1986) has opened new avenues of research in the field. This section of the report is devoted to pinpointing some of such needed research efforts. The observed trend of researches in teacher education has made it quite clear that researchers viewed teacher education from a narrow angle. They studied teacher education in relation to isolated aspects of the total process. They hardly went in for relating policies and practices of teacher education. After all, teacher education cannot be considered in isolation from its national and social obligations. A large number of commissions and committees on education enumerated goals for teacher education in different sets of circumstances. But researchers rarely went in for finding out how far these goals have been realized. They, rather, confined their studies to assessing the functioning of single institutions with respect to the achievement of a small group of students. It is urgently necessary that the gaps between functionality and set targets should be pointed out. This will help in planning teacher education programmes for the desired role of the teacher in the new social order. Now that the National Education Policy (1986) has laid special emphasis on education of teachers and detailed out the role of the teacher in guiding students, building their character, promoting innovation, etc., it has become obligatory on the part of researchers to provide empirical evidence of how far existing teacher education is helpful in promoting such ideals.

If the researches are seen from the framework of categories given in the trend report, one finds that presage-product studies are lacking. Researchers did study teacher effectiveness from the point of view of teacher characteristics, or teacher behaviour and its impact on the achievement of students. But similar studies have not been forthcoming of cases where the teacher educator's characteristics or his classroom behaviour have been studied with respect to student-teachers' attainment in theory of teaching skills. There is a need to train the teacher-educator for training student-teachers. Further studies need to be undertaken where contextpresage-process-product variables are taken into account. Such studies will help in providing a gestaltic view of the teacher-education programme and answer questions like, 'What kind of teachers' using what kind of procedures, most effectively foster healthy mental and behavioural skills in different kinds of children who differ in their background, needs and aspirations? What type of institutions, with what kind of teacher-educators, and following what type of teacher training programmes, promote the desired competency level among student-teachers of a particular background? Further studies made in institutional climates affect student-teachers' and teacher-educators' performance. However, no study has systematically related this factor to the nature and quality of instruction. Only occasionally have studies explored the significance of student-teachers' and teacher-educators' traits in influencing learning, even though these may account for much of the unexplained variance in achievement. Much more needs to be discovered about how teacher educators personal traits influence their teaching in the classroom and student-teachers' competence and satisfaction in learning. The complex interaction of institutional environment, personal traits of teacher educators and student-teachers, instructional methods, and supervisory methods employed and instructional outcomes is a most needed area of research.

The trend of process-product studies reveals that there has been systematization of instruction and a large coverage of objectives of teacher education. In their quest for making instruction more systematic, some researchers developed instructional strategies. Not only did they develop instructional strategies but they also, made attempts to select the best strategy among alternative strategies. Further, researches in interaction analysis provided to student-teachers an experience in objective evaluation of the lessons they observed and helped them in understanding the dynamics of classroom teaching. On the other hand, microteaching studies have been aiming at development of teaching skills in student-teachers. Simulated studies were incorporated for the development of application and decision-making abilities. Above all, the studies in training of student-teachers in alternative models have enhanced the chances of getting rid of outdated approaches in practice teaching programmes. The teaching for training in models such as Concept Attainment, Inquiry Training, Advance Organizer Model, etc., has helped in recognizing the fact that there should be different models for teacher education, depending upon the context of the teacher education programme. All this shows that researchers in teacher education have been following a trend of larger and comprehensive coverage of objectives. This is a welcome trend, but the severe criticism that is levelled against this type of studies is that they have made teacher education simply a mechanical process, rather than a process implying training, of a humane teacher. There is some substance in this criticism, insofar as there may be a lot of risk inherent in this kind of highly specified skill training. After all, the teacher's function is not limited to the four walls of the classroom. He is emotionally attached to the learner as well as the subject he teaches. Because of this attachment and the skills required, he develops an individual 'Style of Teaching'. Researchers must direct their studies towards probing such styles of teaching and communication abilities which may differ from subject to subject and situation to situation in different teachers.

While viewing studies from a methodological point of view, it can be said that researchers have not generally interpreted their studies in terms of implications; they have not made explicit what their findings imply and how they should be used. What is needed in research is that one not only describes the characteristics of teachers and student-teachers of institutions, but also tests strategies for improvement of teacher education with respect to planning and functioning of the system. Empirical evidence is required to identify the gap between the type of student-teachers that enter the portals of teacher-education institution and the requirements of the existing education in the institution; the changes in the teacher-education programme that can be easily made at micro and macro levels so that it is conducive to the society in general and the teaching community in particular.

The trend research work done in the area of curriculum context reveals that this has been one of the most neglected areas in teacher education. The work that has been done is haphazard and ill-conceived, unconnected with the real problems of teacher education. The major problem that has been troubling the educationists is the weightage to be fixed for different theory and practical aspects of courses at B.Ed. level. Educationists have chalked out a programme in the form of 'Curriculum Framework' and fixed a particular system of weightage for the different aspects, but all this they did on the basis of their thinking and experience, in the absence of empirical research data. Such a framework may not provide for a particular aspect of the teacher education course that will help student-teachers to acquire a certain degree of competence to deal with pupils of different ages and abilities. Many problems of this nature need to be addressed to make the curriculum relevance-based.

The measure of good teaching still remains complex and unclear. The development of teaching theories remains in its infancy. Even after four surveys, teaching theory in the Indian context has not been thought out. Of course, this may be partially because of definition, design and instrumentation. Another plausible reason that one infers from the researches done in teacher education so far is that teacher effectiveness has perhaps been considered in the abstract, without reference to the particular subject content involved. As more knowledge is gained about the structure of an individual discipline, both teaching methods and methods of evaluating their effectiveness can be found. Researchers, therefore, need to plan their studies so as to answer the questions, 'What are the conditions under which one learns to learn and how can students be helped to develop attitudes, habits and skills conducive to life-long learning?' Answers to questions like these will help in pursuing the proposed objective in the National Education Policy about 'Accountability of Teachers' to the society in general and the profession in particular. But this does not mean that teacher accountability is solely dependent upon his ability to effect desired changes in learners. This, in fact, raises further questions for researchers: 'What factors help the teacher to become an object of student respect and a source of positive personal influence on the formation of students' intellective values and attitudes? What factors promote social organisational conditions conducive to a teacher's smooth functioning with his peers, head and management authorities?' These questions demand attention.

Changes in society and world over have made it necessary that teacher education be looked at not only from the angle of teacher-student interaction but also from social and psychological perspectives. In other words, teacher-education institutions need to prepare teachers for their social obligations. It is essential that researchers probe into the role of the teacher outside the classroom and related factors. There is need to know more about the teacher's role expectations, the relationship between the individual teacher's role expectation and the social responsibilities of the teacher; the relationship between the teacher's concept of his role and his performance as observed by other members of the society. Such knowledge will help in developing new models of teacher education and trying them for training teachers of the new social order.

The National Education Policy has stressed strong, unified and responsible teachers' associations to protect the dignity and rights of teachers. The role of such teachers' associations, as envisaged by the NEP, is to develop awareness among teachers of their professional growth and development. It entails upon researchers to probe issues concerned with the linkage between the institutional decision structure and the degree of participation by teachers; the educational impact of involving teachers in decision-making; the type of activities in which teachers must participate in order to influence policy; the linkage between teachers' policy-influencing activity and their satisfaction with their working conditions. Research into such questions would help to analyse the relationship between academic governance and policy making.

A problem that is yet to draw the attention of researchers is correspondence education-in the field of teacher preparation. It has been steadily expanding with far greater remote control systems than prevailed a few years ago. Some of the institutions and centres have national networks and it is open to graduates working in different establishments. The products of this system can hardly be distinguished in terms of degree requirements, but certainly they have undergone an entirely different kind of exposure to teacher preparation. It is necessary that researchers probe the qualitative differences in the products of the two systems and advise the universities and the government to adopt such systems as are qualitatively strong and have lower unit cost.

With the advent of the Navodaya Vidyalayas and the Academic Staff College, in-service education of teachers has become a continuous programme. For a very practical reason, it can be provided most widely by an inflow of enriched material into the educational institutions in the form of teachers' handbooks in different context areas. It will help teachers in self-learning as well as give them the freedom to seek guidance from time to time, at their convenience. Such handbooks are equally desired for pre-service education of teachers. After all, future teachers will be able to make their pupils independent in learning in everyday life only if they themselves enjoyed the same independence during their training. Researchers must take up studies in this field and develop material for education of the teachers of different disciplines and different levels of education.

Changes in society have made it all the more necessary to have provision for separate institutions for students of specific age-groups and abilities. The institutions of non-formal education, for exceptional children, adult learners, etc. have to be different from those for general and formal education. For such institutions, specialized teachers are needed and provision has to be made to prepare such teachers to deal with special types of learners. The general teacher-education admission procedure, curriculum, evaluation process, practical work, etc. cannot cover everything in these courses. In this context, it is necessary that researchers identify problems and needs of teachers of such courses so as to advise the functionaries and managers concerning the organisation of specialized teacher-education programmes.

The provision for socially useful productive work and community services in teacher-education programmes has been thought ideal for developing skills and values among student teachers. But such courses have simply become rituals for passing the examination. The responsibility for this lies also with researchers who had not planned their studies to find out training as well as evaluation procedures for such value-oriented tasks. It is necessary that researchers should conduct studies in this direction and help planners chalk out programmes of community work so that they become an integral part of teacher education.

In the end, it can be said that there is need for more comprehensive and sophisticated research and better dissemination of results so that these can be used later on, for the improvement of teacher-education programme within the framework of the total educational system in the country.

The study was confined to 72 higher secondary schools located in seven major cities of Rajasthan. Initially 205 science teachers with a minimum experience of three years were selected. The student sample consisted of 3450 science students. In order to measure

UNIT-VIII

National Organisations in Teacher Preparation

Role and Functions of National Organisations—NCTE

During the IX Plan period, the NCTE, set up in the VIII Plan as a statutory body, would be functioning on a firm footing. As contemplated in the NPE-1992 "all necessary resources and capabilities will be provided to NCTE for improving the quality of teacher education". Infrastructural facilities would be provided to perform its twin functions i.e. maintenance of norms and standards on the one hand and professional upgradation of teachers and teacher educators on the other.

The major task before the NCTE in the IX Plan period would be to develop teacher, education curriculum frame work, Undertake, complete and publish State Level Studies on Teacher Education (focusing on status, issues and futuristic projections, develop a Resource Centre and Institutional Database on teacher education provide professional inputs to DIETs/CTEs/IASEs/SCERTs, commission research and survey on Teacher Education and publish quality resource materials.

In view of the widespread concern at the continued existence of substandard teacher training institutions in various parts of the country and the growing tendency of commercialisation of training of teachers, one of the foremost tasks of NCTE would be to develop a strong and credible accreditation machinery for curbing substandard institutions, weeding out commercial practices and enforcing standards in teacher training institutions. Simultaneously, there is need for encouragement and support to the good teacher training institutions in the non-government sector.

One of the relatively neglected areas is the development of a professional cadre of teacher educators in the country. There are about 30,000 teacher educator's working in 1200 primary teacher education institutions and about 600 secondary teacher training institutions. They are responsible for pre-service, recurrent inservice, and continuing education of more than 30 lakh teachers in the whole country. It is therefore essential and urgent to improve the competencies and quality of these teacher educators. It is through them that DIETs, CTEs, IASEs, SCERTs and other such institutions will contribute towards the improvement and universalisation of quality of elementary level education and providing effective education at the level of secondary and higher secondary schools.

One of the major problems existing at present at the elementary teacher training level is that most of these teacher educators are trained to teach in secondary schools. Many of them have never taught in primary schools at all and are not familiar with techniques of handling children in the age group of 6-11 years. In consequence, they are not in a position to perform the task of primary teacher training effectively. This phenomenon exists on account of the fact that the secondary school teachers cadre and primary teacher educators cadre are treated administratively equivalent and transferable. This problem has, therefore, to be resolved both by taking administrative measures on the one hand and by providing intensive inservice courses to prepare them to become effective primary teacher educators on the other, It is expected that NCTE would take the initiative to evolve a well considered policy and appropriate strategies for teacher educators which addresses issues such as their qualifications, mode of recruitment, emoluments, deployment, career advancement professional development, status and motivation. Minimum levels of learning at the primary and upper primary levels would require NCTE to develop corresponding competency based teacher education in elementary teacher training institutions.

Necessary literature would be developed after consultation with national level agencies (NCERT, IGNOU, NIEPA) and with state level authorities.

Dissemination of values like human rights, secularism, pursuit of excellence, national integration, composite culture, social cohesion, community participation would be one of the priority areas. NCTE may develop such material both in printed and video form to disseminate these values.

The Centrally Sponsored Scheme on teacher education should have mechanism which can seek optimal participation by different agencies working in the field of teacher education like NCTE, NCERT NIEPA, IGNOU, NOS and UGC. The mechanism may be so designed that it has horizontal as well as vertical linkages so that a comprehensive management structure may be designed that would ensure links with State and District level bodies. NCTE could play a catalytical role in developing such a mechanism.

Activities relating to research need to be examined critically. Research has to be functional, field based and result oriented. Universities, SCERTs, Institutes of Advanced Study in Education and CTEs should make joint efforts to outline research needs in each State, A State task force may be constituted to coordinate research activities. Central funding may be provided to each State to commission need based and field related research work. Coordination of research especially related to teacher education at various levels-District, State and National and by various agencies like DIETs, CTEs, IASEs, SCERTs and University Departments need a mechanism which would ensure that research findings are appropriately and promptly disseminated and communicated in language, understood by teachers and have a focus which should help in formulation/revision of policy. NCTE could assume this important role.

Experiments done by the Space Application Centre, Ahmedabad, IGNOU, Institute of Management Studies and NCERT show that interactive one Way video and two way audio linkages can be established in India without much difficulty. As a consequence, IGNOU has already established a up-linkage station for facilitating video interaction. NCERT is on its way. NCTE should also develop video interactive linkages, with SCERTs, Colleges of Education, Institutes of Advanced Studies in Education CTEs and DIETs. In the first phase, a pilot programme may be launched connecting about 2030 institutions. In the second stage, such networks can also be established within States in a phased manner.

Some of the thrust areas of NCTE for TEIs during IX Plan period would be:

- Maintenance of norms and standards
- Curriculum Renewal
- Developing mechanism of monitoring and providing professional support to teacher education institutions
- Studies on Teacher Education
- Promoting distance education for in-service teacher education
- Developing a system of In-service education for teacher educators.
- Promoting research and innovations in TEI
- Developing resource learning materials for teachers
- Developing a Resource Centre and Database on Teacher Education
- Building institutional capabilities
- Support to professional association of teachers for professional upgradation

One of the mandate of the NCTE is to maintain standards in all teacher education institutions; and at all levels of training. It involves laying down norms and guidelines for institutions, for designing new courses, for, appointments of teachers, for fees chargeable by institutions and periodic review for enforcing accountability. The infrastructure of NCTE at the Headquarters and its regional committees would also be augmented both in the Head Office and Regional Committees. In the IX Plan suitable resources would be provided to NCTE to enable it to work as a dynamic professional body and execute its roles envisaged in VIII Plan. An outlay of 57 crores is proposed for NCTE's programmes and activities in IX Plan.

NCERT

The NCERT is a research and development (R&D) organisation in the school education sector and is responsible for experimentation and improvements in curricular, designs, syllabi and prototype instructional materials. Since the curriculum, syllabi and instructional materials form a basis for teacher training programmes, NCERT addresses itself to the task of formulation and organisation of teacher training programmes as school curriculum and teacher training have developmental linkages. Besides, present day effective transaction of school curriculum requires technology based teaching aids within as well as outside the classroom, especially in the context of open learning system and NCERT has, over the years, created a first rate infrastructural facilities and production potential for teacher training through the distance learning mode. These facilities will enhance teacher effectiveness and will also be made available to the NCTE, to promote its programmes of qualitative improvement in teacher education over and above the NCERT's inputs in this direction. It is visualised that the NCERT and NCTE will function to supplement and complement each other's defined role and functions and to provide effective teacher education to school education system. The major programmes and activities which NCERT takes up, through its Regional Institutes of Education at Ajmer, Bhopal, Bhubaneswar, Mysore and Shillong, Department of Teacher Education and other academic departments of the National Institute of Education will remain associated with the following:

A. Pre-Service Teacher Education

The NCERT will continue to design and offer innovative preservice teacher education programmes. The NCERT through As Regional Institutes of Education shall continue to offer programmes like four year integrated B.Sc. B.Ed/B.Sc.Ed. and M.Ed. (elementary education), etc-The institutes may also develop and offer innovative and need based Certificate/Diploma level programmes in specialised areas like Special Education, Measurement and Evaluation Guidance and Counselling, Educational Technology, Research Technology in future to meet the needs of school education in their respective regions. In the accomplishment of this task, it will follow the policies of the NCTE.

B. Undertaking Educational Research

Research is an integral function of the NCERT and is central to all its activity. Towards this end the NCERT has an Educational Research and Innovations Committee (ERIC) which is a Standing Committee of the Council to conduct, promote and commission research in all aspects of education by providing appropriate financial support. The NCERT shall continue to support and promote research in all sectors of education, including teacher education. The NCTE is already collaborating with NCERT to organise a Survey of Teacher Education. A blue print has already been finalised.

C. Undertaking Experimentation with a view to Developing Alternative Inservice Training Modalities such as Teacher Training through Teleconferencing Mode

The NCERT has organised two pilot training programmes in Karnataka and Madhya Pradesh for training of Primary Teachers using teleconferencing involving 2-way audio and one-way video, through the DIETs. All aspects of this inservice training model which takes care of the inadequacies of the cascade model has a great potential. Through its network of RIEs with the DIETs and the technical support of the CIET, the inservice training will be an important programme of the NCERT.

D. Capacity Building of State level and District level Teacher Education Institutions

108. The task of capacity building is enormous. A multiplicity of institutions is perhaps needed to make some dent in the system. The NCERT have already networked RIEs with DIETs

in their respective states within their jurisdiction towards this end and it will continue to perform the existing functions such as:

- organising orientation/training programmes for the faculty of these institutes;
- providing a forum for heads of these institutions for sharing of experiences;
- preparing source materials; for the faculties of these institutes.

E. Extending Academic and Technical Support to MHRD in the Formulation and Implementation of the Various Components of the Centrally Sponsored Scheme At Re-organising and Restructuring Teacher Education.

As in the past, the support will be extended to:

- Special orientation programme for primary teachers (SOPT)
- Academic technical support to the scheme of District Institutes of Education and Training (DIETs)
- Academic technical support to the scheme of colleges of teacher education (CTEs) and Institutes of Advanced Studies in Education (IASEs)
- Capacity building of State Councils of Educational Research and Training (SCERTs)

National Action Plan for Inservice Education of Primary Teachers Through Distance Education

There have been some important efforts in using the cascade model for enhancing training capability, both in PMOST and SOPT. While cascading increases coverage, it leaves a lot to desire as far as quality of training is concerned. Besides the transmission loss, the quality of available trainers decreases progressively from the national to the local training centres. Interactive distance education offers new opportunity to cover large numbers with improved quality of training. India has significant experience, expertise and capability in distance education. More than 50 Universities in India offer courses through distance education. The National Open School and a few State Open Schools offer school level courses through distance education. Although the distance education programme largely depends on the printed material supported by personal contact classes, many programmes are supported by audio, video, television and radio programmes and interactive teleconferencing.

Interactive Teleconferencing has been pilot tested for inservice training course of primary teachers in one-week programme in Karnataka for about 850 teachers and in Madhya Pradesh for about 1450 teachers in 1996. India is all set for a pilot experiment in application of interactive television in distance education for inservice training of primary teachers with a coverage of 13000 teachers in 8 months in two States. In yet another initiative, under DPEP Phase. II, during the next five years, IEPT will be provided through distance education in 95 districts under a World Bank funded project.

The National Action Plan for In-service Primary Teacher Training (NAP) will provide an institutional framework for inservice education and sustainable renewal of primary teachers and capacity building of the system through interactive distance education.

The long term and ultimate) goal of the NAP is universalisation of education through training of teachers and capacity building. In more specific terms, its goals are:

i. Build capacity of the system for providing sustainable inservice education to primary teachers, and others directly associated with primary education in general and primary teachers in particular.

ii. Design and develop courses and programmes that are adaptable to local needs,

iii. Provide short inservice training to all qualified primary teachers once in a year,

iv. Upgrade through inservice education, all unqualified primary teachers to required level of qualification and professional training by the end of the ninth plan,

v. Provide short term training to all encadered teacher trainers and others involved or to be involved in inservice teacher training atleast once in two years,

vi. Provide short term training to all supervisory staff of the Government and Panchayati Raj Institutions at least once in two years,

vii. Improve capability of training institutions involved or to be involved in IEPT for greater sustainability,

viii. Establish a training network linking national, regional, state, district and block level centres for training delivery through distance education,

ix. Improve inter-institutional (interdepartmental and inter-ministerial) linkages, collaboration and coordination for greater effectiveness and sustainability,

The NAP will feed into the ninth five year plan of India. However, the NAP contains a 10 year perspective, and to that extent it will guide the developments in inservice education of primary teachers through both ninth and tenth five year plans.

The numbers of persons to be trained per year total 2.5 million under the Ninth Plan and 4.15 million under the Tenth Plan. The numbers are broken down as follows:

a) primary teachers: an average of 2.23 million per year under the Ninth Plan and an average of 2.5.million per year under the Tenth Plan;

b) non-formal education tutors: 0.24 million and 0.30 million under the Ninth and Tenth Plans respectively;

c) teacher educators: 48,0010 per year under both Ninth and Tenth Plans;

d) supervisory staff: 60,000 per year under the Ninth Plan and 2,560,000 per year under the Tenth Plan.

The National Action Plan would draw upon the existing infrastructure for teacher education built during seventh and eight Plans. It would also take advantage of expansion of teacher training facilities at block level. It does not propose to create any additional buildings or infrastructure but proposes to strengthening the infrastructure by introducing State-of-the-Art communication technology in teacher training. It is infact a capacity building exercise which would enable the Nation to impart necessary skills to its teachers at regular interval.

The implementation of NAP during ninth plan would entail an expenditure of Rs. 671.14 crore. Out of this, technology cost accounts for Rs.287 crore and training cost will account for Rs.328 crore. Possibilities are being explored for timing up with International Funding Agencies for covering the cost involved in state-of-art communication technologies.

Appropriate mechanism, would also be worked out for sharing the training cost among the Centre, states and training institutions. The infrastructure being created under NAP could also be utilised for upgradation of field professionals in the departments of Women and Child Development, Health, Rural Development and Agriculture.

Further since the object and purposes of launching the National Action Plan are similar to those of Special Orientation Programme for Primary School Teachers (SOPT), launched during the VIII Plan it is proposed to progressively subsume the SOPT programme within the overall ambit of NAP. However, SOPT programme in the existing mode would continue till this materialises. Keeping the trend of expenditure during VIII Plan in view, an outlay of Rs.75 crore is proposed for SOPT during IX Plan.

Support for Teacher Education in North Eastern Region

Out of a total strength of around three million teachers in elementary sector, atleast 10% belong to category of untrained teachers. It is interesting to note that of the total untrained teachers engaged at the school level, 35% are from the North Eastern States of the country. With the present teacher training facilities it is practically impossible to reach out such a large number of teachers using the traditional mode. Perhaps, distance education is the only alternative, through which the large segment of untrained teachers in these geographically remote regions in the country could be provided with certain amount of quality training inputs.

Keeping the above in mind, Indira Gandhi National Open University (IGNOU) and National Council of Educational Research and Training (NCERT) have arrived at an agreement to launch jointly a diploma programme called "Diploma in Primary Education (DPE)" for untrained school teachers of North East.

As we have seen, while analysing the present scenario on Teacher Education, special emphasis is needed for speeding up the completion of various projects taken up under the Centrally Sponsored Scheme of Restructuring and Reorganisation of Teacher Education in North Eastern States. Keeping in view the special requirements of the region it is propose to set apart a sum of Rs.10 crore during IX Plan to supplement the resources provided to these states under the centrally sponsored scheme of teacher education and to provide such special assistance, as may be necessary, to augment teacher training facilities in the region.

Coordination among National Institutions

.As already observed, for ensuring the success of the Centrally Sponsored Scheme of Teacher Education as also for effective implementation of National Action Plan it would be essential that all National Institutions whose sphere of activity includes teacher education such as NCTE, NCERT, NIEPA, IGNOU and NOS should work in tandem. However, when a number of national level-institutions work in the same field there are bound to be problems of coordination and role clarity. Accordingly, the need for constituting an Advisory Committee at the apex level is being increasingly felt to perform the function of a coordinator for, the purpose of achieving synergy in the efforts being made by these institutions in furthering the cause of teacher education. This advisory committee could be headed by Education Secretary with Joint Secretary (EE) being its Member Secretary. This would include the Heads of NCTE, NCERT, IGNOU, NIEPA and NOS as the other members.

NAAC

The NATIONAL ASSESSMENT AND ACCREDITATION COUNCIL (NAAC) is an autonomous body established by the University Grants Commission (UGC) of India to assess and accredit institutions of higher education in the country. It is an outcome of the recommendations of the National Policy in Education (1986) that laid special emphasis on upholding the quality of higher education in India.

The system of higher education in India has expanded rapidly during the last fifty years. In spite of the built-in regulatory mechanisms that ensure satisfactory levels of quality in the functioning of higher education institutions, there have been criticisms that the country has permitted the mushrooming of institutions of higher education with fancy programme and substandard facilities and consequent dilution of standards. To address the issues of deterioration in quality, the National Policy on Education (1986) and the Plan of Action (POA-1992) that spelt out the strategic plans for the policies, advocated the establishment of an independent national accreditation body. Consequently, the NAAC was established in 1994 with its headquarters at Bangalore.

Governance

The NAAC functions through its General Council (GC) and Executive Committee (EC) where educational administrators, policy makers and senior academicians from a cross-section of the system of higher education are represented. The Chairperson of the UGC is the President of the GC of the NAAC, the Chairperson of the EC is an eminent academician in the area of relevance to the NAAC. The Director of the NAAC is its academic and administrative head, and is the member-secretary of both the GC and EC. The NAAC also has many advisory and consultative committees to guide its practices, in addition to the statutory bodies that steer its policies. The NAAC has a core staff and consultants to support its activities. It also receives assistance from a large number of external resource persons from across the country who are not full time staff of the NAAC.

Vision and Mission

The activities and future plans of the NAAC are guided by its vision and mission that focus on making quality assurance an integral part of the functioning of higher education institutions.

The vision of the NAAC is:

- To make quality the defining element of higher education in India through a combination of self and external quality evaluation, promotion and sustenance initiatives.
- The mission statements of the NAAC aim at translating the NAAC's vision into reality, defining the following key tasks of the organisation:
- To arrange for periodic assessment and accreditation of institutions of higher education or units thereof, or specific academic programme or projects.
- To stimulate the academic environment for promotion of quality of teaching-learning and research in higher education institutions.
- To encourage self-evaluation, accountability, autonomy and innovations in higher education.
- To undertake quality-related research studies, consultancy and training programme.
- To collaborate with other stakeholders of higher education for quality evaluation, promotion and sustenance.

Guided by its vision and striving to achieve its mission, the NAAC primarily assesses the quality of institutions of higher education that volunteer for the process, through an internationally accepted methodology.

The Methodology

For the assessment of a unit, the NAAC follows a three-stage process which is a combination of self-study and peer review. The three stages are:

- The preparation and submission of a self-study report by the unit of assessment.
- The on-site visit of the peer team for validation of the self-study report and for recommending the assessment outcome to the NAAC.
- The final decision by the Executive Committee of the NAAC.
- The self-study report to be validated by peers is the backbone of the whole exercise. Manuals have been developed to suit different units of higher education, with detailed guidelines on the preparation of the self-study report and the other aspects of assessment and accreditation.

NUEPA

The National University of Educational Planning and Administration (NUEPA), established by the Ministry of Human Resource Development, Government of India, is a premier organisation dealing with capacity building and research in planning and management of education not only in India but also in South Asia. In recognition of the pioneering work done by the organisation in the field of educational planning and administration, the Government of India have empowered it to award its own degrees by way of conferring it the status of Deemed to be University in August, 2006. Like any Central University, NUEPA is fully maintained by the Government of India.

The National University has its origin dating back to 1962 when the UNESCO established the Asian Regional Centre for Educational Planners and Administrators which later became the Asian Institute of Educational Planning and Administration in 1965. After 4 years of its existence, it was taken over by the Government of India and renamed as the National Staff College for Educational Planners and Administrators. Subsequently, with the increased roles and functions of the National Staff College, particularly in capacity building, research and professional support services to governments, it was again renamed as the National Institute of Educational Planning and Administration (NIEPA) in 1979.

The National University comprises ten Departments. It has an outstanding multi-disciplinary faculty and a library which is well stocked with a large number of books, national and international journals and official documents in the area of educational planning and administration. In addition to its multifarious activities, the National University offers Full-time Integrated M.Phil.-Ph.D., Full-time Direct Ph.D. and Part-time Ph.D. programmes in educational policy, planning and administration from a broader inter-disciplinary social science perspective. The research programmes of NUEPA cover all levels and types of education from both national and international development perspectives.

Vision

Evolving a humane learning society through advancement of knowledge.

Mission

To become a centre of excellence in educational policy, planning and management by promoting advanced level teaching, research and capacity building in national and global contexts.

Objectives

- To organize pre-service and in-service training programmes in the area of educational planning and administration and allied disciplines;
- To undertake, aid, promote and coordinate research in various aspects of educational planning and administration and allied disciplines, including comparative studies in planning techniques and administrative procedures in the different States of India and in other countries of the world;
- To provide academic and professional guidance to agencies, institutions and personnel engaged in educational planning and administration;

- To offer M. Phil, Ph. D. and Post-Doctoral Programmes and award degrees in educational planning, educational administration, educational finance, comparative education, school education, higher education, professional education, policy research, gender in education, discrimination in education, education and globalization, educational management and information system, etc.;
- To act as a clearing house of ideas and information on research, training and extension in educational planning and administration services and other programmes;
- To prepare, print and publish papers, periodicals and books in furtherance of these objectives and especially to bring out a Journal on Educational Planning and Administration;
- To organize training, conferences, workshops, meetings, seminars and briefing sessions for educational personnel of the Central and State Governments and Union Territories;
- To offer, on request, consultancy service to Governments, including State Governments, educational institutions and institutions/ organisations in India & abroad.
- To organize orientation and training programmes and refresher courses for teacher-educators and for University and College Administrators engaged in educational planning and administration;
- To organize orientation programmes, seminars and discussion groups for persons including legislators in the field of educational planning and administration at the level of policy making in Central and State Governments;
- To award consultancy work/services to other organisations/ individuals;
- To collaborate with other agencies, institutions and organisations, including the University Grants Commission, the Universities, Institutes of Management

and Administration and other allied institutions in India and abroad, in such way as may be considered necessary for the promotion of these objectives;

- To provide, on request, facilities for training and research in educational planning and administration to other countries, especially of the Asian Region, and collaborate with them in programmes;
- To offer fellowships, scholarships and academic awards in furtherance of the objects of the National University;
- To confer honorary fellowships on eminent educationists for their contribution in the field of educational planning and administration;
- To undertake extra mural studies, extension programme and field outreach activities to contribute to the development of society;
- To disseminate and advance knowledge by providing instructional, research and extension facilities in such branches of learning as it may deem fit and to provide to students and teachers the necessary facilities and atmosphere for the promotion of innovations in education leading to restructuring of courses, new methods of teaching and learning, and integral development of personality, studies in various disciplines, inter-disciplinary studies, and National tegration & International understanding;
- To conduct the above-mentioned programmes and ses in its off-Campuses, and off-shore campuses; and
- To do or perform all such other acts, functions and things as may be deemed necessary, desirable or incidental by the National University in furtherance of the above objectives of the National University.

UGC

From ancient Bharat to modern India, higher education has always occupied a place of prominence in Indian history. In ancient times, Nalanda, Taxila and Vikramsila universities were renowned seats of higher learning, attracting students not only from all over the country but from far off countries like Korea, China, Burma (now Myanmar), Ceylon (now Sri Lanka), Tibet and Nepal. Today, India manages one of the largest higher education systems in the world*.

The present system of higher education dates back to Mountstuart Elphinstone's minutes of 1823, which stressed on the need for establishing schools for teaching English and the European sciences. Later, Lord Macaulay, in his minutes of 1835, advocated "efforts to make natives of the country thoroughly good English scholars". Sir Charles Wood's Dispatch of 1854, famously known as the ' Magna Carta of English Education in India', recommended creating a properly articulated scheme of education from the primary school to the university. It sought to encourage indigenous education and planned the formulation of a coherent policy of education. Subsequently, the universities of Calcutta, Bombay (now Mumbai) and Madras were set up in 1857, followed by the university of Allahabad in 1887.

The Inter-University Board (later known as the Association of Indian Universities) was established in 1925 to promote university activities, by sharing information and cooperation in the field of education, culture, sports and allied areas.

The first attempt to formulate a national system of education in India came In 1944, with the Report of the Central Advisory Board of Education on Post War Educational Development in India, also known as the Sargeant Report. It recommended the formation of a University Grants Committee, which was formed in 1945 to oversee the work of the three Central Universities of Aligarh, Banarasand Delhi. In 1947, the Committee was entrusted with the responsibility of dealing with all the then existing Universities.

Soon after Independence, the University Education Commission was set up in 1948 under the Chairmanship of Dr. S Radhakrishnan "to report on Indian university education and suggest improvements and extensions that might be desirable to suit the present and future needs and aspirations of the country". It recommended that the University Grants Committee be reconstituted on the general model of the University Grants Commission of the United Kingdom with a full-time Chairman and other members to be appointed from amongst educationists of repute.

In 1952, the Union Government decided that all cases pertaining to the allocation of grants-in-aid from public funds to the Central Universities and other Universities and Institutions of higher learning might be referred to the University Grants Commission. Consequently, the University Grants Commission (UGC) was formally inaugurated by late Shri Maulana Abul Kalam Azad, the then Minister of Education, Natural Resources and Scientific Research on 28 December 1953.

The UGC, however, was formally established only in November 1956 as a statutory body of the Government of India through an Act of Parliament for the coordination, determination and maintenance of standards of university education in India. In order to ensure effective region-wise coverage throughout the country, the UGC has decentralised its operations by setting up six regional centres at Pune, Hyderabad, Kolkata, Bhopal, Guwahati and Bangalore. The head office of the UGC is located at Bahadur Shah Zafar Marg in New Delhi, with two additional bureaus operating from 35, Feroze Shah Road and the South Campus of University of Delhi as well.

University Grants Commission Act, 1956

1. (1) This Act may be called the University Grants Commission Act, 1956. (2) It shall come into force on such date as the Central Government may, by notification in the Official Gazette, appoint.

2. In this Act, unless the context otherwise requires- (a) "Commission" means the University Grants Commission established under section 4; (b) "executive authority" in relation to a University, means the chief executive authority of the University (by whatever name called) in which the general administration of the University is vested; (c) "Fund" means the Fund of the University Grants Commission constituted

under section 16; (d) "member' means a member of the University Grants Commission and includes the Chairman (and Vice-Chairman]; (e) "prescribed' means prescribed by rules made under this Act; Short title and Commencement; (f) "University" means a University established or incorporated by or under a Central Act, a Provincial Act or a State Act, and includes any such institution as may, in consultation with the University concerned, be recoginsed by the Commission in accordance with the regulations made in this behalf under this Act.

3. The Central Government may, on the advice of the Commission, declare by notification in the Official Gazette, that any institution for higher education, other than a University, shall be deemed to be a University for the purposes of this Act, and on such a declaration being made, all the provisions of this Act shall apply to such institution as if it were a University within the meaning of clause (f) of section 2.

Establishment of the Commission

4. (1) With effect from such date as the Central Government may, by notification in the Official Gazette, appoint, there shall be established a Commission by the name of the University Grants Commission. (2) The said Commission shall be a body corporate having perpetual succession and a common seal, and shall by the said name sue and be sued.

5. (1) The Commission shall consist of – (i) a Chairman, (ii) a Vice-Chairman, and (iii) ten other members, to be appointed by the Central Government.

(2) The Chairman shall be chosen from among persons who are not officers of the Central Government or of any State Government.

(3) Of the other members referred to in clause (iii) of sub-section (1) – (a) two shall be chosen from among the officers of the Central Government, to represent that Government; Application of Act to institutions for higher studies other than Universities Establishment of the Commission Composition of the Commission University Grants Commission of 1956 (b) not

less than four shall be chosen from among persons who are, at the time when they are so chosen, teachers of Universities; and (c) the remainder shall be chosen from among persons- (i) Who have knowledge of, or experience in, agriculture, commerce, forestry or industry; (ii) who are members of the engineering, legal, medical or any other Learned profession; or (iii) who are Vice-Chancellors of Universities or who, not being teachers Of Universities, are in the opinion of the Central Government, educationists or repute or have obtained high academic distinctions: Provided that not less than one-half of the number chosen under this clause shall be from among persons who are not officers of the Central Government or of any State Government.

(4) The Vice-Chairman shall exercise such of the powers, and discharge such of the duties, of the Chairman as may be prescribed.

(5) Every appointment under this section shall take effect from the date on which it is notified by the Central Government in the Official Gazette.

6. 1(1) A person appointed as Chairman, Vice-Chairman or other member after the commencement of the University Grants Commission (Amendment) Act, 1985 shall, unless he sooner becomes disqualified for continuing as such under the rules that may be made under this Act, – (a) in the case of Chairman, hold office for a term of five years or until he attains the age of sixty-five years, whichever is earlier; (b) in the case of Vice-Chairman, hold office for a term of three years or until he attains the age of sixty-five years, whichever is earlier; (c) in the case of any other member, hold office for a term of three years: Terms and conditions of service of members 1. Subs. by Act 70 of 1985, for sub-section (1) of Section 6 (w.e.f. 20-12-1985) University Grants Commission [ACT 3 8 Provided that– (i) a person who has held office as Chairman or Vice-Chairman shall be eligible for further appointment as Chairman, Vice-Chairman or other member, and (ii) a person who has held office as any other member shall be eligible for further appointment as Chairman, Vice-Chairman or other member: Provided further that a person who has held office for two

terms, in any capacity, whether as Chairman, Vice-Chairman or other member [excluding a member referred to in clause (a) of sub-section (3) of section 5], shall not be eligible for any further appointment as Chairman, Vice-Chairman or other member.

(2) A member may resign his office by writing under his hand addressed to the Central Government; but he shall continue in office until his resignation is accepted by the Central Government.

1[(3) If a casual vacancy occurs in the office of the Chairman, whether by reason of his death, resignation or inability to discharge his functions owing to illness or other incapacity, the Vice-Chairman holding office as such for the time being shall, withstanding anything contained in sub-section (2) of section 5, act as the Chairman and shall, unless any other person is appointed earlier as the Chairman, hold the office of the Chairman for the remainder of the term of office of the person in whose place he is to so act: Provided that where no Vice-Chairman is holding office at the time, when the vacancy in the office of the Chairman occurs, the Central Government shall, notwithstanding anything contained in subsection (2) of section 5, appoint any other member to act as the Chairman and the person so appointed shall not hold the office of the Chairman for a period exceeding six months.

(4) If a casual vacancy occurs in the office of the Vice-Chairman or any other member, whether by reason of his death, resignation or inability to discharge his functions owing to illness or other incapacity, such vacancy shall be filled up by the Central Government by making a fresh appointment and the member so appointed shall hold office for a term of three years.

(5) The office of the Chairman and the Vice-Chairman shall be whole-time and salaried and subject thereto, the terms and conditions of service of the Chairman, Vice-Chairman and other members shall be such as may be prescribed.

7. The Commission shall meet at such times and places and shall observe such rules of procedure in regard to the transaction

of business at its meetings as may be provided by regulations made under this Act.

8. No act or proceedings of the Commission shall be deemed to be invalid by reason merely of any vacancy in, or any defect in the constitution of the Commission.

9. (1) The Commission may associate with itself, in such manner and for such purposes as may be determined by regulations made under this Act, any person whose assistance or advice it may desire in carrying out any of the provisions of this Act. (2) A person associated with it by the Commission under sub-section (1) for any purpose shall have a right to take part in the discussions relevant to that purpose, but shall not have a right to vote at a meeting of the Commission, and shall not be a member for any other purpose.

10. Subject to such rules as may be made by the Central Government in this behalf, the Commission may appoint a Secretary and such other employees as it may think necessary for the efficient performance of its functions under this Act and the terms and conditions of service of the employees shall be such as may be determined by the Commission.

11. All orders and decisions of the Commission shall be authenticated by the signature of the Chairman or any other member authorised by the Commission in this behalf, and all other instruments issued by the Commission shall be authenticated by the signature of the Secretary or any other officer of the Commission authorised in like manner in this behalf.

Powers and Functions of the Commission

12. It shall be the general duty of the Commission to take, in consultation with the Universities or other bodies concerned, all such steps as it may think fit for the promotion and coordination of University education and for the determination and maintenance of standards of teaching, examination and research in Universities, and for the purpose of performing its functions under this Act, the Commission may-

(a) inquire into the financial needs of Universities;

(b) allocate and disburse, out of the Fund of then Commission, grants to Universities established or incorporated by or under a Central Act for the maintenance and development of such Universities or for any other general or specified purpose;

(c) allocate and disburse, out of the Fund of the Commission, such grants to other Universities as it may deem [necessary or appropriate for the development of such Universities or for the maintenance, or development, or both, of any specified activities of such Universities] or for any other general or specified purpose: Provided that in making any grant to any such University, the Commission shall give due consideration to the development of the University concerned, its financial needs, the standard attained by it and the national purposes which it may serve, [(cc) allocate and disburse out of the Fund of the Commission, such grants to institution deemed to be Universities in pursuance of a declaration made by the Central Government under section 3, as it may deem necessary, for one or more of the following purposes, namely:-(i) for maintenance in special cases, (ii) for development, (iii) for any other general or specified purpose;]

["(ccc) establish, in accordance with the regulations made under this Act, institutions for providing common facilities, services and programmes for a group of universities or for the universities in general and maintain such institutions or providen for their maintenance by allocating and, disbursing out of the Fund of the Commission such grants as the Commission may deem necessary".]

(d) recommend to any University the measures necessary for the improvement of University education and advise the University upon the action to be taken for the purpose of implementing such recommendation;

(e) advise the Central Government or any State Government on the allocation of any grants to Universities for any general or specified purpose out of the Consolidated Fund of India or the Consolidated Fund of the State, as the case may be;

(f) advise any authority, if such advice is asked for, on the establishment of a new University or on proposals connected with the expansion of the activities of any University;

(g) advise the Central Government or any State Government or University on any question which may be referred to the Commission by the Central Government or the State Government or the University, as the case may be;

(h) collect information on all such matters relating to University education in India and other countries as it thinks fit and make the same available to any University;

(i) require a University to furnish it with such information as may be needed relating to the financial position of the University or the studies in the various branches of learning undertaken in that University, together with all the rules and regulations relating to the standards of teaching and examination in that University respecting each of such branches of learning;

(j) perform such other functions as may be prescribed or as may be deemed necessary by the Commission for advancing the cause of higher education in India or as may be incidental or conducive to the discharge of the above functions. (a) "affiliation" together with its grammatical variations, includes, in relation to a college, recognition of such college by, association of such college with, and admission of such college to the privileges of, a university; (b) "college" means any institution, whether known as such or by any other name which provides for a course of study for obtaining any qualification from a university and which, in accordance with the rules and regulations of such university, is recognised as competent to provide for such course of study and present students undergoing such course of study for the examination for the award of such qualification; (c) "prosecution" in relation to a course of study, includes promotion from one part or stage of the course of study to another part or stage of the course of study; (d) "qualification" means a degree or any other qualification awarded by a university; (e) "regulations" means regulations made under this Act; (f) "specified course of study" means a course of study in respect of which regulations of the nature mentioned in sub-section (2) have been made; (g) "student" includes a person seeking admission as a student; (h) "university" means a university or institution referred to in sub-section (1) of section 22.

(2) Without prejudice to the generality of the provisions of section 12 if, having regard to – (a) the nature of any course of study for obtaining any qualification from any university; (b) the types of activities in which persons obtaining such qualification are likely to be engaged on the basis of such qualification; (c) the minimum standards which a person possessing such qualification should be able to maintain in his work relating to such activities and the consequent need for ensuring, so far as may be, that no candidate secures admission to such course of study by reason of economic power and thereby prevents a more meritorious candidate from securing admission to such course of study; and (d) all other relevant factors, the Commission is satisfied that it is necessary so to do in the public interest, it may, after consultation, with the university or universities concerned specify by regulations the matters in respect of which fees may be charged, and the scale of fees in accordance with which fees shall be charged in respect of those matters on and from such date as may be specified in the regulations in this behalf, by any college providing for such course of study from, or in relation to, any student in connection with his admission to, and prosecution of, such course of study: Provided that different matters and different scales of fees may be so specified in relation to different universities or different classes of colleges or different areas.

(3) Where regulations of the nature referred to in sub-section (2) have been made in relation to any course of study, no college providing for such course of study shall – (a) levy or charge fees in respect of any matter other than a matter specified in such regulations; (b) levy or charge any fees in excess of the scale of fees specified in such regulations, or (c) accept, either directly or indirectly, any payment otherwise than by way of fees; or any donation of gift (whether in cash or kind), from, or in relation to, any student in connection with his admission to, and prosecution of, such course of study.

(4) If, after making, in relation to a college providing for a specified course of study, an inquiry in the manner provided

by regulations, and after giving such college a reasonable opportunity of being heard, the Commission is satisfied that such college has contravened the provisions of subsection (3), the Commission may, with the previous approval of the Central Government, pass an order prohibiting such college from presenting any students then undergoing such course of study therein to any university for the award of the qualification concerned.

(5) The Commission shall forward a copy of the order made by it under sub-section (4) to the university concerned, and on and from the date of receipt by the university of a copy of such order, the affiliation of such college to such university shall, in so far as it relates to the course of study specified in such order, stand terminated and on and from the date of termination of such affiliation and for a period of three years thereafter affiliation shall not be granted to such college in relation to such or similar course of study by that or any other university.

(6) On the termination of the affiliation of any college under sub-section (5), the Commission shall take all such steps as it may consider appropriate for safeguard the interests of the students concerned.

(7) The provisions of this section and the regulations made for the purposes of this section shall have effect notwithstanding anything inconsistent therewith contained in any other law for the time being in force. Government, the Commission, or any other organisation receiving any funds from the Central Government, to a University which is established after the commencement of the University Grants Commission (Amendment) Act, 1972, unless the Commission has, after satisfying itself as to such matters as may be prescribed, declared such

13. (1) For the purpose of ascertaining the financial needs of a University or its standards of teaching, examination and research, the Commission may, after consultation with the University, cause an inspection of any department or departments thereof to be made in such manner as may be prescribed and by such person or persons as it may direct.

(2) The Commission shall communicate to the University the date on which any inspection under sub-section (1) is to be made and the University shall be entitled to be associated with the inspection in such manner as may be prescribed.

(3) The Commission shall communicate to the University its views in regard to the results of any such inspection and may, after ascertaining the opinion of the University, recommend to the University the action to be taken as a result of such inspection.

(4) All communications to a University under this section shall be made to the executive authority thereof and the executive authority of the University shall report to the Commission the action, if any, which is proposed to be taken for the purpose of implementing any such recommendation as is referred to in sub-section (3).

14. If any University [grants affiliation in respect of any course of study to an college referred to in subsection (5) of section 12A in contravention of the provisions of that sub-section or] fails within a reasonable time to comply with any recommendation made by the Commission under section 12 or section 13, [or contravenes the provision of any rule made under clause (f) or clause (g) of sub-section (2) of section 25, or of any regulation made under clause (e) or clause (f) or clause (g) of section 26,] the Commission, after taking into consideration the cause, if any, shown by the University [for Such failure or contraventions may withhold from the University the grants proposed to be made out of the Fund of the Commission.

15. The Central Government may, after due appropriation made by Parliament by law in this behalf, pay to the University Grants Commission [ACT 3 16 Commission in each financial year such sums as may be considered necessary for the performance of the functions of the Commission under this Act.

16. (1) The Commission shall have its own Fund; and all sums which may, from time to time, be paid to it by the Central Government and all the receipts of the Commission (including any sum which any State Government or any other authority or person may hand over to the Commission) shall be carried

to the Fund and all payments by the Commission shall be made therefrom.

(2) All moneys belonging to the Fund shall be deposited in such banks or invested in such manner as may, subject to the approval of the Central Government, be decided by the Commission.

(3) The Commission may spend such sums as it thinks fit for performing its functions under this Act, and such sums shall be treated as expenditure payable out of the Fund of the Commission.

17. The Commission shall prepare, in such form and at such time each year as may be prescribed, a budget in respect of the financial year next ensuing showing the estimated receipts and expenditure, and copies thereof shall be forwarded to the Central Government.

18. The Commission shall prepare once every year, in such form and at such time as may be prescribed, an annual report giving a true and full account of its activities during the previous year, and copies thereof shall be forwarded to the Central Government and the Government shall cause the same to be laid before both Houses of Parliament.

19. (1) The Commission shall cause to be maintained such books of account and other books in relation to its account in such form and in such manner as may, I consultation with the Comptroller and Auditor-General of India, be prescribed.

(2) The Commission shall, as soon as may be after closing its annual accounts, prepare a statement of accounts in such form, and forward the same to the Comptroller and Auditor-General by such date, as the Central Governments may, in consultation with the Comptroller and Auditor-General, determine.

(3) The accounts of the Commission shall be audited y the Comptroller and Audito General at such times and in such manner as he thinks fit.

(4) The annual accounts of the Commission together with the audit report thereon shall be forwarded o the Central

Government and the Government hall cause the same to be laid before both of Parliament and shall also forward a copy of the audit report to the Commission for asking suitable action on the matters arising out f the audit report.

DEC

Statute

(1) Consistent with the duty of the University to take all such steps as it may deem fit for the promotion of the Open University and distance education systems in the educational pattern of the country and for the coordination and determination of standards of teaching, evaluation & research in such systems; and in pursuance of the objects of the University to encourage greater flexibility, diversity, accessibility, mobility and innovation in education at the University level by making full use of the latest scientific knowledge and new educational technology, and to further cooperation between the existing Universities; it is considered necessary and expedient to establish a Distance Education Council as an authority of the University under Section 16 of the Act.

"It shall be the duty of the University to take all such steps as it may deem fit for the promotion of the open university and distance education systems and for the determination of standards of teaching, evaluation and research in such systems, and for the purpose of performing this function, the University shall have such powers, including the power to allocate and disburse grants .... as may be specified by the Statutes"

(2) There shall be a Distance Education Council (DEC) which shall .... be responsible for the promotion and coordination of the open university and distance education system, and for the determination of its standards.

Powers & Functions of the Distance Education Council

(a) It shall be the general duty of the Distance Education Council to take all such steps as are consistent with the provisions of this Act, the Statutes and the Ordinances for the promotion of the open university/distance education systems, its coordinated development, and the determination of its standards, and in particular.

i. to develop a network of open universities/distance education institutions in the country in consultation with the State Governments, Universities, and other concerned agencies;

ii. to identify priority areas in which distance education programmes should be organized and to provide such support as may be considered necessary for organizing such programmes;

iii. to identify the specific client groups and the types of programmes to be organized for them, and to promote and encourage the organisation of such programmes through the network of open universities/distance, education institutions;

iv. to promote an innovative system of University level education, flexible and open, in regard to methods and pace of learning, combination of courses, eligibility for enrolment, age of entry, conduct of examination and organize various courses and programmes;

v. to promote the organisation of programmes of human resource development for the open university/distance education system;

vi. to initiate and organize measures for joint development of courses and programmes and research in distance education technology and practices;

vii. to recommend to the Board of Management the pattern and nature of financial assistance that may be sanctioned to open universities/distance education institutions and the conditions that may have to be fulfilled by them to receive such assistance;

viii. to take such steps as are necessary to ensure the coordinated development of the open university/distance education system in the country;

ix. to establish and develop arrangements for coordinating and sharing the instructional materials prepared by different open universities/distance education institutions, and the student support systems with a view to avoiding duplication of efforts;

x. to evolve procedures for sharing of courses and programmes and for the payment of royalty or other charges to the members of the network whose courses and programmes are used by other members;

xi. to prescribe broad, norms for charging fees from students who join various programmes offered by the network of open universities/distance education institutions;

xii. to collect, compile and disseminate information relating to the courses and programmes offered by various open universities/distance education institutions;

xiii. to advise State Governments, universities and other concerned agencies on their proposals to set up open universities, or to introduce programmes of distance education;

xiv. to appoint Review Committees from time to time to study and assess the performance of the open universities/distance education institutions participating in the network on any aspect relevant to the functioning of the network;

xv. to prescribe a broad framework for courses and programmes including their pattern and structure;

xvi. to evolve norms, procedures and practices in respect of admission, evaluation, completion of courses requirements, transfer of credits, etc. of students admitted to the programmes of the open university/distance education network and for the award of certificates, diplomas and degrees to them;

xvii. to evolve guidelines for the organisation of student support services for the open university/distance education programmes;

xviii. to take such measures as are necessary, consistent with the objects of the University to provide an innovative, flexible and open system of University education, for the promotion, including introduction and continuation, of courses and programmes which conform to the standards prescribed by the DEC, to maintain such standards in the institutions offering distance education programmes and to prevent, through such measures as are considered appropriate, institutions from offering courses and programmes which do not conform to the standards laid down by the Council;

xix. to appoint Committees for advising and assisting the DEC in the performance of any of its functions or exercise of any of its powers.

(b) The Distance Education Council shall:

i. appoint Committees which shall assess, in consultation with the concerned open universities/distance education institutions, the development grants required by them for a five-year period and make recommendations to the Board of Management for sanctioning such grants;

ii. sanction grants to open universities/distance education institutions for specific projects on the basis of reports by duly appointed committees and in accordance with guidelines prescribed for the purpose and report such approvals to the Board of Management.

ICSSR

Icssr at a Glance

Indian Council of Social Science Research (ICSSR) was established in the year of 1969 by the Government of India to promote research in social sciences in the country. The Council was meant to:

- Review the progress of social science research and give advice to its users;
- Sponsor social science research programmes and projects and administer grants to institutions and individuals for research in social sciences;
- Institute and administer scholarships and fellowships for research in social sciences;

- Indicate areas in which social science research is to be promoted and adopt special measures for development of research in neglected or new areas;
- Give financial support to institutions, associations, and journals engaged in social science research;
- Arrange for technical training in research methodology and to provide guidance for research;
- Coordinate research activities and encourage progrmmes for interdisciplinary research;
- Develop and support centers for documentation services and supply of data;
- Organize, sponsor, and finance seminars, workshops and study groups;
- Undertake publication and assist publication of journals and books in social sciences;
- Advise the Government of India on all matters pertaining to social science research as may be referred to it from time to time; and take such measures generally as may be necessary from time to time to promote social science research and its utilization.

MHRD

The Ministry of Human Resources Development (HRD) is an Indian government ministry, responsible for the development of human resources. The ministry is divided into two departments: the Department of School Education and Literacy, which deals with primary education and literacy, and the Department of Higher Education, which deals with secondary and post-secondary education.

The Ministry of Human Resources Development is headed by a minister of cabinet rank as a member of the Council of Ministers.

Department of School Education and Literacy

The Department of School Education and Literacy is responsible for primary education, both formal and non-formal.

Its stated goal is the universalization of elementary education (UEE). The department originated as the Indian Education Department in the 1910 under the British Raj. After independence, a full-fledged ministry, the Ministry of Education, was created in 1947.

The Ministry of Education was merged with the newly-created Ministry of Human Resources Development in 1985. The department aims to achieve universal access and enrolment, universal retention of children up to 14 years of age, and substantial improvement in the quality of education to enable all children to achieve essential levels of learning.

Department of Higher Education

The Department of Higher Education is in charge of secondary and post-secondary education. The Department is divided into six bureaus: University and Higher Education; Minorities Education; Book Promotion and Copyrights; Technical Education; Distance Education and Scholarships; Planning; and UNESCO, International Cooperation, Administration, Coordination, Policy, Statistics, and Languages; and the Integrated Finance Division.

Most the work of the department is through about 90 autonomous bodies that it oversees:

- University Grants Commission (UGC), the 23 Central Universities (Union Universities), the Indian Council of Social Science Research (ICSSR), the Indian Council of Historical Research (ICHR), the Indian Council of Philosophical Research (ICPR), and the Indian Institute of Advanced Studies (IIAS), Shimla.
- All India Council for Technical Education (AICTE), the seven Indian Institutes of Technology (IITs), the three Indian Institutes of Science Education and Research (IISERs), the six Indian Institutes of Management (IIMs), the 20 National Institutes of Technology (NITs), the four Indian Institutes of Information Technology (IIITs), the four National Institutes of Technical Teachers' Training and Research (NITTTRs), and the

four Regional Boards of Apprenticeship/Practical Training

- The three Deemed Universities in the field of Sanskrit (Rashtriya Sanskrit Sansthan (RSkS), New Delhi; Shri Lal Bahadur Shastri Rashtriya Sanskrit Vidyapeeth (SLBSRSV), New Delhi; and Rashtriya Sanskrit Vidyapeeth (RSV), Tirupati), Kendriya Hindi Sansthan (KHS), Agra; the Central Institute of English and Foreign Languages (CIEFL), Hyderabad; the National Council for Promotion of Urdu Language (NCPUL); and National Council for Promotion of Sindhi Language (NCPSL)
- National Institute of Educational Planning and Administration (NIEPA)
- National Book Trust (NBT)
- National Commission for Minority Educational Institutions (NCMEI)
- Attached Offices: Central Hindi Directorate, New Delhi; Commission for Scientific and Technical Terminology (CSTT), New Delhi; Central Institute of Indian Languages (CIL), Mysore
- a public sector enterprise, Educational Consultants (India) Limited (EdCIL)
- National Council of Educational Research and Training (NCERT)
- Central Board of Secondary Education (CBSE)
- Kendriya Vidyalaya Sangathan (KVS)
- Navodaya Vidyalaya Samiti (NVS)
- National Institute of Open Schooling (NIOS)
- Central Tibetan School Administration (CTSA)
- National Foundation for Teachers' Welfare.

And the following post-secondary education bodies :

- University Grants Commission (UGC)-responsible for coordination, determination and maintenance of standards, release of grants.

- Professional councils, responsible for recognition of courses, promotion of professional institutions and providing grants to undergraduate programmes and various awards:
  - * All India Council for Technical Education (AICTE)
  - * Distance Education Council (DEC)
  - * Indian Council for Agriculture Research (ICAR)
  - * Bar Council of India (BCI)
  - * National Council for Teacher Education (NCTE)
  - * Rehabilitation Council of India (RCI)
  - * Medical Council of India (MCI)
  - * Pharmacy Council of India (PCI)
  - * Indian Nursing Council (INC)
  - * Dentist Council of India (DCI)
  - * Central Council of Homeopathy (CCH)
  - * Central Council of Indian Medicine (CCIM).

As well as following inter-university centres (IUCs)

- Nuclear Science Centre, New Delhi
- Inter-University Centre for Astronomy and Astrophysics (IUCAA), Pune
- Inter–University Consortium for DAE Facilities, Indore
- Information and Library Network (INFLIBNET), Ahmedabad
- Consortium for Educational Communication (CEC)
- National Assessment and Accreditation Council (NACC), Bangalore

SCERT

SCERT functions as an R&D institute at the state level by providing guidance, support and assistance to the State Education Department in its endeavor to improve the quality of elementary and secondary education and teacher education. To achieve this goal, the SCERT conducts research Studies, develops information systems, curricular policies, and instructional materials and co-ordinates in-service education for teachers at all levels.

SCERT is concerned with the academic aspects of school education including formulation of curriculum, preparation of textbooks, teachers' handbooks and teacher training. It advises the Government on policy matters relating to school education

The academic activities and programmes of SCERT are carried out by the various departments / units. SCERT plans and co-ordinates all academic projects and programmes in the state.

SCERT has the following departments/Units

Department of Curriculum, Text Books and Evaluation [DCTE]

DCTE is responsible for preparation and revision of curriculum and textbooks, preparation of handbooks for teachers in eight languages and different school subjects for all classes, refresher courses, orientation & training programmes for teachers, headmasters, DEOs& DDEs on curriculum-related topics.

Faculties under the Department of Curriculum, Textbooks and Evaluation are Malayalam, English, Hindi, Mathematics, Chemistry, Biology, Physics, Geography, Social Science, Arabic, Urdu, Sanskrit, Kannada and Tamil.

Department of Teacher Education (Pre-service & in-service) and Extension

DTE aims at integrating the training programmes and research programmes with thrust on quality and gives shapes to the changes to be brought in the training courses.

DTE's areas of action are organising teacher training programmes (both in-service & pre-service) for the TTIs & DIETs, orientation courses for teacher educators in TTI's, preparation of evaluation tools for TTC and revision of the TTC curriculum.

Department of Educational Technology (DET)

DET's aims are to develop common vision of ET and its functioning with the help of experts in the field of IT.

It develops the curriculum, syllabus, text books, hand books for teachers, evaluation tools, and other teaching learning materials for IT education in High School level.

It also provides technological support to all other departments of SCERT. DET is working in association with IT@School project, SIET etc.

It gives academic leadership for the training of IT Master Trainers and School IT Coordinators to implement IT education in schools, using computers as a tool for acquiring and using information and knowledge. Development of story board for resource CDs for various subjects in high school classes is another contribution of DET.

Department of Art, Physical, Health and Vocational Education

DHPVE is established with a view to cater to academic quality in non-scholastic areas like art, health and physical education.

The Department is responsible for orientation courses for the Health Club sponsors and for teachers of other non-scholastic subjects, training programmes for teachers to make the work experience sessions productivity-oriented, pre-vocational training to work experience teachers, remedial training to educationally backward students, preparation of music curriculum for Higher Secondary, State Resource Group training for music and drawing teachers.

Department of Non-formal, Countinuing and Special Education (NFE)

NFE is envisaged for organising educational programmes for marginalized and out-of-school populations to draw them into mainstream education. Special Education, Population Education & National Talent Search Examination come under this department.

Special Education/Integrated Education for the Disabled (IED)

It aims to provide equity in opportunity to the deprived groups, thus helping them to get into the mainstream of the society.

Population Education (POPED)

The activities of POPED are two-fold: population education progrommes supported by the State Govt. and those funded by UNFPA.

It conducts several programs for teachers, students, opinion makers, administrators of school education about adolescent education, help education, AIDS education, Life-skill education etc.

National Talent Search Examination (NTSE)

SCERT plays a major role in preparing students for the NTSE (conducted by NCERT by administering the screening test at state level)

Department of Research Documentation and Dissemination

Research is a significant input to SCERT's training programmes. This unit conducts, sponsors and coordinates inter-disciplinary research with focus on theory, policy relevance, methods and processes of the educational, curricular and training programmes carried out by SCERT.

It is also responsible for the evaluation of the massive teacher training programmes, continuous monitoring and assessment of terminal evaluation and field analysis of textbooks. The Unit provides empirical and analytical basis for policy and plan formulation and implementation.

DTERT

It is the aim of this directorate to produce efficient teachers and impart in-service training on the modern teaching techniques after they have joined service.

Teacher Education

A separate Directorate for Teacher Education, Research and Training has been created and it is functioning since 1990. The Teacher Training Institutes functioning under this directorate are as follows:

District Institute of Education and Training

- Government Teacher Training Institutes
- Government aided non-minority Teacher Training Institutes
- Government aided minority Teacher Training Institutes
- Government recognised unaided minority Teacher Training Institutes
- Anglo Indian Teacher Training Institute
- Minority Language sections in Government Institutions
    - * Urdu
    - * Malayalam
    - * Telugu.

A separate section is functioning in each of the 17 District Institutes of Education and Training exclusively for Scheduled Caste/Scheduled Tribe students. 60% of the total seats available in District Institute of Education and Training and Government Teacher Training Institutes are earmarked for regular students coming from +2 stream and 40% earmarked to the affected students of derecognised Teacher Training Institutes.

As it will take some more years to give regular training to all the affected students, a scheme is being formulated to give training to all such students during the current year itself.

To override the difficulties experienced in the past, orders have been issued for admitting the students in Teacher Training Institutes through single window system from the academic year 2001-2002. The construction of buildings at a cost of Rs.12 crores in the 8 new District Institutes of Education and Training (Kurukkathi, G.Ariyur, Lalgudi, Mannarkudi, Uthamacholapuram, Uthamapalayam, Kaliyampoondi, and Keelapalur) is under progress.

The existing buildings in Government Teacher Training Institutes are old buildings.

In the first phase, new buildings are constructed at a cost of Rs.150 lakhs in four Government Teacher Training Institutes at Royapettah, Ranipet, Gangavalli and Chinnatharapuram.

Research and Training

Directorate of Teacher Education, Research and Training and the 29 District Institutes of Education and Training are jointly imparting training to the teacher educators in order to give a qualitative education to students.

Aim

The aims of the Directorate of Teacher Education, Research and Training are:

a. To improve the teacher education programmes to the level advocated in

b. National Policy on Education by improving the teacher educators' skills and technology;

c. To prepare teaching materials, viz. books, handbooks, exercise books, audio/video cassettes for improving the quality of education;

d. To impart training in new methods to all teachers;

e. To do research work in the field of primary and secondary education etc. and to develop research orientation among the teachers;

f. To spread the knowledge acquired through action research in order to supplement the knowledge acquired through books.

Administrative Measures

The following administrative measures have been taken to achieve the above goals;-

* To remodel teacher education syllabus suitably at all levels in consultation with NCERT and Universities;

* To prepare books, handbooks and exercise books to all standards step by step;
* To prepare audio/video cassettes through education television studio to understand rhymes/songs;
* To prepare basic elementary teaching materials on health education, population education, AIDS education, pre-school education and Institutional Planning.
* To impart in-service training to primary and middle school teachers in subjects, teaching methods and in general topics;
* To make research on the effect of the use of subject books and other teaching-learning materials;
* To encourage teachers and District Institutes of Education and Training to have action research regarding school and class room environments;
* To put to use and spread the results of action research through publication of 'Newsletter' in the Directorate of Teacher Education, Research and Training and the District Institutes of Education and Training;
* To maintain Data Centres in the districts regarding the various plan of action in training programmes.

Inservice Training to Primary School Teachers.

Since the Text Books for 1st Std. students have been revised by the movement for Elementary Education for All, all the 1st standard teachers have been trained on the methods of joyful learning.

In order to make the class room conducive and attractive to children, an appropriate educational methodology of teaching which will promote self learning has been evolved and all the primary school teachers will be trained within a period of three years.

Special Orientation Training to Primary School Teachers

The aim of special orientation training is to introduce skills in minimum level of learning prescribed in National Policy on Education. Training has been given almost to all secondary grade teachers handling classes from 1st to 5th std. and primary school Headmasters. It is proposed to give training under this programme to all teachers handling classes from 6th to 8th standards during this year. Science and maths kits will be prepared under the guidance of experts from Regional Institute of Education, Mysore, National Institute of Education planning and Administration, National council for Education, Research and Training and National Council for Teacher Education for imparting the above training.

Block Resource Centres

The Universalisation of primary education is emphasized by the National Educational Policy. The over aged children, working children, children of disadvantaged sections, school drop-outs and all school age children are being brought into formal primary school system with the aim to achieve the universalisation of primary education.

Block Resource Centres have been established in 8 districts where District Primary Education Programme is being implemented. The District Institute of Education and Training plays a vital role in establishing linkages with these Block Resource Centres to achieve compulsory elementary education.

Hence it is proposed to set up similar Block Resource Centres in the remaining non-District Primary Education Programme Districts. Now 8 Block Resource Centres in Theni District, 10 Centres in Thiruvarur District and 12 Centres in Sivagangai District (30 Block Resource Centres in all) have been set up.

Revision of syllabus for Diploma in Teacher Education

The new text books were introduced for primary/ secondary/ higher secondary students since 1994-95 based on the curriculum and new syllabus containing minimum level of learning and other concepts necessary for life. But, the existing teacher education curriculum prepared in 1990 is an outdated one.

The teacher education curriculum has to be necessarily revamped to suit the present needs; to handle the new text books drawn in terms of minimum level of learning and other essential skills. To prepare a competency based teacher education syllabus based on the guidelines of National Council for Teacher Education, an expert committee headed by the Director of Teacher Education, Research and Training with 12 members has been constituted.

This committee, with the guidance of the experts and the identified sub-committee members, has evolved the competency based commitment oriented performance teacher education curriculum after conducting various workshops in this regard. For the first time the text books for pre-service teacher education based on the revised competency based curriculum has been prepared.

Subjects like crafts, physical education, yoga and integrated education for the disabled have been included in the new syllabus for the Diploma in Teacher Education. Computer syllabi have also been included in the curriculum for trainees of secondary grade and B.T. teachers.

It is proposed to prepare syllabus for all the subjects from Stds VI to +2. Experts in each subject have been identified for this purpose from the directorate of school education and they will prepare the syllabus through discussion in the workshops.

Syllabus for higher secondary vocational courses will be prepared during the current year.

Open School System

The open school system in Tamil Nadu has been introduced as a pilot scheme for the benefit of those who have discontinued their studies before reaching 10th standard to continue their study under this system to quality for 10th standard. The salient feature of the scheme is that the housewives, the women belonging to economically weaker societies, the basic servants of government and private establishments and those who have discontinued their studies due to economic conditions are benefited through this system without attending the formal schools. Those who have passed 8th standard can get through 10th standard under this system.

The books for the open school system have been prepared based on the revised syllabus. The 10th standard certificate issued under open school system has been evaluated to that of the secondary school leaving certificate issued by the Director of Government Examinations and makes one eligible for higher studies including employment.

Educational Television Studio

The aim of education television studio is to prepare audio/ video cassettes for clear understanding by the school children covering the syllabi.

To improve the quality of primary education video programmes will be prepared for the benefit of students of II and III Stds and telecast under 'Kanbom – Karpom" programme. The video programmes will also be used during the in-service training programmes conducted in 29 District Institutes of Education and Training and in Block Resource Centres.

ETV studio is also getting audio/video educational programmes from other organisations like National Council for Educational Research and Training, State Institutes of Educational Technology and foreign educational institutions and by making necessary changes according to our needs supply these programmes to schools.

After analysing various possibilities to reorient / improve primary education it has been proposed to teach the children in schools through visual media like audio/video cassettes. For this purpose, ETV studio in the Directorate of Teacher Education, Research and Training has been modernised with installation of new modern equipments at a cost of Rs. 102 lakhs.

Repairs/improvement works in the ETV studio has been undertaken on a priority basis at a cost of Rs. 16.10 lakhs.

RCI

The Rehabilitation Council of India was set up as a registered society in 1986 under the aegies of the Ministry of Social Justice & Empowerment (then Ministry of Social Welfare) to standardize and maintain uniform standards of training of professionals.

However, it was soon realised that the Society could not ensure proper standardization and acceptance of the standards by other Organisations. The Parliament enacted the Rehabilitation Council of India Act in 1992. The Rehabilitation Council of India became a Statutory Body on 22nd June 1993.

The RCI Act was amended by the Parliament in 2000 to make it more broad based. The Act casts onerous responsibility on the Council. It also prescribes that any one delivering services to people with disability, who does not possess qualifications recognised by RCI, could be prosecuted. Thus the Council has the twin responsibility of standardizing and regulating the training of professional and personnel in the field of Rehabilitation and Special Education.

Objectives

- To regulate the training policies and programmes in the field of rehabilitation of persons with disabilities
- To bring about standardization of training courses for professionals dealing with persons with disabilities
- To prescribe minimum standards of education and training of various categories of professionals/ personnel dealing with people with disabilities
- To regulate these standards in all training institutions uniformly throughout the country
- To recognize institutions/ organisations/ universities running master's degree/ bachelor's degree/ P.G.Diploma/ Diploma/ Certificate courses in the field of rehabilitation of persons with disabilities
- To recognize degree/diploma/certificate awarded by foreign universities/ institutions on reciprocal basis
- To promote research in Rehabilitation and Special Education
- To maintain Central Rehabilitation Register for registration of professionals/ personnel

Bibliography

Bailey, K. and Nunan, D.: *Voices from the Language Classroom*, Cambridge, CUP, 1996.

Balloch, F.: *Teacher Development Resource Book,* Folkestone, English Experience, 1996.

Baron, Cynthia: *Creating a Digital Portfolio*, Indianapolis, Hayden Books, 1996.

Bowen, T. & Marks, J.: *Inside Teaching,* Oxford, Heinemann, 1994.

Brown, H. D.: *Principles of Language Learning and Teaching,* White Plains, NY: Pearson Education Inc, 2007.

Burke, Kay: *Designing Professional Portfolios for Change*, Palatine, Illinois, 1997.

Campbell, Melenyzer: *Portfolio and Performance Assessment in Teacher Education*, Boston: Allyn & Bacon, 2000.

Flowerdew, J., Brock, M. and Hassiya, S.: *Perspectives on Second Language Education,* Hong Kong, City Polytechnic of Hong Kong, 1992.

Forsyth, P.: *Running an Effective Training Session,* Aldershot, Gower, 1992.

Freeman, D. and Richards, J.: *Teacher Learning in Language Teaching,* Cambridge, CUP, 1996.

Green, C.: *Tasks for Teacher Education,* Harlow, Essex: Addison Wesley Longman, 1998.

Hayes, D.: *In-service Teacher Development: International Perspectives,* Hemel Hempstead, Herts.: Prentice Hall, 1997.

James, D.: *Planning Professional Training Days,* Milton Keynes, Open University Press, 1990.

Index